THE HARDEST
DEAL OF ALL

CHARLES C. BOLTON

UNIVERSITY PRESS OF MISSISSIPPI / *JACKSON*

THE HARDEST DEAL OF ALL

THE BATTLE OVER

SCHOOL INTEGRATION

IN MISSISSIPPI, 1870–1980

www.upress.state.ms.us

The University Press of Mississippi is a member of the Association of American
University Presses.

First edition 2005

Library of Congress Cataloging-in-Publication Data

Bolton, Charles C.
    The hardest deal of all : the battle over school integration in Mississippi,
1870–1980 / Charles C. Bolton.
        p. cm.
    Includes bibliographical references and index.
    ISBN 1-57806-717-0 (cloth : alk. paper) 1. School integration—Mississippi.
2. Segregation in education—Mississippi. 3. African Americans—Education—
Mississippi. I. Title.

    LC214.22.M7B65   2005
    379.2′63′09762—dc22   2005004454

British Library Cataloging-in-Publication Data available

For Leslie, Laura, and Ben

CONTENTS

ACKNOWLEDGMENTS

In the decade that I spent researching and writing this book, I was fortunate to receive assistance from many individuals. Anyone who has conducted historical research knows how vital the role of archivists and librarians are to the preservation of and access to the sources of the past. I received patient help and wise advice from the archival staffs of Georgia State University; the American Friends Service Committee Archives in Philadelphia; the Amistad Research Center in New Orleans; the Federal District Courthouses in Jackson and Oxford, Mississippi; the Library of Congress; the Lyndon Baines Johnson Library in Austin, Texas; the Madison County–Canton Public Library, in Canton, Mississippi; Mary Holmes College in West Point, Mississippi; the National Archives in Washington, D.C.; the Southeast Regional Branch of the National Archives in Atlanta; the King Center in Atlanta; the State Historical Society of Wisconsin; the Southern Historical Collection at the University of North Carolina at Chapel Hill; and the University of Mississippi.

At repositories where I spent a great deal of time, I got to know some staff members quite well, as they devoted seemingly endless hours of their time helping me locate materials. I am especially grateful for the help of Tara Zachary at Delta State University; Michael Ballard and Mattie Sink at Mississippi State University; Yvonne Arnold, Toby Graham, Henry Simmons, and Bobs Tusa at the University of Southern Mississippi; Nancy Bounds, Ann Lipscomb Webster, and Hank Holmes at the Mississippi Department of Archives and History; and Alma Fisher and Clarence Hunter at Tougaloo College. In terms of locating sources, I also have to give a special thanks to Leesha Faulkner, who let me search through her personal cache of Mississippi State Sovereignty Commission Papers before the official copies of these documents became publicly available at the Mississippi Department of Archives and History. Finally, both the Aubrey Keith Lucas Faculty Excellence Fund at the University of Southern Mississippi and the Lyndon Baines Johnson Research Foundation provided financial help with research travel expenses.

While conducting research trips to these various locales, I enjoyed the fellowship and encouragement of numerous friends and family, especially Lynn Bolton, Ed Baptist, Kevin Farrell, Tim Rafferty, Glenn Robins, and Tim Tyson. I also received valuable suggestions and criticisms from a number of colleagues who read parts or all of this manuscript at various stages of its creation, including Jim Bissett, Brad Bond, Brian Daugherity, John Dittmer, Charles Eagles, Sean Farrell, Phyllis Jestice, Neil McMillen, and Kim Rogers. The maps were ably prepared by George Roedl, and the manuscript was significantly improved by the expert copyediting of Bob Burchfield.

Many of the sources used for this project were oral histories, and while I have mined the oral sources concerning Mississippi at a variety of institutions, I am particularly appreciative of the work of my colleagues at the Center for Oral History and Cultural Heritage at the University of Southern Mississippi, who have labored to create one of the most impressive collections of oral memoirs available anywhere. Particularly important to the success of this enterprise during the time I worked on this project were Curtis Austin, Stephanie Millet, Sue Rodriguez, Marie Sykes, Shana Walton, and Carolyn Ware.

With teaching responsibilities and administrative duties, the research and writing of this book often had to be fitted into odd hours and weeks off here and there. Thankfully, my wife, Leslie Bloch, offered support, encouragement, and editorial advice every step of the way. She, along with my children, Laura and Ben, also provided a welcome respite from the often lonely task of research and writing.

Finally, it seems only fitting that in a book that examines education that I thank my teachers. Coming of age in the period when segregated schools across the South were forced to integrate, I was among the first generation of white Southerners to experience teaching from a biracial corps of instructors. I learned much from all of them.

INTRODUCTION

September 12, 1966, began as a rainy Monday morning in Grenada, a town in central Mississippi on the border between the Hills and the Delta. That day, about 150 black children attempted to enter the all-white schools of the town for the first time, per an August 26 federal court order by Judge Claude Clayton mandating freedom-of-choice school desegregation. By early afternoon, at least eight black children, one black adult, and a number of white reporters had been beaten by several groups of angry white men and women.[1]

Well before the opening bell rang, whites gathered in the vicinity of John Rundle High and Lizzie Horn Elementary (the two all-white schools shared a campus). Before any children arrived, some of the whites stopped a carload of blacks on their way to work, pounded on the car with wooden clubs, and unsuccessfully tried to pull the occupants out of the car before the driver was able to race away. This weapon-wielding assembly soon saw a group of black children on their way to begin their first day of classes; the mob rushed toward the students, who fled. Many of the children immediately went to regroup at Belle Flower Mount Baptist Church, the physical home of the Grenada civil rights movement. Meanwhile, the white toughs received additional weapons when a truck delivered a shipment of metal pipes to the crowd. An hour later, about forty of the black students set off from Belle Flower, accompanied by a small group of adults, to march to the schools and enroll. Several blocks shy of their destination, the group was met by thirty white men toting sticks, clubs, ax handles, and metal pipes. At least one, Justice of the Peace James R. Ayers, had a gun, which he fired into the air. Most of the black group beat a quick retreat, except for a group of elderly women, who stood their ground. The white thugs ignored the old women but pursued the slowest of the escaping children. Two were beaten, one an eleven-year-old girl, Emerald Cunningham, afflicted with polio. She was pushed down by Ayers, who threatened to kill her with the pistol. While she lay on the ground, another man clubbed her legs with one of the metal pipes.[2]

This early-morning confrontation was only the beginning of the day's violence. Groups of armed whites continued to roam the area around the schools, where at least one hundred black children had managed to enter and were now attending classes. When classes were dismissed shortly after noon (only a half day had been scheduled for the first day of classes), gangs of whites chased and attacked black children leaving the school grounds. At least six black students and one black parent were injured in a series of assaults. In one of the incidents, a white mob broke the leg of Richard Earl Sigh, an elementary student, as he left his new school. Approaching a group of whites yelling at him to "run nigger run," Sigh was first assaulted by a white woman with an umbrella. When he did start to run, a white man kicked him in the leg, and another hit him with a billy club. Once he was on the ground, the white mob kicked him and tried to choke him. Although the whites threatened to kill Sigh, they let him escape, and he staggered back to Belle Flower Church with a broken right leg. Irate groups of whites also turned on the reporters who had begun to gather near the schools as classes were dismissed for the day, assaulting Jack Cantrell and Jim Reid of the *Memphis Press-Scimitar*.[3]

When the noontime violence began, many of the black students successfully retreated inside the school, protected by the Mississippi Highway Patrol and local law officers, although angry and armed whites continued to linger around the school grounds. The arrival of United Press International (UPI) reporter Robert Gordon, just in town from Jackson, revived the ire of the mob. A man in "the uniform of a service station attendant" punched Gordon in the face after he identified himself as a newspaper reporter, and then a number of other white men fell on him, beating him with "their fists and some unknown objects," according to Gordon. Escaping from the group, he ran across the street to the school, but a Grenada policeman told him to get off school grounds. When he did, the white mob chased him down and beat him again, until two Grenada police officers got him away from the attackers. Soon after, the Mississippi Highway Patrol—which had been in town at the beginning of the morning but received reinforcements after the initial signs of trouble—along with local Grenada law enforcement officials, provided protection as the remaining black students walked back to the safety of Belle Flower Church.[4]

Only a relatively small number of white men and women were actually involved in the violence that engulfed Grenada on September 12. In addition to Justice of the Peace Ayers, the white gangs included some individuals from nearby counties; a group of men cruising in a blue and white truck from the local Don Belk Texaco, which one white witness claimed was "the focal point for the groups of white males who roamed through the area"; and the son of constable Grady Carroll. The elder Carroll was already under federal indictment following an assault in July on a civil rights attorney.

Local law enforcement officials and other local whites generally allowed the mob to rampage without much opposition. The Grenada city police and the Grenada County sheriff's deputies basically stood by while whites beat Emerald Cunningham, Richard Sigh, the white reporters, and others. As the woman with the umbrella and several men pounded on Sigh, a Grenada officer did arrest one of the male attackers—for carrying a concealed weapon. When the white crowd, including the gas station employee, started hassling Robert Gordon, four or five local law enforcement officers turned their backs and walked away as the beating began. Although one white woman prevented at least two attacks by placing herself and her German shepherd between the white attackers and the black children and by telling the assailants she was "ashamed to see a group of grown white men acting like a bunch of animals," most whites who lived in the area looked away as violence erupted on their streets. One white woman claimed that when she heard the first hint of trouble around 8 A.M., "she immediately went to the back portion of her house and remained there, since she did not want to witness anything uplesant [sic]."[5]

While some white Grenadians tried to ignore the school controversy that had spilled onto their streets, a number of whites applauded the white mob and only regretted that it had not been allowed to complete its work. When the Grenada City Council met in emergency session on the evening of the 12th, five hundred citizens waited outside in the halls and on the grounds of city hall to confront the council; many in the crowd believed the city leaders had called in the Highway Patrol reinforcements, putting an end to the violent effort to halt school desegregation. (In fact, the patrol chief, following directives from Governor Paul B. Johnson Jr., had sent in reinforcements at midmorning when the white crowds began to grow around the recently desegregated schools.) Concluding its meeting, the council tried to mollify the white assembly by announcing the resignation of the city manager, J. E. McEachin, perceived by many as a racial liberal who had allowed the civil rights business to get out of hand. But the "angry and unrully [*sic*]" assembly of whites was not placated. Several people in the crowd yelled out: "To hell with the Highway Patrol and if you get them away from here, we will take care of the damn niggers." The white citizens also heckled a *Memphis Commercial Appeal* reporter and demanded that the council fire two other perceived racial liberals in the city government: prosecuting attorney Bradford Dye and police chief Pat Ray. Someone from the crowd even suggested that Dye's head be cut off. Although some whites may have questioned Chief Ray's segregation bona fides, many of his officers had proved earlier in the day that they were certainly not soft on school desegregation. While a certain segment of white society in Grenada seemed poised to resist school desegregation by any means necessary, others deplored the use of violence. A week after the Grenada riot, three hundred whites in the town, including most of the town's elected officials, signed a petition denouncing "the use of violence in the settlement of our problems."[6]

Although Grenada's moderate white citizens condemned the violent efforts to halt school desegregation, they remained committed to racial discrimination and did not embrace the Grenada civil rights movement that had propelled the effort to desegregate the schools. Indeed, the same white petitioners who took a stand against the violence that erupted on September 12 also noted that the primary problem confronting the city was not the violent resistance to school desegregation by whites but the two-month-old boycott by blacks of Grenada merchants. Mississippi congressman John Bell Williams also condemned the violence in Grenada, but he blamed "SNCC, COFO, CORE, SCLC, and other professional trouble-makers [who] have been working for months in Grenada trying to provoke just the kind of incident that occurred the other day." Williams was correct that the Southern Christian Leadership Conference (SCLC) had helped to launch a broad-based civil rights campaign in Grenada during the summer of 1966. SCLC workers had arrived as part of the march through Mississippi started by James Meredith, who wanted to encourage black Mississippians to exercise their voting rights, newly guaranteed by the Voting Rights Act of 1965.

But Williams failed to understand that the Grenada movement was enthu-
siastically supported by all segments of the local black community—adults,
teenagers, children, even a number of teachers, and at least one principal
from the town's black schools. In the days after the Meredith march, town
leaders had initially agreed to a number of the movement's demands, but as
the glare of national publicity and the number of "outside agitators" in
town diminished, white officials backed off from their earlier promises to
carry out basic civil rights reforms, such as desegregation of public facilities
required by the Civil Rights Act of 1964.[7]

The black citizens of Grenada, however, continued the fight. During July,
August, and early September, Grenada blacks tested public accommodations, initiated a boycott of town merchants, and held almost-nightly
marches around the downtown square with its Confederate monument. The
marches became the scene of frequent violent confrontations that summer
when whites started their own countermarches on the town square. Local
law enforcement, with help from the Highway Patrol, generally kept the two
groups separated, though the officers failed to prevent all of the white attacks
on the black protesters, and on occasion, the officers' peacekeeping efforts
actually involved assaults on the black protesters. In one of the worst incidents, in early July helmeted Highway Patrol officers beat scores of the about
two hundred black protesters—assembled on the lawn of the jail to protest
the earlier arrest of fellow civil rights demonstrators—with billy clubs and
the butts of their shotguns after the protesters would not disperse when
ordered to. One hundred white counterprotesters at the same scene were not
subjected to violence by the authorities; they were merely "chased away" by
Grenada sheriff's deputies. During this same evening, Constable Grady Carroll
fired a submachine gun at Henry Aronson as the civil rights attorney entered
Belle Flower Church. On a number of occasions, black protesters on the
town square were injured by flying objects (such as ball bearings and chain
links) hurled from the white crowd that gathered nightly to jeer the black
marchers.[8] Thus, the riot in Grenada on September 12 did not happen in a
vacuum. It was the culmination of a long summer of black-white confrontation in Grenada.

Even so, the violence associated with the beginning of school desegregation in Grenada was an aberration. Indeed, both the state and federal governments moved swiftly to stop the white perpetrators. The state government,

though somewhat reluctantly, played an important role in containing the Grenada violence quickly and possibly prevented a real bloodbath. Soon after one hundred additional Highway Patrol officers arrived in town (augmenting fifty patrolmen already on the scene), order was restored. The patrolmen, in full riot gear and armed with tear gas and shotguns, generally followed their orders to enforce the federal court's school desegregation ruling, which meant protecting the black children now attending John Rundle and Lizzie Horn, a task that local law enforcement officials who sympathized with the white mob were clearly unwilling to perform. On September 12, patrolmen helped lead the black children stranded in the newly desegregated schools through the white crowd to safety. The following day, when whites returned to continue their campaign to harass black students and their parents, the Highway Patrol preserved order around the schools for the most part, although they ignored a few instances of property damage, perhaps because they believed they had to allow white toughs to vent their frustration a bit, as long as they did not physically assault black parents and children or white reporters. For example, the patrol stood by as whites broke the car windows of several vehicles bringing black students to the desegregated schools and watched as one white group smashed the camera of an ABC newsman. The federal government responded even more forcefully to the Grenada riot. The day after the violence, the Department of Justice successfully sued for an injunction to prevent city officials from "willfully" failing to protect the black students entering previously segregated schools under a federal court order. Four days later, federal agents arrested thirteen local white men, including Justice Ayers, on conspiracy charges associated with the attacks on the black youth. Eight of the men, including Ayers, were eventually tried in federal court, although they were acquitted by an all-white jury.[9]

The violence surrounding the desegregation of schools in Grenada in 1966 was not repeated in other locales on other days as the state's separate school system began to crumble in the mid-1960s. Even so, most white Mississippians shared the passionate and firm opposition to ending segregated schools that animated the white mobs in Grenada. Indeed, the state's dual educational system had long represented the most treasured part of the segregated world for whites in the state. Buck Wells of Hattiesburg remembered that of all the civil rights reforms in the 1960s, "the most serious one, and the one that hurt the most was the fact when people had to send their little children, the small children in grade schools, had to integrate them with 50 percent black children. That hurt more than any of the other integration deals. Now voter rights and the right to ride in the front of the bus, all of that was just really not near as serious."[10]

For white Mississippians, then, one-race schools represented the very heart of segregation. Losing the battle to preserve segregated schools would make it impossible to prevent social equality and miscegenation and was tantamount to losing the war over the continuation of racial separation. As a result, white Mississippians waged a long battle to preserve the state's dual system from the attacks of black Mississippians and, by the mid-twentieth century, the federal government. Black opposition to the state's system of segregated schools, on the other hand, sprang not from some abstract desire to "mix" black and white children but from an ongoing struggle to secure a quality education for their children, the kind of schooling that separate schools could never deliver in Mississippi. This book is about both of these struggles, white and black, and about how these competing visions of what constituted quality schooling affected the development of public education in Mississippi from its beginnings in 1870 through the transition to a unitary school system in the 1970s. To paraphrase Buck Wells, the battle over school integration in Mississippi was indeed the hardest deal of all.

Mississippi public education was actually created as a biracial enterprise during Reconstruction, with the newly emancipated slaves playing a leading role in agitating for the development of a system of public schools. Despite such a promising beginning, the institution of public schools in Mississippi was only really established in the state around the turn of the twentieth century, during the height of the retreat from the Reconstruction ideals of a biracial society and the establishment of Jim Crow and black disfranchisement. As a result, Mississippi created two school systems, even though it could not really even pay for one. What the state ended up with was a mediocre white school system, though whites viewed it as top quality primarily because it remained all-white, and a sorely impoverished black system, which, despite its inadequate funding, still provided important education to black Mississippians.

By 1940, after more than three decades of building a dual school system, the disparity between black and white education in Mississippi had grown to immense proportions. Black Mississippians, who had long complained about the unequal arrangements of the so-called separate but equal school system, continued to agitate for a truly equal allocation of public education resources, whether schools remained separate or not. By the late 1930s and early 1940s, increasing numbers of whites also recognized the shortcomings of the dual schools and resolved to do something about improving the inequities heaped on black schools. The motive for white concern revolved primarily around an understanding that racial segregation was increasingly scrutinized, and no one could claim, with a straight face at least, that Mississippi had a separate but equal education system. In the 1940s and early 1950s, the state considered accepting federal aid to education and developed a state-supported equalization program to try to solve the dilemma of separate but unequal schools. Neither approach proved successful.

In 1954, the U.S. Supreme Court's landmark decision in *Brown v. Board of Education* seemingly ended Mississippi's system of separate education for whites and blacks. Enforcement of the *Brown* decision, however, proved difficult, and for ten years white Mississippians resisted all efforts to desegregate their schools. Instead, the state offered to retain its equalization program, which continued to prove ineffective. While blacks in Mississippi kept up their long struggle to end the inequitable dual school system, now with federal law on their side, white Mississippians used private and state-sanctioned economic and physical intimidation to maintain the segregated system they so deeply cherished. By 1964, however, a combination of persistent black efforts and federal pressure finally brought the first school desegregation to four Mississippi communities: Biloxi, Jackson, Harmony (Leake County), and Clarksdale.

White resistance to integrated education, however, did not disappear. Between 1965 and 1969, all Mississippi school districts were desegregated on a token basis through a mechanism known as freedom of choice, which supposedly allowed students to choose to go to any school in their school district. For whites, freedom of choice was seen as a minor retreat, one that allowed them to claim they had complied with the *Brown* decision, even as they continued to maintain dual schools. White Mississippians also continued their effort (and improved on it somewhat) to equalize black and white education, a further sign of their continuing devotion to dual schools. Black Mississippians, for their part, pressed forward and used the approved mechanism of freedom-of-choice school desegregation to demolish partially the dual school system (primarily by eliminating many previously all-white schools).

Mississippi's dual school system was finally abolished because of another landmark Supreme Court decision handed down in October 1969, *Alexander v. Holmes*. By the fall of 1970, all of the state's school systems had been integrated. Yet because the transition to unitary schools occurred under duress, whites generally either abandoned the public schools (in black-majority areas) or worked to find ways to limit the impact of school integration by preserving as much white supremacy over education as possible (in white-majority areas). As a result, schools were not truly integrated in Mississippi in 1970. They were transformed largely on white terms, and whites primarily wanted to continue, as much as possible, to keep their children out of the same classrooms blacks attended. In the process, blacks lost more than they gained with the coming of school integration, including a diminution of what little control they exercised over black education, as well as the elimination of key community institutions and important jobs in the public schools.

Despite a period of adjustment to the new reality of integrated education, in the years that followed 1970 black and white children in many Mississippi communities—typically those where blacks did not outnumber whites—attended school together on something more than a token scale, a significant development in a state that had fiercely resisted such interaction for quite a long time. The end of segregated schooling also allowed Mississippi politicians to make improvements to public education in ways not possible during the long era of dual schools. Even so, the integration of black and white education remained far from complete, and the racial considerations that affected so much of the development of public education over the years continues to cast a long shadow over the state's ability to educate its citizens in the twenty-first century.

In Mississippi, the project of public education foundered on the rock of racial discrimination. Both the long crusade to create and maintain a dual school system based on racial segregation and the twenty-year battle to transition to a unitary school system severely influenced the development of Mississippi's public education system and tragically affected the fortunes of the state's children. In recent years, there has been a great deal of discussion about the failures of public schools, not just in Mississippi but across the United States.[11] In part, these anxieties are to be expected, given the often unrealistic expectations Americans have had for public education. Indeed, throughout U.S. history, the project of public schooling has been invested with weighty and sometimes contradictory responsibilities, everything from ensuring an informed citizenry in a democratic republic to Americanizing the waves of immigrants arriving in the United States, from providing a literate workforce for an industrializing society to delivering both universal education and comprehensive social services. Even under ideal conditions, public schools in the United States perhaps could never solve all these problems or achieve all the grand objectives people set for them. Among the many social, economic, and political forces that have shaped public education in the United States, one of the most important in many parts of the country has been racial discrimination. This factor is perhaps easiest to trace in a state like Mississippi, where the impact of race on the evolution of public education is so easy to see because it has been so prominent for much of the state's history. Yet the ways in which racial concerns ultimately weakened the institution of public education in Mississippi are not unique to the Magnolia State.

ABBREVIATIONS

AFL-CIO   Mississippi AFL-CIO Records, 1947–86, Southern Labor Archives, Georgia State University, Atlanta

AFSC   American Friends Service Committee Archives, Philadelphia

ARC   Amistad Research Center, New Orleans

BIENNIAL   *Biennial Report and Recommendations of the State Superintendent of Public Education*, Mississippi State Department of Education, Jackson

DSU   Charles W. Capps Jr. Archives, Delta State University, Cleveland, Mississippi

FBI-GRN   FBI Files: Grenada, Mississippi, Public School Riots, 1966–67, McCain Library and Archives, University of Southern Mississippi, Hattiesburg

FDCOX   Federal District Court, Oxford, Mississippi

FIS   Freedom Information Service Records

GEBR-MS   General Education Board Records, Early Southern Program: Mississippi

JCS   John C. Stennis Papers, Congressional and Political Research Center, Mississippi State University, Starkville

LBJ   Lyndon Baines Johnson Library, Austin, Texas

LC   Library of Congress, Washington, D.C.

LF   Leesha Faulkner Civil Rights Collection, McCain Library and Archives, University of Southern Mississippi, Hattiesburg

MC-CPL	Oral History Collection, Madison County–Canton Public Library, Canton, Mississippi
MCHR	Mississippi Council on Human Relations Papers, Mississippi Department of Archives and History, Jackson
MCLA	McCain Library and Archives, University of Southern Mississippi, Hattiesburg
MDAH	Mississippi Department of Archives and History, Jackson
MFDP	Mississippi Freedom Democratic Party
MHC	Oral History Collection, Mary Holmes College, West Point, Mississippi
MOHP	Mississippi Oral History Program, McCain Library and Archives, University of Southern Mississippi, Hattiesburg
MS-FB	Records of the Assistant Commissioner for the State of Mississippi, 1865–69, Records of the Bureau of Refugees, Freedmen, and Abandoned Lands, RG 105, National Archives, Washington, D.C.
MSU	Mitchell Memorial Library, Mississippi State University, Starkville
NA	National Archives, Washington, D.C.
NAACPLDF	National Association for the Advancement of Colored People Legal Defense and Educational Fund
PBJ	Paul B. Johnson Jr. Papers, McCain Library and Archives, University of Southern Mississippi, Hattiesburg
RG	Record Group
SCRLR	Southern Civil Rights Litigation Records
SHC	Southern Historical Collection, University of North Carolina at Chapel Hill Libraries, Chapel Hill
SHSW	State Historical Society of Wisconsin, Madison
TCA	Tougaloo College Archives, Tougaloo, Mississippi
UM	Department of Archives and Special Collections, J. D. Williams Library, University of Mississippi, Oxford
WHCF	White House Central Files
WHSF-SMOF	White House Special Files, Staff Members and Office Files, Nixon Project, National Archives, Washington, D.C.

THE HARDEST
DEAL OF ALL

CHAPTER ONE

TOO MANY SCHOOLS, TOO LITTLE MONEY

Mississippi's Dual Education System, 1870–1940

In the twentieth century, Governor William Winter did more than any other chief executive to advance the cause of public education in the state of Mississippi. His own education began in 1929 in the isolation and poverty of rural Grenada County. Because the nearest white public school was more than seven miles away, his mother, trained as a teacher, established a one-room schoolhouse in an abandoned outbuilding on the Winter farm. Two children attended during Winter's first year of schooling, joined by seven others the following session. By the 1931–32 academic year, Grenada had developed a transportation system to serve the white hinterlands of the county, and the future governor was fortunate to move to "an excellent school system" in the town of Grenada, where he completed his elementary and secondary education.[1]

As Winter settled into the relative comfort of the white schools of Grenada during the 1930s, Annie Stewart and other black students in Grenada saw the yellow buses pass by as they walked to the town's black schools. At times, some of the white children would spit on their black counterparts from the bus windows. Most of Stewart's treks to school were made during the winter since she generally only attended school between December and March, the slack times of the local agricultural cycle. On the coldest days, school was dismissed for lack of wood to heat her ramshackle school building.[2]

The experiences of Winter and Stewart in 1930s Mississippi suggest the ever-widening gap between the two parts of the state's dual education system, an increasingly "excellent" one for whites and a makeshift operation for blacks. Yet as Winter's story reveals, the state's entire public education system, both black and white, had a history of inadequacies to overcome, especially in its most rural areas, where the vast majority of the population lived. The shortcomings that permeated Mississippi's public education system could be traced to the effort to establish a dual school system. Creating two good public school systems in a state with a robust economy would have been an ambitious undertaking. In Mississippi, one of the poorest states in the Union, the state succeeded only in creating a mediocre school system for whites and an unbelievably impoverished school system for blacks. Although the logic of segregation meant that a poor state like Mississippi spent too little money for too many schools, white Mississippians still regarded their schools as quality institutions, primarily because they remained one-race schools, a fact ultimately more important than any other measure.

Before 1870, Mississippi had no real public education system. In the antebellum era, Mississippi's white leaders never embraced the notion that one of the state's duties was to provide free public schools for its children, an idea that carried the day in much of the nation outside the South during the 1840s and 1850s. The children of Mississippi's white elite generally received formal instruction at private expense, while the mass of the state's white children remained mired in illiteracy. A number of state politicians, such as A. G. Brown, who built his career in the 1840s on the support he garnered from poor whites, argued, with some limited success, for the necessity of building a public school system to raise his political constituency from the depths of ignorance and poverty. Beginning in 1848, the Mississippi legislature passed a number of public education laws, but they all proved ineffectual. Some covered only a limited number of counties, while others allowed a majority of "heads of families" to "file a written protest" and block the creation of a local system of tax-supported common schools. Antebellum leaders not only failed to construct a public school system to serve the white population but also crafted legislation that officially denied enslaved blacks access to education. Even so, some slaves did manage to learn to read and write through their own efforts or those of their masters.[3]

Emancipation revitalized the issue of public education in Mississippi. As black freedom and the dislocations of the Civil War undermined long-standing social relations, black Mississippians, like freedpeople throughout the South, clamored for schools. Once the conflict ceased, these desires only intensified. One official of the Freedmen's Bureau noted in the summer of 1865 that black Mississippians "all desire to learn to read and write, and spare no pains, and will render any service that may be required to those who will assist them in their attempts for knowledge." Indeed, though impoverished, the freedpeople contributed their meager resources to the venture of establishing schools and paying teachers. Although no black schools had been established in Jackson, the capital city, by the fall of 1865, in October 1865 a Freedman's Bureau official noted the "disposition on the part of the colored people to support schools at their own expense." Through the efforts of black Mississippians, and with the help of the Freedman's Bureau and Northern religious societies such as the American Missionary Association, by the summer of 1867 sixty-one black schools had been built in fifty Mississippi communities, teaching as many as forty-five hundred African American children.[4] While this number represented but a small fraction of the total eligible black school population, the rapid growth of these institutions and their avid support by the newly freed slaves confirmed that black Mississippians in the immediate postbellum world believed that education represented one of the cornerstones of a successful transition to freedom.

White Mississippians, however, were not so certain about the benefits of black education. Few agreed with the sentiments expressed by Robert W. Flournoy of Pontotoc County. Flournoy had represented his northeast Mississippi county in the 1861 secession convention, voting against the measure. Accepting the decision of the state's majority to withdraw from the Union, he organized a volunteer military company that was soon dispatched to Richmond. After arriving there, however, Flournoy realized he could not take up arms against the United States; he resigned his commission, returned to Pontotoc, and remained there throughout the war as a strong Unionist advocate. When the war ended, Flournoy launched a newspaper, *Equal Rights*, that advocated, among other things, "mixed" schools for black and white children. As Flournoy explained, "when children can play together, as black and white children do, I see no reason why it would poison them to go to school together."[5]

Almost all Mississippi whites disagreed with Flournoy's egalitarian sentiments on grounds of white supremacy and fears of miscegenation, but a minority nevertheless advocated education for blacks out of a combination of paternalism, self-interest, and a fear that Yankees would take the lead in the endeavor and "corrupt" the freedpeople. Edward Fontaine, an Episcopal minister who served as an ordnance officer for the Confederacy during the Civil War and who owned a plantation near Jackson, worried about Northern teachers educating the ex-slaves, but he also urged his fellow planters "to lose no time in setting schools for the colored children in operation upon their lands if they wish them cultivated by the better class of colored laborers. If no higher motive can prompt them to discharge this duty, self interest will compel them to do it," for blacks "will seek employment where they can send their children to school." Some planters heeded this advice. In the fall of 1866, the owner of Retirement Plantation turned to the Freedman's Bureau for help in setting up a school "for the benefit of my freedmen's children [about fifty] on the place." He had already allowed construction of a building that would serve as both church and school for his black workers and was seeking a teacher to lead a daytime school for the children and a night school for the adults. White citizens in Canton, Columbus, Corinth, Jackson, and other locales also donated funds to help construct black schoolhouses.[6]

The white opposition to black education in Reconstruction Mississippi, however, dwarfed the scattered white support. As Joseph Warren, superintendent of Mississippi schools for the Freedmen's Bureau, noted in 1865, white disapproval of black schooling "is so much more active a principle than faint and uninterested approval." Whites offered a host of reasons against educating the freedpeople. Some believed that blacks had no capacity for learning, so any money expended on educating them would be a huge waste. Others countered the economic argument advanced by Edward Fontaine by claiming that a "learned negro is a nuisance;—for while he is ignorant, stupid and loutish he may be compelled to labor; but as soon as he comes to know something, the white people cannot make so profitable use of him." As the former slaves struggled to create schools, whites showed their displeasure with the project in numerous ways: they refused to lease or sell buildings that might be used as black schoolhouses or refused to board white teachers who came south to serve as teachers; whites arrested black teachers as vagrants under Mississippi's Black Code; and black schools were attacked by white adults and children while in session or destroyed under the cover of darkness. These efforts in part succeeded in frustrating black education efforts. The Reverend J. P. Bardwell, working with the American Missionary Association in 1866, believed that "the fear of offending the whites deters many [freedpeople] from sending their children to school."[7]

While the majority of white Mississippians opposed education for the newly freed slaves, this position received little representation in the constitutional convention that met in 1868 to establish a post-Confederate government for the state. The convention was dominated by native and Northern white Republicans but also seated sixteen black delegates. One of the most hotly debated parts of the new constitution, Article VIII, dealt with public education. Most of the delegates supported the creation of some type of public school system, but little agreement existed on the specifics. The convention debated two measures supported by the black delegates, one that would have required integrated schools and another calling for compulsory attendance in the new public schools, but both were defeated. At the same time, the black delegates helped beat back a measure that would have required segregated schools. In the end, the convention agreed merely to require a state system of education, leaving it to the state legislature to define the details.[8]

When the first legislature of the new government convened in the winter of 1870, dominated by a similar group of white and black Republicans, it created a system of "free" public schools in which "all children between the ages of 5 and 21 shall have equal advantages." The divisive issue of whether these schools should be integrated was left to local option. Twenty-five parents in any county could establish a school that would receive public funds. Recognizing the opposition of whites to mixed schools, and indeed to the very idea of black education, neither blacks nor whites in the legislature pressed the issue of mixed schools, even those who strongly supported the principle of black equality. They recognized that the alternative to separate schools was likely no black schools rather than integrated ones. Lieutenant Governor Ridgely C. Powers, a transplanted white Northerner, noted that he had "no sympathy with the great outcry that is leveled against the rights of men, solely on the ground of color," but he agreed that the details of establishing public schools should be left to local people, who might "provide separate schools for white and black, or for good and bad children, or for large and small, or male and female children." Although two mixed-race schools operated in Jefferson County briefly in 1870 and 1871, all other local residents in the state chose to establish schools under the new law for one race only.[9]

By 1875, a number of all-black and all-white schools dotted the Mississippi landscape, although most of these new educational enterprises faced inadequate funding and, in the case of black schools, continued white hostility. Financing public schools proved difficult in a state still recovering from the ravages of war. Between 1870 and 1875, property values in Mississippi fell dramatically, shrinking the primary source of public education funding. Although many of the state's school buildings were donated structures, at times counties struggled to raise enough revenue simply to pay the salaries of their teachers. While some white taxpayers (who were generally the wealthiest Mississippians, the ones who had property) did not support taxation to pay for anybody's education, the vast majority of white taxpayers particularly resented the notion that any of their monies would finance black schooling.[10]

Throughout the five years of Republican oversight during Reconstruction, black public education had a rocky beginning. In white-majority areas of the state, such as east-central and northeast Mississippi, the Ku Klux Klan, which began to appear in the state during 1870, directed much of its anger at the entire enterprise of black public education. Black schoolhouses were damaged or completely destroyed in at least seventeen counties. School board members, superintendents, and teachers were threatened and attacked. Most of the victims were blacks or white Republicans, but some white Democrats who had dared work as teachers in the black schools also faced the Klan's wrath. By 1872, federal action had greatly weakened the Klan, and the most coercive forms of opposition to black education in east-central and northeast Mississippi ended, but the damage done to fledgling black schools in the area lingered for years.[11] In the state's black-majority districts, such as the Mississippi Delta, blacks exercised significantly more political power during Reconstruction and in some cases controlled the machinery of the new public schools. For instance, in Tunica County, at the north end of the Delta, blacks held a three-to-two majority on the county school board, and a black man, Edward Carter, served as superintendent of education from 1872 until 1875. While such power dampened displays of overt white hostility to black education, such as those found in east-central Mississippi, the white minority in the Delta refused to consider their schools as part of the same system as those of the black majority. Indeed, during his tenure, Carter found that he had little control over the white schools in Tunica County. When he went to inspect the white school in Austin, for example, the teacher and her pupils ran the school leader off the property.[12]

If the state's public education system struggled under the regime of its Republican founders, the experiment in public schooling suffered a more serious setback once the Democrats overthrew the Republicans in a violent coup d'état in 1875. The Democrats immediately set about dismantling the Republicans' entire education project of the preceding five years. According to the new Democratic state superintendent of education, the Republican creation of public schools was nothing less than "an unmitigated outrage upon the rights and liberties of the white people of the state. It was enacted to demoralize our people and to proselyte our children in the interest of a political party hostile to the dignity, interests and sensibilities of the white people of Mississippi."[13]

To bolster their point about the inherent evil of Republican-created public education, the Democrats could point to corruption at the top of the state's public education system. Soon after seizing control of the state, Democrats moved to impeach the black Republican state superintendent of education, Thomas W. Cardoza, for embezzling state funds. Although Mississippi's Reconstruction government had been relatively free of corruption (certainly more financially honest than the conservative Democrats who followed), Cardoza apparently was indeed guilty of embezzling state funds while circuit clerk in Warren County and as treasurer for Tougaloo College, which received small state appropriations under the Republican administrations. Shortly after Cardoza's impeachment trial began in the Mississippi Senate in February 1876, the school leader resigned. Cardoza's shady tenure only made it easier for Mississippi Democrats to do what Democrats did in every other southern state: reduce financial support for public education. The decreased funding for education was part of the larger Democratic effort to dismantle the activist state government created by Mississippi Republicans by drastically reducing taxes and state expenditures in all areas.[14]

After ensuring the impoverishment of the state's already-feeble public education system, the Democrats moved in 1878 to rewrite the 1870 education law to codify the racial segregation of the schools that already existed in fact. For the most part, Democratic legislators preserved the structure of public education created by their Republican predecessors. The 1878 law, however, contained important additions that mandated racial segregation and opened the door for widespread racial discrimination. The new law required "that the schools in each county shall be so arranged as to offer ample free school facilities to all educable youths in that county but white and colored children shall not be taught in the same school-house, but in separate school-houses." The law also detailed the geographic parameters of racial segregation by requiring that black and white schools be located at least two and a half miles apart, "unless there was an impassable barrier between them." In addition, the 1878 school law gave county superintendents the sole power to test teachers and award the appropriate teaching certificate, a measure that allowed white superintendents to shortchange black teachers whenever financially expedient.[15]

The Democratic legislature's declaration that Mississippi's public schools would remain racially separate was merely the first step in establishing white supremacy over public education. Achieving that goal did not happen overnight, but by the 1890s white supremacy and racial segregation were deeply embedded in Mississippi public education. For instance, black and white teachers initially continued to work together after the Democrats overthrew Mississippi's Republican government. When the Mississippi Teachers' Association held its first meeting in August 1877, both blacks and whites attended the conference. Ten years later, the association's annual meeting was still biracial. By the late 1880s, however, most white educators came to see the benefits of white supremacy, especially in a state with few resources. As early as the 1887 convention, white speakers from the Mississippi Delta could be heard complaining about the expense of "the education of the colored people, the burden of which rests upon the few whites." By 1889, the organization, by then known as the Mississippi State Teachers' Association and later called the Mississippi Education Association (MEA), had successfully barred all black teachers. After their exclusion from the Mississippi State Teachers' Association, black teachers did not have a professional organization until they established the Mississippi Association of Teachers in Colored Schools (MATCS) in 1906.[16]

A closer look at the Jackson public schools offers an example of how black control over black schooling eroded in the decade following the Democrats return to power in 1875. In 1872, Jackson had five public or "free" schools, three for blacks and two for whites. One was a black public school staffed by a group of Ohio Quakers. The city board of aldermen managed the schools and had unanimously adopted a policy in 1869 outlawing racial discrimination in the distribution of school funds, requiring that "no payment of funds for school purposes be made with the sanction of this body, unless all children, without regard to race or color, be entitled to receive the benefits therefrom." By 1875, only one black school remained, and it was housed in the St. James Hotel. In the late 1870s, this school, by then known as West Ward Colored School, moved to a benevolent hall on the corner of Farish and Griffith streets. While the black school in Jackson was not located in a public building and had not become firmly established, in these early years blacks continued to have a voice in the operation of their schools. In 1882, the three black trustees of West Ward, selected by Jackson's mayor and board of aldermen, were James Spellman, a forty-two-year-old Connecticut native who worked in an office; Peyton Robinson, a gardener in his late fifties; and Wilson Alexander, a forty-year-old farmer. These three men served on the Jackson school board with six white trustees, three from each of the two white schools.[17] Over the next several years, a move to improve the city's white public schools coincided with an effort to transform the school board into a body that only bothered with white education. In 1888, the Jackson Graded School opened, a consolidation of the two white schools, in a new building located directly behind the governor's mansion. In the same year, although the city's politicians continued to select trustees for both the white and black schools, city school board meetings became meetings of only the white trustees of Jackson Graded School.[18]

While the West Ward trustees still exercised control over the selection of teachers and the day-to-day operation of their school, in 1888 they were essentially excluded from all discussions about the allocation of public resources for public education. For the next four years, the white-only school board, as much as possible, simply pretended that West Ward was not a part of the Jackson public school system. Ironically, that approach soon had to be adjusted because of the passage of a new school segregation law, one that would conform to the state constitution of 1890. The amended school law of 1892 required that "separate schools shall be maintained for children of the white and colored races." The law also mandated the establishment of separate white and black school districts within a school administrative unit. With the law requiring that school districts "establish" and "maintain" a dual school system, the Jackson Graded School Board, with the blessing of Jackson's mayor and board of aldermen, moved to take legal control of the West Ward School. Its first act was to approve a slate of teachers at the black school for fall term 1892. The all-white school board also focused on maintaining a strict color line between the city's white and black schools. For example, after a group of white parents lodged a complaint in September 1892 that Mary Bloxum's nine-year-old son was "tainted with negro blood," the board investigated. They concluded, based on "common rumor" and the "appearance of the child," that the boy should be removed from the white school.[19]

Although Jackson's all-white school board had acquired legal authority to run Jackson's black school and uphold the color line, the law apparently imposed no burden on the white authorities there, or elsewhere in Mississippi, to pursue educational progress for the district's black students, a goal they increasingly strove for on behalf of their own children. The Mississippi Supreme Court in 1893 essentially absolved the white school boards in the state, then assuming or beginning to exercise power over the black schools, of any obligation to distribute equally the limited resources available to improve public education. The 1893 case sprang from an 1890 lawsuit by three black property owners in the southwest Mississippi town of Brookhaven who refused to pay their taxes and sued the town over the local board of aldermen's decision to issue $9,000 in bonds to build a white school. Clara Washington owned one acre of town property in Brookhaven, as did Hartwell Scott. The other plaintiff, Paul Gage, held two town lots. The plaintiffs protested the fact that they had to pay taxes to fund white schools, even though "no school house has been provided for the negro or colored children" of Brookhaven. A Lincoln County chancery judge rejected the plaintiffs' claims, and the Mississippi Supreme Court affirmed the decision on appeal. The plaintiffs' appeal argued that Brookhaven's bond issue to assist only the white schools violated the requirement in the 1868 constitution for a "uniform system of free public schools." The supreme court noted that the recently approved 1890 constitution had not included the "absurd provision" of the earlier constitution. The court also asked how it could be illegal to establish a separate school for whites when that was exactly what the constitution of 1890 mandated. Whether public funds were also used to improve black schools was apparently immaterial.[20]

From the beginning, then, there was little hope that separate schools in Mississippi were ever intended to be equal schools. In 1899, the U.S. Supreme Court, in *Cumming v. Richmond County Board of Education*, sanctioned the logic of the Brookhaven decision by declaring that individual states could determine the exact parameters of what constituted a separate but equal education.[21] In Mississippi, with the blessing of the federal mandate in *Cumming*, separate but equal education quickly became a fiction. Disfranchisement of black (and many poor white) Mississippi voters coincided with the coming of de jure segregation, so black Mississippians could offer very little resistance to unfair treatment from a government they had no say in creating.

Before white control of education had been firmly secured in the 1890s, white and black education, while unequally funded, remained almost everywhere, except perhaps in the state's largest towns, equally inadequate. As Sidney D. Redmond, a black physician, attorney, and businessman in Jackson, recalled in the 1940s, during his youth in rural Hinds County in the 1880s, "gross discriminations" between white and black education did not exist. School statistics from the period bear out Redmond's recollection. A comparison of black and white Mississippi public schools in the 1894–95 school year illustrates not only the emerging inequalities between white and black education (already greatest in the Delta) but also the overall dismal state of public education in Mississippi at that time (see table 1). In general, all rural schools in the state had short terms, few supplies, and poorly paid teachers leading large classes in one-, two-, or three-teacher operations. Urban areas, on the other hand, were generally able to provide a better education for both black and white students than rural districts. As late as 1904, while the average annual school term in Mississippi's cities and towns was 166 days (8.3 months), the corresponding figure for all the state's rural districts was only 110 days (5.5 months). Black teachers everywhere in the state, however, taught more students for less pay; at the same time, black teachers in Mississippi towns frequently received higher salaries than white teachers in all rural areas except the Delta. Overall, the gap between rural black and white

Table 1. Statistics for Mississippi Black and White Schools, Selected Districts, 1894–95

School district	No. of schools	No. of teachers	Enrollment	Student to faculty ratio	Teacher salaries (avg. monthly)
Cities/towns:					
Jackson	W: 1	W: 16	W: 732	W: 46/1	W: $51.56
	B: 1	B: 9	B: 649	B: 72/1	B: $35.00
Natchez	W: 1	W: 16	W: 566	W: 35/1	W: $47.05
	B: 1	B: 13	B: 798	B: 61/1	B: $43.30
SW MS:					
Amite County	W: 47	W: 65	W: 2,254	W: 35/1	W: $26.52
	B: 42	B: 57	B: 2,899	B: 51/1	B: $19.91
Franklin County	W: 35	W: 50	W: 1,570	W: 31/1	W: $32.42
	B: 18	B: 24	B: 1,045	B: 44/1	B: $23.61
East-Central MS					
Choctaw County	W: 52	W: 63	W: 2,306	W: 37/1	W: $22.44
	B: 23	B: 26	B: 1,103	B: 42/1	B: $18.86
Attala County	W: 88	W: 91	W: 3,472	W: 38/1	W: $29.26
	B: 53	B: 53	B: 2,830	B: 53/1	B: $18.15
Delta:					
Bolivar County	W: 44	W: 45	W: 747	W: 17/1	W: $52.00
	B: 67	B: 124	B: 5,347	B: 43/1	B: $28.00
Coahoma County	W: 25	W: 26	W: 478	W: 18/1	W: $42.23
	B: 38	B: 40	B: 2,622	B: 66/1	B: $22.26
NE MS:					
Lee County	W: 53	W: 63	W: 2,972	W: 47/1	W: $32.96
	B: 27	B: 28	B: 1,679	B: 60/1	B: $20.63
Lafayette County	W: 75	W: 88	W: 3,023	W: 34/1	W: $31.78
	B: 45	B: 51	B: 2,364	B: 46/1	B: $17.78
South MS:					
Jones County	W: 51	W: 82	W: 3,344	W: 41/1	W: $21.64
	B: 9	B: 9	B: 492	B: 57/1	B: $22.14
Covington County	W: 49	W: 61	W: 1,814	W: 30/1	W: $23.81
	B: 19	B: 22	B: 1,043	B: 47/1	B: $17.49

Source: *Annual Report of County Superintendents*, 1894–95, RG 50, vol. 18, MDAH.

schools remained relatively small, especially compared to the much wider chasm that would soon exist between the two school systems.[22]

A dramatic upgrade of Mississippi's white schools, however, began to occur soon after these statistics were compiled, a trend that continued for the next several decades. White politicians in Mississippi justified plans for a whites-only education upgrade with claims that blacks were inferior; that the funds used for black schools were essentially wasted; that education for blacks would lead to all kinds of calamities; and that the money spent on black education, especially in a poor state like Mississippi, could better be used to support white public education. State legislator E. A. Rowan began arguing in the late nineteenth century that giving any educational advantages to blacks would mean "crippling the facilities for educating whites." In addition, Rowan asked how much sense it made for the state to make literacy a disfranchising mechanism while still requiring the state to maintain common schools for blacks. For Rowan, such logical inconsistency could only lead to one outcome: "Should the white people continue to educate the negroes they will, in [the] course of time, be able to override the suffrage barriers, and will want to run the state government." James K. Vardaman, governor of Mississippi from 1904 to 1908, promoted increased funding for and modernization of white education as the cornerstone of his progressive administration. Vardaman, however, received little support from the legislature for increased education expenditures. As an alternative to new spending, Vardaman advocated eliminating or reducing spending for black schools. In 1906, Vardaman told the Mississippi legislature that he wanted to "put a stop to the worse than wasting of a half million dollars annually—money taken from the toiling white men and women of Mississippi—and devoted to the vain purpose of trying to make something of the negro which the Great Architect of the Universe failed to provide for in the original plan of creation." Vardaman believed that education "ruined" plantation laborers; he also thought that black education would lead "to rapes and murders, which precipitated the unpleasantries of hangings and burnings." In other words, black education ultimately undermined one of the primary reasons for preserving racial segregation: to prevent social equality and miscegenation.[23]

Both Rowan and Vardaman also catered to class fears in the white-majority areas of Mississippi by pointing out that the same Delta whites who blocked new expenditures for white schools diverted the sizable funds the region received for black education to create white school systems superior to any found in the poorer Hill counties. Although state school funds were distributed on the basis of how many school-aged children lived in each county, Delta districts used most of the money they received for the region's black majority to invest in educating the Delta's relatively small white population. At the same time, poorer Hill counties had to use their meager funds in part to support black education. Segregationist champions, such as Vardaman, advocated that the school fund be divided between black and white schools based on how much each race actually paid in taxes, a scheme that would have meant more money for white schools, especially in those areas outside the Delta. Despite repeated attempts to enact such a provision, Delta politicians, who recognized that such plans would cripple white schools in their area, repeatedly blocked the efforts.[24]

While the most extreme measures advocated by Vardaman and others were never adopted, their overall scheme was gradually put in place over the next three decades. The white schools were modernized, primarily through consolidation. State and local funding for white education increased dramatically. State support for black education stagnated, seriously impeding— though not halting—the development of black education.

The most important of the Progressive Era reforms to improve white rural schools in Mississippi and other southern states was school consolidation, which allowed small schools to combine to form larger, graded schools, with at least one teacher for each grade. At the same time, control of these consolidated schools passed from local school trustees to centralized, usually countywide, school authorities who gained the power to raise taxes on a district- or countywide basis. The modernized school districts used their newly available local funds to improve white schools by extending the school term, raising teacher salaries, and instituting a system of public transportation of students to the larger, more amply furnished, consolidated schools. White Mississippians frequently objected to consolidation because of the additional taxes or the loss of local control. The protests occasionally turned violent, as anticonsolidation whites burned schools and physically assaulted school officials. Despite losing a few local battles, the consolidators ultimately won the war for a reform that increasingly gained popularity as a mechanism for bolstering the educational opportunities available to the white youth of Mississippi's rural districts.[25]

The Mississippi legislature's initial school consolidation measure, passed in 1910, provided for the creation of rural school districts that could levy taxes and issue bonds. Over the next thirty-five years, whites took advantage of the new law to initiate a massive consolidation of their schools, a project financed largely by a substantial increase in local property taxes. In the 1909–10 school year, Mississippi had 4,256 rural white schools; by 1946 the state had 861 consolidated white schools and only 164 that had not yet been consolidated. State leaders hailed the changing structure of white education as a dramatic improvement. As the Mississippi Board of Development noted in 1944, "There is as much difference between the modern Mississippi consolidated school plant and the one-teacher school it has replaced as there is between the modern automobile and the 1890 horse and buggy."[26]

As a general rule, whites did not extend this basic yet costly technique of school modernization to black education. During the 1909–10 school year, the state had 3,006 black schools, a number that by 1946 had swollen to 3,737, only 100 of which had been consolidated.[27] Between 1910, when the state enacted consolidation legislation, and 1930, only 15 black schools were consolidated in the entire state, and almost half of these were in Forrest County, located in south Mississippi. This county clearly had the early progressive edge among the state's counties, at least in terms of assisting the development of black education. Before consolidation, the county had 26 black schools, only 2 of which were located in structures that one might identify as schoolhouses; the remainder held classes in one-room shacks or even sawmill sheds. The average length of the school term in these institutions was just forty days; the average white school term at the time was not much better, only fifty-nine days. When a new county superintendent, John Gay, took office in 1918, he helped convince the county authorities to consolidate not only the white schools but also the black ones. Forrest County officials moved to improve black education perhaps in an effort to keep the black population that had only recently moved to the area to work in the timber industry from leaving, at a time when the opportunities for migration out of the state had become more attractive. Whatever the reasons, the county soon had a $75,000 high school for blacks in Hattiesburg, built with bond money authorized by white voters in the city, as well as five additional consolidated schools around the county, all built with help from the Julius

Rosenwald Fund, a northern philanthropy, which provided building funds but required local matching funds. The county even provided transportation for black students to the new consolidated schools in "auto trucks," a segregated service almost unheard of elsewhere in the state.[28]

Although they spent only a small sum of money on their black schools, Forrest County officials created perhaps the best public educational facilities for blacks in the entire state during the 1920s and 1930s, an achievement that offers a sad commentary on the continuing poverty of black education in the state at the time but also provides a revealing example of the impact of school consolidation. In the 1930s, the five consolidated black schools in Forrest County located outside of the city of Hattiesburg had modern desks and blackboards, "deep wells," drinking fountains, and other amenities not found in the typical one-room schoolhouse. Accompanying the improvements in the school plant was an upgrading of the system's black teachers. By 1940, twenty-six of the twenty-eight teachers working in the county's five consolidated black schools had done some college work, and all were high school graduates, making the faculty in the Forrest County black schools easily the most educated black faculty in the state. By comparison, a more typical district in the state, such as Amite County in southwest Mississippi, had only sixteen high school graduates among its fifty-five black teachers in 1940. Consolidation in Forrest County also meant the extension of the school term, initially to seven months and by 1940 to eight months. These improvements drew area blacks to the public schools; during the 1930s, over 70 percent of eligible black children attended school in Forrest County, a significant achievement in a state—without a compulsory attendance law—that regularly failed to attract large numbers of black or white students to its schools. Consolidation of black schools meant a greater investment by whites in black schools, and even if that investment still lagged far behind monies expended on white schools, at least the disparities did not reach the absurd proportions they did in other counties. In 1940, Forrest County's per capita expenditure on its black schools was $18.20, while $37.84 went to each white child; in the same year, Amite County officials spent only $3.51 per black student, while lavishing $30.24 on every white student.[29]

More typically, school consolidation was for whites only, and it widened the inequalities between the education of the two races throughout Mississippi. For one thing, white teachers in the consolidated schools began to get more training for their profession and more pay. White teacher salaries in rural districts increased more than 90 percent between 1890 and 1937, while black teacher salaries in the same areas remained essentially stagnant. Other inequities created by white school consolidation were readily apparent to black Mississippians. Sidney Redmond of Hinds County understood that the failure to consolidate black rural schools along with their white counterparts in his county led to easily-recognizable educational inequities: "the sending of the Negro boy and girl on a several mile trudge, to an old 'tumbled down,' one or two teacher-room shack, where one teacher has to try to teach 5, 6, or 7 grades, while the white child whizzes by in a bus, bought and paid for with the taxes paid by all the people, to a 12 grade school house, of 12 or 15 rooms, of commodious proportions, manned by 15 or 20 sell [*sic*] paid teachers—where the work is so divided and systemized that real results are possible."[30]

While providing little benefit for blacks, the consolidation of white schools created additional burdens for black schools and black taxpayers. In some places, county officials actually moved black schools to make way for the new, larger white schools. Hinds County officials, for example, rebuilt the rural Liberty Grove School in the 1940s—as "another little frame 2 or 3 room shack"—a short distance from its original location so that they could erect a large white consolidated school on Liberty Grove's initial site. Black landowners around the state had to pay the additional taxes imposed on residents to effect consolidation of white schools without receiving any of the educational benefits for their children. Despite the claims of whites that they subsidized black education, the fact was that Progressive reforms such as consolidation created a situation in which blacks with property often financed white education. In the late 1930s, black landowners in Prentiss chafed under the realization that "we are assessed with a 15 mill levy for the White Consolidated schools and are to have more for a bond issue, and have repeatedly [been] denied a consolidated school for we Colored." The landowners asked, without success, to be exempted from the new taxation.[31]

The white-only reforms that widened the gap between black and white education were backed by increased expenditures for white education at both the state and local levels (see table 2). Despite continual increases in the amount of money spent on public education in Mississippi, the state actually did not have enough money to construct even one adequate school system. Indeed, by 1939 Mississippi was spending a greater percentage of its public funds on public education than any other state in the Union. But it was not enough. Mississippi education officials estimated in 1939 that even if the state spent all of its public monies on education, it would still need an additional $9 million to reach the national spending average on education. Far from having any hope of achieving national parity in education spending, Mississippi could not even keep up with the similar funding increases ongoing in the early twentieth century in other southern states. In 1930, despite a growing education budget, Mississippi continued to rank near the bottom of the southern list for spending on white education, coming in slightly ahead only of Georgia. In fact, the amount neighboring Tennessee spent per capita for black education in 1930, the highest in the region, was actually slightly better than Mississippi's spending on white education.[32]

The sad reality of Mississippi's economy, combined with the fact that blacks had no political voice in the state, ensured that black education received only the most token amounts from state and local treasuries. In the 1930s and early 1940s, while funding for white education continued to grow, the state only slightly increased the amount of money spent on black schools. By 1942, the spending ratio on white and black education, which in 1914 had stood at more than five to one in favor of white education, had grown to almost eight to one (see table 3). Much of the disparity arose from the distribution of local funds, which became increasingly important sources of capital for public education (see table 2). To receive a share of the local levies and to receive their equal share of the state funds, allocated to each

Table 2. *State and Local Spending on Public Education, Mississippi, 1909 and 1942 (percentage of total funds spent on public education)*

	State funds	Local funds
1909	$1,320,000 (69%)	$600,000 (31%)
1942	$7,240,000 (43%)	$9,590,000 (57%)

Sources: *Biennial Report and Recommendations of the State Superintendent of Public Education* (Jackson: Mississippi State Department of Education, 1911); and *Biennial Report and Recommendations of the State Superintendent of Public Education* (Jackson: Mississippi State Department of Education, 1943).

district on the basis of its white and black populations, black Mississippians had to depend on the goodwill of their white employers and neighbors. As J. A. Travis, one of the white officials who supervised black education for the State Department of Education, noted in 1939, "The most valuable asset to the average Negro School is sympathetic support of the white people of the community." Sometimes that support was forthcoming, as when a group of Calhoun County whites, after attending a Christmas program at a local black school, agreed in the late 1930s to help repair the roof at the institution. But all too often white officials refused to use local tax funds to improve black schools in their areas. In 1917, for example, the elected superintendent of the Carroll County schools resolved to do very little for black education in his district because of his fear that additional aid to black schools would result in the loss of his political post.[33]

At the same time, since whites at the local level completely controlled the dual school system, they often "took" from the share provided by the state for black education and simply transferred it to the white schools. Public officials sanctioned such theft. In 1916, the outgoing superintendent of education in Lauderdale County confessed to a scheme of requiring salary kickbacks from the black teachers in his district. When he was indicted for misappropriating funds, his defense was that the diverted money was intended for the Lauderdale County schools, specifically to upgrade his office and to buy new furnishings for various white schools. Had he been able to prove such a use for the "misappropriated" money, this defense would have led to an acquittal, but unable to secure the necessary evidence,

Table 3. Per Capita Spending on Black and White Public Education, Mississippi, 1914–15, 1929–30, and 1942–43

	1914–15	1929–30	1942–43
Per capita, black	$1.53	$5.94	$6.16
Per capita, white	$8.20	$31.33	$47.95

Sources: Henry Allen Bullock, *A History of Negro Education in the South* (New York: Praeger, 1967), 172; "Public School Enrollment and Expenditures in Six Southern States," 1944, General Education Board Records, Early Southern Program: Mississippi, reel 78.

the court sentenced the superintendent to four years in the state penitentiary.[34] This kind of subterfuge was not actually necessary. Indeed, many school districts, especially those with large black populations, simply diverted, on a regular basis, the funds appropriated to them by the state for black education to finance the schooling of their white minorities. Only twenty-one of Mississippi's eighty-two counties in 1937 spent as much or more on black education as the funds they received from the state based on the size of their black population; most of these counties were located in southeast and northeast Mississippi, areas with small black populations (see map 1). On the other hand, at least thirty-three counties spent less than 75 percent of their allocation intended for the black population on black education; fourteen of these were in the Delta, while eleven others were black-majority counties in other parts of the state.

The disparity in the public funding of black and white education in Mississippi was not merely a result of a politically enfranchised yet economically impoverished group stealing from their poorer, powerless neighbors. The failure to provide public assistance to black schooling also resulted from the belief among whites in Mississippi, and most whites elsewhere, that black education had to be structured in a way that recognized the difference between white and black intellectual abilities. Such ideas had been present among the Northern missionaries who came south to help establish black education in the Reconstruction years, and these notions continued to flourish as the natural complements to the separate but equal doctrine. So-called white education progressives championed the creation of a separate type of education for blacks, one that recognized the "mental differences" between the races. In 1903, at the Sixth Conference for Education in the South, Mississippi education reformer R. B. Fulton noted that the primary problem in the area of black education was "to determine what racial differentiation in the mode of education should be made for the negro race in view of his racial peculiarities and his social condition and family life." Most whites who supported improvements in black education agreed with the suggestion most famously proffered by Booker T. Washington that some kind of industrial or vocational education represented the curriculum best suited for former slaves.[35]

While educators and politicians also advocated vocational education for rural, poor white Mississippians in the early twentieth century, the notion

Mississippi, 1940
% Black Population

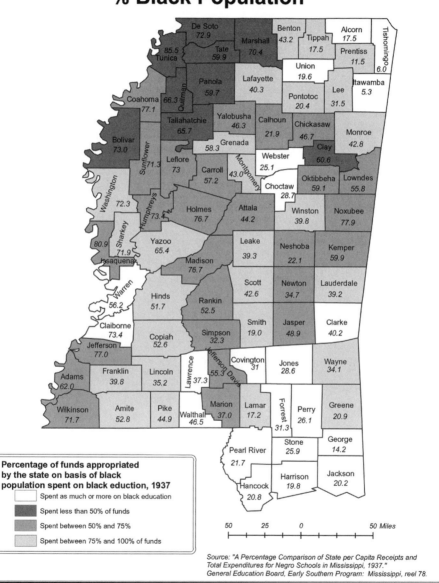

Percentage of funds appropriated
by the state on basis of black
population spent on black eduction, 1937

☐ Spent as much or more on black education

■ Spent less than 50% of funds

▨ Spent between 50% and 75%

▨ Spent between 75% and 100% of funds

50   25   0   50 Miles

Source: "A Percentage Comparison of State per Capita Receipts and
Total Expenditures for Negro Schools in Mississippi, 1937."
General Education Board, Early Southern Program: Mississippi, reel 78.

that black intellectual capacities precluded anything but a vocational track for all blacks became deeply entrenched and fixed in whites' minds and in Mississippi's official public policy concerning black education. Consider these pronouncements from the Mississippi State Department of Education in the early 1940s. Agency officials claimed that Mississippi was "making progress" in "training the Negroes of Mississippi." The state's black elementary schools taught students not only how to read and write but also "how to talk, how to use numbers, how to use their hands in doing their work and in earning a living, how to be clean and healthy, how to be honest, truthful, courteous, and how to take care of property." According to the white men who supervised black education, the high school curriculum for blacks "should emphasize, above everything else, health and economic efficiency." It should also "be adapted to the needs of the students and should equip them for the vocations in which they are to engage—agriculture, carpentry, plastering, blacksmithing, auto mechanics, domestic service, etc."[36] Thus, even the white friends of black education in Mississippi continued to see black schooling as a fundamentally separate project from the parallel enterprise of teaching white youth. By definition, the two undertakings could never be equal. It was a small step from that position to the justification that little reason existed to provide equal funding for two such fundamentally different initiatives.

The state of Mississippi, and individual white citizens, did continue to provide some resources to the project of educating the state's black majority. These funds, however grudgingly doled out by whites, provided important resources for the growth of black education in the state. Equally crucial to the advancement of black schooling in Mississippi in the first half of the twentieth century was the financial assistance provided by northern philanthropists and the valiant efforts of black citizens to provide for themselves.[37]

A number of northern philanthropies aided the development of black public education in Mississippi during the first third of the twentieth century, including the Julius Rosenwald Fund, the Anna T. Jeanes Fund, the John F. Slater Fund, and the General Education Board. The northern benefactors who provided these monies generally embraced the industrial or vocational model of black education, which made the acceptance of the Yankee funds palatable to white Mississippians. Black Mississippians, for their part, gladly accepted the additional financial support for their efforts to educate their children, although they did not always completely accept their funders' notion that their children required a separate curriculum specifically suited to black intellectual abilities.[38]

The various northern philanthropies played different roles in advancing black education in Mississippi. The General Education Board provided funds for a variety of projects, including teacher education, the development of black agricultural high schools, and black higher education, which at that time in Mississippi primarily meant Alcorn A&M College in southwest Mississippi. The Slater Fund provided donations for schools designated as county training schools; these institutions supplied instruction, including an industrial curriculum, through at least the eighth grade and ensured that "in the last year some training, however elementary, for the work of teaching" would be undertaken. In a state like Mississippi, which made very little provision for training black teachers, the aid from the Slater Fund helped improve the educational qualifications of black teachers, though in no way up to the standards white teachers were increasingly held. The Jeanes Fund, initially established through a $1 million endowment provided by a wealthy Philadelphia Quaker, Anna T. Jeanes, allowed southern states to hire individuals who served as supervisors for rural black schools. Jeanes supervisors, as they came to be called, were typically college-educated women who would visit the schools in their county on a regular basis and do everything from helping to teach certain subjects to checking on attendance to helping raise funds for the schools. By 1938, Mississippi had fifty Jeanes supervisors working in fifty-five counties, and their dedicated efforts had a positive impact on some of the state's most impoverished black schools.[39]

Of all the northern philanthropic efforts, however, the Julius Rosenwald Fund, which provided monies to aid in the construction of black elementary schools, had perhaps the most visible impact in Mississippi. Julius Rosenwald, the Chicago merchant responsible for transforming Sears, Roebuck and Company into America's top retail firm in the early twentieth century, was convinced by Booker T. Washington to invest in building common schools for blacks in the South, which would serve as feeders for Tuskegee and similar institutions throughout the region. Between 1914 and 1932, the Rosenwald Fund contributed over $4.3 million to this effort.

During the same period, Mississippi received over $539,000 of these funds to help construct 557 black schoolhouses as well as seventy-six additional school-related buildings, such as teachers' homes and industrial shops.[40]

White school officials controlled the Rosenwald Fund contributions, an arrangement that did not always lead to the best use of the additional revenue. On the one hand, white school officials sometimes took little care to see that the northern windfall reached its intended target. For example, the Rosenwald Fund's overseers had ongoing concerns about Bura Hilbun, the Mississippi State Department of Education supervisor of rural schools who oversaw the distribution of Rosenwald capital in the state for much of the 1920s. S. L. Smith, the Rosenwald Fund's director for southern schools, described Hilbun as "very careless in all kinds of reports and records—causing us much inconvenience and concern." Soon after Hilbun left his state education post in 1928 to take a job in Theodore Bilbo's second gubernatorial administration, reports began to surface about unpaid matching funds to both Yazoo and Tunica counties for Rosenwald school projects, as well as other missing monies controlled by Hilbun from the General Education Board and various relief funds established to help victims of the Mississippi River flood of 1927. Although indicted by a Hinds County grand jury in 1929, Hilbun was acquitted on charges of receiving money under false pretenses, while two trials on embezzlement charges both ended in mistrials.[41]

Although the fraud of a Hilbun was the exception rather than the rule, even well-meaning white school officials generally failed to use the additional monies provided by northern sources to modernize the black schools in the same manner new school funding had been steadily transforming the white schools during the same period. For example, when P. F. Williams, the superintendent of education in Coahoma County, moved to improve black education in the 1920s, in part supported by the revenue available from the Rosenwald Fund and other northern philanthropies, he ignored his own recent and successful consolidation of most of the county's white schools. Rather, he developed a plan that, while providing some new opportunities for black education, perpetuated some of the worst features of the old system. When Williams began his reorganization program, the county had eighty black schools, most located in black churches. Williams transformed these facilities into seventy elementary schools, many of them located in new structures financed in part by the Rosenwald Fund. None of these elementary schools, however, was larger than a three-teacher operation. To his credit, Williams also helped create a series of junior high schools around the county (for grades six through eight) and also launched the state's first agricultural high school for blacks. Like Williams, most whites who bothered at all about improving black education generally chose to replace dilapidated one-room schoolhouses with newer ungraded ones, where one or two teachers still taught several different grades. The Rosenwald Fund helped finance this construction. Indeed, during the 1920s the state of Mississippi used the Rosenwald monies to support a building project that duplicated for black Mississippians the outmoded one-, two-, or three-room schoolhouses increasingly rejected by whites as inadequate. For example, less than a fourth of the 123 Rosenwald-assisted projects in Mississippi between 1920 and 1922 housed more than three teachers.[42]

Clearly, the additional money provided by the Rosenwald Fund did not help modernize black education in the same way additional state and local funds for the county's white schools had helped end the era of the one-room schoolhouse. Even so, the Rosenwald schools represented a major improvement. In fact, the Rosenwald Fund provided the seed money that spurred a dramatic improvement in the physical plant of the state's black school system.

One key aspect of the Rosenwald school construction project was that the money provided by the Rosenwald Fund had to be matched by state or local funds, as well as by contributions from black residents. An early fund director, Francis W. Shepardson, noted in 1922 "that the main thing sought in the [school construction] plan was to get the Negroes to work for themselves." Whites often agreed to temporary local tax increases to raise the required matching funds, a relatively cheap method of building black schools. In Tunica County, for instance, which had a large black population but which had spent few local resources on black education before World War I, whites agreed in the late 1920s to impose a three-year county levy that raised $33,000 as matching funds for the construction of twenty-four Rosenwald schoolhouses. The contribution of blacks to Rosenwald-built schools was generally quite substantial. For example, the 633 Rosenwald buildings constructed in Mississippi between 1914 and 1932 cost over $2.8 million. Of this amount, blacks contributed 30 percent, the Rosenwald

Fund gave 19 percent, whites contributed 11 percent, and 40 percent came from county funds. Thus, in order to build schools for their children, blacks submitted to a system of "double taxation" in the early twentieth century.[43]

Black parents used the second, self-imposed tax to complete the modernization of black education whites refused to fund. School consolidation is a good example. Such reform for black schools generally occurred only when blacks were willing to invest their own funds in the project. Local officials bankrolled school consolidation, which meant larger, graded schools, but white leaders had no incentive (since most blacks were disfranchised) and no legal obligation to aid black citizens. By the late 1930s, county governments sometimes did contribute funds to help build larger, consolidated black schools, but most local authorities still expected blacks to raise most or all of the monies to ameliorate their children's education. For example, when blacks in white-majority Jasper County moved to create a six-teacher consolidated school in Shady Grove during the late 1930s, they received $150 from the county board of education, a few contributions from local whites, and 4,500 feet of wood from the nearby Masonite Corporation. The bulk of the funds to build the new school were amassed by blacks themselves. The principal of the school held fish fries and "went out on a speaking tour to every little church in every little corner and raised money." In Lafayette County, black trustees for the Taylor school organized a fund-raising drive in January 1937 to collect $3,000 to build a five-room school. The three trustees secured $10 donations from those who had available cash and pledges of free labor or timber from those unable to give money. By the summer of 1937, the building program had gathered $1,000 and numerous promises for in-kind donations, and work on the new schoolhouse commenced that fall. Similarly, after whites in Monroe County voted down a bond issue to build a consolidated black school in the neighborhood of Union Grove during the early 1940s, "the colored people of the community . . . started raising money by subscription and giving suppers and picture shows." The building was completed in 1945, but the black community did not finish paying for their new school until 1949. Black Mississippians also took advantage of used or unclaimed resources to complete their school-building projects. In the northeast Mississippi county of Benton, the first modern black school, Old Salem, was started in the 1940s after blacks in the county secured leftover lumber from Camp McCain near Grenada and gravel for the foundation from an abandoned gravel pit in Marshall County.[44]

Beyond building projects, a host of smaller contributions from the black community aided their children's schooling in a variety of ways. Edna Scott's father, a renter in Mound Bayou, scraped together the extra funds in the 1930s to keep her four-month school open for a couple of extra months. Other parents did the same, sometimes "they would go together, and pay this teacher in either groceries or in money, whatever they had." In the age before public transportation for students attending black schools (not provided by the state for black public schools until the 1940s or later), parents used their own vehicles to haul black children to classes. Edna Scott's father, for instance, at one time was transporting as many as fourteen children to the local black schools. Mississippi had an active black Parent-Teacher Association (PTA), first formed in 1923 by a group of women in Natchez, and school patrons regularly turned out at their local schools both to raise much-needed funds or provide in-kind labor and to celebrate black educational accomplishments. Black parents did everything from improving the school grounds to making minor repairs and providing general upkeep of the physical plant to raising extra funds for extracurricular activities, such as music programs and athletic teams. Students also contributed what they could. In the 1920s, for example, a group of students in Mound Bayou picked cotton and donated their wages to improving their school.[45]

Because they required community support for their very existence, Jim Crow schools played an important role in black neighborhoods and, despite their inadequacies compared to the white schools, were a source of community pride in black achievement.[46] Although the creation of Mississippi's dual school system limited the amount of public resources dedicated to black schooling—a fact clearly detrimental to the entire project of black education—segregated learning did help preserve some measure of local black control over the education of black children. In many communities, local black school trustees continued to exercise a good deal of control, outside of state and local funding, over their neighborhood black schools, precisely because local white school leaders tended to pay little attention to the black side of the dual system. Some school districts, of course, had white officials who did consider oversight of the black schools within their job descriptions; some, like Charles Johnson, superintendent of the majority-black Canton schools in the 1930s, even tried to divert some resources to improve the physical plant of black schools. Johnson regularly visited the black schools in his district, and often he "would take extra books, chalk, etc."

Yet black schools were frequently considered so separate from the larger project of (white) public education that many black schools were able to take the small public contributions, add in the substantial donations from black parents, and run their schools without much interference from whites. Indeed, in Canton a decade before Superintendent Johnson arrived, no one on the white school board "knew anything about the Negro school." In another case, according to Dave Dunaway, a white principal in the Greenville schools, the white superintendent often "simply tried to get him a good man to run the black schools and just say, 'Ya'll do want you want to. Just don't bother us.'" In Bolivar County in the early 1900s, the black schools were run by a "colored deputy," J. M. Williams, who had so much autonomy from the white school board that some people in the county noted that he was "not governed by the school law in attending to school matters." Even if black school trustees often remained powerless in the sense of being unable to tap into state and local revenues to furnish their schools adequately, they still had an important voice in how their schools operated on a day-to-day basis.[47]

One of the duties of local black school trustees was to recommend a teacher or teachers for their school, subject to approval of the local white superintendent. Since whites did not generally see the value of educating blacks, they often cared little about who actually did the job. At the same time, poorly educated teachers were usually the only ones available to fill available teacher slots, and these teachers, with less education than their white counterparts, could be hired for a cheaper rate of pay. Before 1940, Mississippi made little effort to provide for the training of black teachers. At the turn of the twentieth century, a normal school for blacks existed in Holly Springs, supported in part by public dollars, but during the Vardaman administration, with his talk of wasted tax funds for black education, the legislature decided not to make an appropriation to the Holly Springs institution, and it folded. That left Alcorn A&M College as the primary public institution where potential black teachers in Mississippi could receive college-level education, but Alcorn had been created as the state's land-grant institution for blacks, and teacher training was not part of its basic mission. A Southern Education Board investigator noted in 1911 that Alcorn "offers no special courses for the training of teachers." The observer also realized that "nothing is being done by the state to make it a more effective training school." For those who could afford the tuition, a number of private colleges in the state, such as Rust College in Holly Springs and Tougaloo and Jackson colleges in the capital city, supplemented the makeshift teacher education program available at Alcorn. For the first half of the twentieth century, at the same time that a college degree was increasingly a requirement for white teachers, a sizable part of the black teaching corps had no college training; until the 1940s, many, especially those in the state's rural districts, had received no education beyond the eighth grade. In the late 1920s, 63 percent of the state's rural black teachers did not have a high school degree; 28 percent had no education beyond the eighth grade. Emily May Carouthers remembered that in the early twentieth century, she attended school one year in Buena Vista with her cousin Jeremiah, and "then he turned around [the next year] and taught me at the same school . . . he had finished eighth grade." During the 1930s and 1940s, increasing numbers of black children had access to a high school education; by 1944 all but eight Mississippi counties had black high schools. As a result, a high school education increasingly became the minimum credential needed to teach in a black school. This training was supplemented by summer institutes held at various locales around the state, but many black teachers prior to 1945 still entered the classroom with little or no college education.[48]

Although black teachers were poorly trained by white standards, they generally represented the most educated segment of local black communities. They applied, often with incredible perseverance and self-sacrifice, their talents to the task of improving the lives of black youth. Black teachers frequently worked beyond the state-funded short school term for no payment or simply food and board as compensation. Others worked at second jobs, which frequently provided more income than teaching, to make ends meet. Black teachers regularly offered extra instruction after school hours to help slow students catch up or challenge brighter ones to learn more.[49]

At times, black teachers also challenged the racial assumptions of segregated education. Of course, black teachers were employed by a Jim Crow system that ultimately saw little value in educating black Mississippians beyond the most rudimentary level, and as employees of that system and as advocates of additional support for black schooling, black teachers intelligently avoided any kind of direct challenge to the racial status quo. Bernice White, who grew up in rural Washington County in the Delta, remembered that her teachers "never talked about white or black issues," but she also realized her teachers were "kept from that." Despite the constraints, many black teachers found ways to "teach equality." They talked about African American history, for instance. As early as the 1930s, teachers in Meridian sponsored a "Negro History Week." The teachers organized the presentations and, to avoid unwelcome white attention, held the meetings at local churches rather than at the schools. Aaron Henry, who attended Coahoma County Agricultural High School, remembered that his teachers never attacked segregation directly or advocated integration; rather, "[t]heir aim was to instill in us racial pride, and they led us to believe in our personal worth and made us understand that we were equal to any other man. They tried to show us that racial superiority was a myth." What white Mississippians failed to realize was that any education, even an "inferior" one, was inherently subversive of their white supremacist agenda.[50]

Indeed, educated black Mississippians had long recognized the inadequacies and injustice heaped on black education, but it was not until the 1930s and 1940s that the prospects for changing the flawed dual school system seemed promising. Shifts in national demographics, national politics, and the national mood put white Mississippians on the defensive about their education system, which was clearly separate but most certainly not equal. Some whites in the state, including a number of political leaders, began to see possible benefits in improving black education. Reform might forestall an increasingly likely legal challenge to the whole notion of separate but equal arrangements and might be necessary to secure a share of the increasingly available federal education monies, funds sorely needed by a state as poor as Mississippi. By the 1940s, positive changes to black education did begin to occur in Mississippi, but the state's dual educational edifice remained firmly entrenched.

CHAPTER TWO

A LAST GASP TO MAINTAIN A SEGREGATED SYSTEM

Mississippi's Failed Effort to Make Separate Education Truly Equal

B y the late 1930s, Mississippi had succeeded in significantly improving the state's white public education system; even so, the state's white schools, especially in rural areas, remained largely second rate and still in need of costly improvements. The dramatic transformations in white education, however incomplete, had only been possible because of the almost total neglect of black public education. While black Mississippians had objected to state plans to provide unequal school facilities for their children from the beginning of the white educational improvement campaign begun in the early twentieth century, it was not until the late 1930s that any segment of white Mississippi began to agree that the state's minimal support for black public education would no longer suffice. White concern over the dismal state of black education sprang largely from fears that the entire edifice of racial segregation, and the separate but equal doctrine that justified American apartheid, was vulnerable. Indeed, by the end of World War II, changes in the region's demographics and economy threatened to undermine the racial status quo, while the federal government seemed increasingly sympathetic to the cause of black civil rights.[1] White political leaders and others in Mississippi, like those throughout the South, began to recognize that a little more emphasis on the equal part of the separate but equal equation might be prudent if segregation was to be preserved. The gap between rhetoric and reality was perhaps greatest in the area of public education, where even the most charitable comparison of black and white public schools stood as a glaring refutation of the notion that separate could ever be equal in the state.

White Mississippians began to explore two options for creating a separate but more truly equal education system: federal aid and a state-sponsored equalization campaign. While both brought modest yet needed improvements to black (and white) education, neither mechanism succeeded in creating an equalized dual school system. Beginning with Franklin D. Roosevelt's New Deal, federal money was available to the states in increasing amounts. For a poor state like Mississippi, such funds represented a potential windfall to address the state's inability to fund state services like public education adequately. The use of federal money, however, raised the specter of federal oversight and the possible destruction of the state's Jim Crow arrangements.

State-funded equalization was also fraught with problems. First, as one of the poorest states in the nation, Mississippi had limited resources to expend on closing the huge gap between black and white education created during the first half of the twentieth century. Second, Mississippi, like other southern states, developed its equalization program as a bulwark against perceived threats to segregation. Consequently, equalization proposals were designed to make only minimal adjustments in state spending on black education in the hope that such an effort would deflect a possible challenge to separate but clearly unequal arrangements. In 1950, the editor of the *Grenada (Miss.) Grenada County Weekly* expressed succinctly the rationale behind the state's recent efforts to improve black education: "I claim that we had better do a little than to be MADE to do a heap."[2] Third, white Mississippians never wholly embraced an honest and fair equalization program because of concerns that growing numbers of blacks in the state favored abolishing school segregation, which equalization was designed to support. Although many black Mississippians actually endorsed equalization if carried out justly, white leaders ultimately hesitated to spend millions to upgrade black schools without an explicit pledge of support from black leaders to maintain Jim Crow education. In addition, the practical motivations that led Mississippi political leaders to consider federal aid to education or to favor even inadequate equalization schemes did not necessarily alter local attitudes of racial discrimination committed to preserving white educational prerogatives. Consequently, when local school officials did seek to tap into federal funds, they often used most of the extra money to continue the effort to improve white schools in their area. And since local officials often implemented the state equalization mandates, an already insufficient effort became exceedingly lame in actual operation.

The creation of Mississippi's separate but unequal school system had been possible because whites had stripped black Mississippians of all political power, a powerlessness regularly reinforced by violence against those who dared challenge white supremacy. Even so, some black Mississippians dared to agitate for black school improvements, and those who did protest perhaps kept an already unjust system of school funding from sinking to even lower depths of discriminatory treatment. For example, in 1908 the Mississippi legislature passed a law providing for the establishment of white agricultural high schools to teach agricultural and homemaking skills. When the Jasper County school board moved the following year to set up such a school for whites, a black landowner in the county, Robert Goins, sued the county board of supervisors after it imposed a one-half-mill tax on all taxable property to support the new institution. Surprisingly, given the Jim Crow justice that often prevailed in the courts of Mississippi during this period, the local chancery judge agreed with Goins's objections and enjoined the supervisors from levying the tax and building the school. When the local Jasper County officials appealed to the Mississippi Supreme Court, the defendants argued that school officials did not have a duty "to furnish all children identical advantages." Their definition of separate but equal was that "equality of facilities means the providing at public expense of the opportunity to attend a school established by the State suitable to the grade of advancement of the pupil who attends." Apparently, the local white authorities believed that blacks had no need for advanced studies, even in the types of vocational subjects to be offered at the agricultural high schools, exactly the kind of farming and domestic skills whites thought most suitable for blacks. The Mississippi Supreme Court, however, disagreed. It upheld the lower court ruling, and in its 1910 session the legislature rewrote the agricultural high school legislation to provide for black agricultural high schools. As a result, a number of these institutions were established around the state, and many of them became the premier educational facility for blacks in the primarily rural areas they served.[3]

In the state's more urban areas, blacks in the first third of the twentieth century also petitioned school authorities to upgrade black educational facilities, though with only intermittent success. Blacks in Jackson, for instance, waged a constant campaign for improvements to the city's black schools in the early twentieth century, but city leaders and school officials generally wanted to devote most of their efforts to constructing a first-class system of schools only for the city's white children. Though most whites were inclined to give little or no thought to the needs of black education in the city, a steady stream of black complaints kept some pressure on white leaders to improve Jackson's black public schools.

As the Jackson population began to expand significantly around the turn of the century, the need for additional schools in the city became a pressing concern for both blacks and whites. While city officials scrambled to find the funds to build additional white schools, they generally ignored or put off the pleas of black Jacksonians to provide adequate school facilities for their children. Between 1902 and 1917, Jackson constructed five elementary schools and an elaborate $75,000 high school for white children. Education officials boasted in 1917 that "the public schools of Jackson are of such a high order that we take very great pleasure in showing to the world that the Capital City of the State has a public school system second to none in the State." Such a claim could only be made because school officials did not consider the black schools under their authority to be part of "the public schools of Jackson." Indeed, the expansion of the black public schools in Jackson proceeded at a much slower pace. In 1902, Smith Robertson, the city's only black school, was seriously overcrowded. That year the school board agreed to build four additional classrooms at the school. When nothing had happened four years later, a committee of black citizens implored the school board to abandon plans for an annex at Smith Robertson and build another black school. The board members rejected this advice and finally fulfilled their earlier pledge to construct the four-classroom addition, completed in 1907. Two years later, however, Smith Robertson burned, causing all the school's first through fourth graders to take an unscheduled six-month furlough because temporary quarters could only be located for the higher grades. Smith Robertson was rebuilt, and at least in part because of continued pressure from black citizens, a second black school was finally constructed in 1912, Jim Hill School. The Jackson school board continued the project of constructing an unequal black and white school system for the next several decades, and though white schools received the bulk of resources, black pressure prodded whites to offer some modern facilities for the city's black students, including a black high school, Lanier, completed in 1925.[4]

Before the 1940s, however, black protest against Mississippi's creation of a patently unequal dual school system remained necessarily intermittent and sporadic. Given the racial climate in Mississippi and the nation, black Mississippians wisely focused their efforts not on objections that would remain largely unheard but on building up black education largely through their own efforts, without much help from the state. By the time of World War II, the conditions for black protest had improved, and blacks in Mississippi began to press more stridently for the state to improve black education. In the spring of 1941, a group of black teachers from the MATCS met with white political leaders to complain about short terms for black schools and unequal salaries for black teachers. The meeting left the black teachers "without 'promises' and without hope," so the following fall the teachers' organization created a legislative committee to "use whatever method is available to law-abiding citizens in a democracy to secure better educational opportunities for our children and better salaries for our teachers." During World War II, the membership of the MATCS began raising funds to file a teacher salary equalization suit, similar to the ones already initiated in other states. Although the association set aside $500 for the effort, its inability to secure a local lawyer eventually sidetracked the attempt.[5]

Black demands for educational improvements grew even louder by the end of the war. In January 1945, T. R. M. Howard, a black doctor from Mound Bayou, bluntly announced to the black Greenwood Civic League what most of his listeners already knew: the state's black educational system was a "failure." And he asked, "Will it interfere with any good Southern tradition to do something about this problem?" A 1945 survey conducted by the MATCS's *Mississippi Educational Journal* revealed that 95 percent of the organization's membership favored court action if the 1946 legislature did not address the teacher salary equalization issue. A statewide mass meeting of black leaders held in Jackson in early 1946 drafted a message for the legislature outlining many of the educational problems that required legislative solutions: unequal teacher salaries, inadequate black school facilities, insufficient teacher-training institutions, and limited higher education offerings. As the black leaders noted, no additional taxes would even be necessary to begin the upgrade of black education; an equal distribution of levies already collected would itself allow for significant betterment.[6]

During the late 1930s and 1940s, for the first time since Reconstruction serious public discussions also occurred among white Mississippians about how to improve black education. This awakening of concern among whites was spurred by the earliest rumblings of the first national criticism of the South's racial arrangements in almost half a century. In the wake of the U.S. Supreme Court's 1938 *Gaines v. Canada* decision, which held that Missouri's failure to provide a law school for blacks violated the *Plessy v. Ferguson* doctrine of separate but equal, Fred Sullens, the fiery editor of the *Jackson (Miss.) Daily News* and certainly no foe of segregation, warned white Mississippians that "if the Missouri contention should be sustained, it will play havoc with the whole system of public instruction throughout the South. Here in Mississippi we ought to have at least a little common honesty in expenditure of the public school fund."[7]

Educators were among the earliest white supporters of the efforts to improve black schooling. In the late 1930s, the all-white MEA appointed a committee to study black education in the state, and in 1940 the committee issued a report outlining a number of deficiencies and suggested improvements. The Delta Council, composed of the area's leading planters and businesspeople, in a 1943 resolution also endorsed improvements in black education, undoubtedly spurred in part by the out-migration of their black laborers, which had accelerated during World War II. In 1940, former legislator Mildred Topp noted that "the pittance we devote to negro education should bring shame upon every one of us." Topp thought that if white civic organizations knew the extent of the inequity, they would take action to improve black education. A number of white groups did begin to devote attention to the problems of black education, including a group of Methodist women who met in Jackson during the fall of 1948 "to study the present status of Negro education in Mississippi and see what steps can be taken to improve our state facilities."[8]

Those white Mississippians who began to call for greater equalization between white and black public schools generally made sure to confine their support for reforms within the unshakeable boundaries of preserving white privilege and saving school segregation. For instance, when Percy H. Easom, the supervisor of black education for the State Department of Education and a white man truly interested in advancing the cause of black schooling in the state, asked the state legislature for improvements in the training of black teachers in 1938, he carefully couched his request for change in the language of white supremacy: "it is not so much a question of what the colored people deserve as it is a question of what the white people of Mississippi deserve. The white people deserve to have something done to improve the status of their colored people. Do not the white people depend upon the colored people for their labor supply, for their tenant farmers, for their cooks, for their nurses, for their brickmasons, for their plasterers, for their chauffeurs, etc.?" As the threats to segregated education began to appear more visibly on the horizon, Easom began to emphasize not only the benefits of equalization but also the danger to continued segregation if improvements to black education were not made. In a speech before the Indianola Rotary Club in 1946, Easom reiterated his theme of how black educational advances benefited whites, but he also suggested that segregation could only be preserved if whites made a sustained attempt to address long-ignored black educational needs.[9]

As both national and local criticism of the shortcomings of Jim Crow education mounted in the late 1930s and 1940s, the state of Mississippi looked for ways to improve black schooling, to make separate education more truly equal. Federal aid to education was touted by some white leaders as the best means of preserving a segregated, but more equalized, education. Superintendent H. M. Ivy of Meridian recognized that a federal aid bill under debate in the U.S. Congress in the late 1940s would provide $7 million for the state's black schools, "almost treble the amount now being spent for that purpose," a sizable down payment on necessary improvements to black schools if Jim Crow had any chance of surviving court scrutiny in the post-*Gaines* era. Robert Mayo, Hinds County superintendent, accurately identified the state's three options for addressing the educational equalization issue: "lowering of expenditures for white education," hiking local taxes to fund an equalization campaign, or accepting "federal aid without federal control." Only the last of these, according to Mayo, represented a truly viable possibility.[10]

Few white Mississippians, however, or other southerners for that matter, had ever believed that Mayo's "federal aid without federal control" could ever become a reality. As early as 1876, a proposal by Representative Gilbert Walker of Virginia for the distribution of proceeds of public land sales to the states for education on the basis of illiteracy rates, highest in the states of the former Confederacy, failed to pass Congress because of southern fears that the legislation might lead to federal oversight of southern institutions. During the 1880s, similar legislation introduced by Senator Henry W. Blair of New Hampshire passed the Senate three times, but the House never even brought the measure up for a vote. The Blair bill would have spent $77 million of federal funds on public education over eight years, with 75 percent of the largesse going to the South. White southern Democrats, however, joined others in their party in opposing this and most other new federal expenditures. They particularly disliked the requirement in the Blair bill that mandated equal spending between the races of not only federal education funds but also of state education funds required to match the federal dollars on a one-to-one basis. Republicans lost interest in the issue by 1890, and though the question was briefly revived after World War I, a serious renewal of interest in the topic did not occur until during the Great Depression.[11]

During the hard times of the 1930s, individual agencies of Roosevelt's New Deal brought much-needed relief and improvement to black and white schools in Mississippi. For example, in 1933–34 the Federal Emergency Relief Administration gave the state almost $1.5 million "to keep the rural schools open." During the same academic year, 72 of Hinds County's 106 black schools received aid from the short-lived Civil Works Administration (CWA) for various remodeling projects and for the employment of adult education teachers. In the next several years, both the Public Works Administration (PWA) and Works Progress Administration (WPA) also provided assistance in improving Mississippi schools. While black schools, primarily in the state's more urban areas, received some of these New Deal funds, school districts often acquired the aid, which generally required local matching funds, primarily for the benefit of their white schools. Sympathetic school officials, such as the Hinds County superintendent who applied for the substantial CWA project that revamped his county's black schools, did exist, but many school officials seeking federal aid thought little about the needs of their black patrons. For instance, Hattiesburg school officials secured funds from the CWA and PWA for eight school improvement projects in 1933 and 1934, but only one of these projects went to the city's three black schools. White school officials in the south Mississippi town failed to seek federal aid to revamp the black Third Ward school, which had a roof in need of serious repair and insufficient classroom space for its almost four hundred students. The white school board also ignored the need of the black schools for an athletic facility, which blacks ended up building in 1935 with their own funds.[12]

The New Deal programs demonstrated how federal aid could augment Mississippi's small education budgets, but white fears about the long-term implications of federal school financing remained. Between 1937 and 1950, Congress considered a number of comprehensive educational aid measures, but most went down to defeat. White southerners, while hungrily calculating how federal dollars might help their financially strapped region improve and ultimately preserve Jim Crow schools, continued to worry that federal funds might also provide an entree for the federal government to step in and destroy their system of segregation. These concerns helped doom most congressional proposals for federal support of public education, especially after President Harry S. Truman and the Democratic Party offered their support for black civil rights in 1948 and once the National Association for the Advancement of Colored People (NAACP) in 1949 reversed its earlier stance of calling for merely an equal distribution of any federal aid to education in favor of demanding that the government deny any federal funds to segregated schools.[13]

By the early 1950s, many Mississippians clearly perceived the possible dangers to segregation posed by receiving financial support from a federal government increasingly at odds with the South on the question of preserving segregation. In fact, the one federal education initiative Congress actually enacted during this period, providing federal assistance to areas affected by the location of federal military facilities during World War II and after, did increasingly threaten to provide a launching pad for a federal assault on racial segregation in education. During World War II, the federal government provided aid under the Lanham Program to communities affected by the location of federal facilities in their midst; part of these funds were distributed as grants to school districts. Between 1941 and 1944, fifteen Mississippi school districts received over $500,000 under this program. In 1950, Congress enacted a similar program of providing federal aid to schools affected by the continuing federal presence associated with the cold war military buildup. Public Laws 815 and 874 eventually provided more than $16 million between 1951 and 1961 to help construct and operate public schools in at least twenty-five Mississippi school districts that had federal installations. While the state and the local school districts welcomed the assistance, the threat that federal aid would bring federal control loomed as an ever-present shadow. When amendments to federal-impact aid measures were proposed in 1951, language in the revisions suggested that the schools funded with the monies be "comparable" to those already in existence in the states. Of course, in the South this wording could clearly be interpreted as endorsing segregated schools, and President Truman objected to what he considered a "backward step" in the federal government's effort "to extend equal rights and opportunities to all our people." While Truman did not think the school aid law should require integrated schools, he did believe that "we should not impair our moral position by enacting a law that requires a discrimination based on race. Step by step we are discarding old discriminations; we must not adopt new ones." As white Mississippians and other white southerners correctly perceived, the leap from concerns about avoiding the appearance of racial discrimination to active intervention to prevent racial oppression could be a small one. In fact, such a transformation loomed just over the horizon. In the 1960s, federal aid to education did indeed prove to be the Trojan horse white southerners had long feared.[14]

Though federal aid ultimately proved a problematic solution to Mississippi's school financing woes in the 1940s and 1950s, state leaders still resolved to address the issue of inadequate funding of black schooling, despite a lack of sufficient state resources. Like other southern states in the 1940s, Mississippi pursued a strategy of educational equalization that sought to ensure a more equal distribution of resources between separate black and white schools.[15] Correcting the disparities between white and black education that had been created over the previous decades was an expensive proposition, however, and the state essentially did not have enough money for the job. Although Mississippi would spend significant amounts of state funds to improve education after World War II, the state could not finance one school system adequately, much less two. Mississippi already spent a considerable part of its citizens' earnings on public education, ranking ninth among all states in percentage of income expended on education in 1945. Because of the state's relative poverty, however, Mississippi remained dead last in terms of actual tax dollars used for public education.[16]

The first significant move in Mississippi's equalization campaign came in 1944 when Governor Thomas L. Bailey appointed a legislative committee to study the state's public school system. Bailey, a former schoolteacher, had long supported education improvements as a representative and Speaker of the Mississippi House, and when the committee's report appeared in early 1946, he backed its recommendations: improve the training of black teachers, provide for a general increase in teachers' salaries based on the training and experience of individual teachers, and appropriate $3 million for the building of public schools. The 1946 legislature approved the committee's suggestions. To improve black teacher training, the state allocated additional funds for Alcorn A&M College; bolstered the finances of the Mississippi Negro Training School, established by the legislature in 1940 on the old site of the private Jackson College; and created a new institution, Mississippi Vocational College, to educate black teachers in the Delta. The legislature also increased the overall budget for the state's public schools, with much of the increase targeted for raising teachers' salaries. In response to the committee's call for new school buildings, the legislature allocated the suggested $3 million. To help pay for the new schoolhouses, the legislature required that counties provide matching funds and authorized them to levy additional taxes if necessary.[17]

The measures to aid school construction and to increase teachers' salaries made no mention that the funds should be spent either in whole or in part on black education; however, Fred Sullens later claimed that, at least for the school construction resources, there "was a sort of gentleman's agreement, fully understood among lawmakers who voted for the appropriation, that this money would be used for the improvement of Negro schools." Blacks certainly believed that most of the state funds appropriated for school construction would be used to revamp or replace their woefully inadequate facilities. At the 1946 meeting of the MATCS, the organization's president, E. S. Bishop of Corinth, heralded the $3 million fund as " 'heavenly' news to those of us who have found it necessary to give 'box suppers' and 'fish frys,' which helped us get the meager funds to build the many shacks in which we teach." In the same address, Bishop noted that his only concern was "the fair and equitable distribution of these funds without discrimination."[18] Given Mississippi's long history of denying blacks their fair share of the state's education money, such concerns seem unremarkably appropriate.

If lawmakers did have a "gentlemen's agreement" that their $3 million school construction appropriation would be spent primarily on black schools, they did little to see that those charged with dispersing the state funds—the State Building Commission and local officials—had a similar understanding. State Superintendent of Education J. M. Tubb realized that while school districts might have had a "moral obligation" to spend money on black schools, the state program for school construction had not created any "legal obligation" to undertake such an endeavor. Without such compulsion, most of the $3 million appropriation of 1946 went to white schools. By October 1947, the State Building Commission had approved use of more than $2.8 million of the funds, but only 35 percent had been allocated to black schools. The needs of white schools, while certainly not as glaring as those of blacks, were also quite substantial, and county officials and the State Building Commission responded to pressures from white school patrons for a lion's share of the state's largesse. As A. H. Ramsey, the superintendent of the largely black Bolivar County school system in the Delta, noted, in many districts "the white schools made a run on the Building Commission and secured their allocation for white schools."[19]

As with school consolidation in years past, black Mississippians who sought to take advantage of the state appropriation and improve the educational facilities for their children ultimately had to depend on the goodwill of local whites. Some communities, such as Yazoo City, New Albany, Philadelphia, Laurel, and Biloxi, did provide funds to construct modern schoolhouses for black children, but most rural districts made little effort to raise local funds or apply for state monies to aid black school construction. For example, in the largely black Tunica County system, the school board's "improvements" during the late 1940s for its forty-eight black schools, including sixteen located in churches and four in private homes, amounted to the construction of three two-teacher schools and one-room additions to two existing schools. At other times, simple indifference by local whites could sabotage the state's equalization program, as the following example from northeast Mississippi illustrates. In 1946, a man in Booneville donated five acres of land for a black school in Jumpertown, eleven miles northwest of Booneville. A group of black men in the Jumpertown neighborhood had agreed to donate $300 in labor to build the school. With these contributions in hand, the proposed Jumpertown school could receive $2,500 from the state. But the State Building Commission rejected the planned school after the county superintendent of education "sent a very crude drawing of the proposed buildings." Needing only to get a qualified draftsman to make the architectural sketches for the school, the local superintendent absentmindedly hampered black efforts to take advantage of the 1946 school construction law.[20]

Mississippi's effort to solve the problem of unequal salaries for white and black teachers foundered on a similar failure of state leaders to provide a clear and unequivocal mandate to local officials. In 1946 and 1948, the state appropriated additional funds for public schools so that school districts could raise teachers' salaries but left the distribution of any increase solely in the hands of local school officials. As with the school building program, local leaders generally used the extra money to benefit whites more than blacks. Of course, the actual workings of any salary adjustments varied from district to district. In many rural locales where the black school term remained shorter than the white one, black teachers automatically received less of the benefit of rising salaries, since increases were usually made to a teacher's monthly salary. In 1948, 40 percent of the state's black teachers still taught in schools that had only five- or six-month terms. In more urban areas, black teachers frequently received a more equal share of the funds slated for teachers' salaries.[21] Statewide, between 1945 and 1950 pay for white teachers increased by 63 percent, from an average of $1,108 to $1,806; during the same period, salaries for black teachers rose on average 78 percent, from $399 to $711. But in 1950, black teachers still earned only 39 percent of what their white counterparts received, up slightly from the 36 percent of five years earlier.[22] Clearly, the program of general state increases in teachers' salaries did little to narrow the pay disparity between white and black teachers, especially when the monies were filtered through the hands of local white officials, who had little motivation to use their additional funds on salary equalization when white teachers also needed a pay raise.

The results of the state's 1946 educational improvement project led to widespread criticism from blacks and even some whites. A "State-wide Mass Meeting of Negro citizens" assembled in Jackson in February 1948 to protest the unequal workings of the equalization program. Noting "the great problems involved in an equitable distribution of the resources of the State," the group called for the creation of a biracial commission to oversee the process, a request denied by Governor Fielding L. Wright, soon to be the vice presidential candidate in the Dixiecrat revolt. A group of white citizens from Jackson labeled the disbursement of school construction funds "unfair and unchristian [sic]," and Jackson editor Fred Sullens warned white Mississippians that "our educational theory of 'all for the white folks and nothing for the Negro' must be abandoned."[23] But the protest that really got the attention of the state's white leaders was an equal pay lawsuit launched by a black teacher in Jackson.

When the legislature failed to act on salary equalization in 1946, black teachers resolved to carry out their earlier threat of legal action. In 1947, the MATCS secretly invited the NAACP's Thurgood Marshall to talk to them about initiating a lawsuit. Informed that such an action would require at least $5,000, the teachers voted to increase their annual dues by $1 to raise the capital, but in order to allay any possible white suspicions, they officially claimed the increase was for the creation of a benevolent fund. With the $5,000 amassed, the teachers only needed a willing plaintiff, and most looked to the teachers in the state's largest school district in Jackson to take the lead. In November 1947, the all-black Jackson Teachers Association adopted a resolution requesting equal salaries for black and white teachers in the district and promising legal action if the school board failed to act. The group delayed relaying their bold pronouncement to the local school board, however, until a plaintiff could be found.[24]

In February 1948, Gladys Noel Bates, a young Jackson teacher, stepped forward. Her father, Andrew Noel, a U.S. railway mail clerk and an active participant in local civil rights groups such as the Progressive Voters' League and the NAACP, had helped prod his daughter to take up the challenge of becoming an equalization plaintiff. But Bates herself had long been engaged in the struggle for black civil rights, first as a participant during the 1930s in the local NAACP chapter's Youth Council and then as a member of the local branch's board of directors. After graduation from Tougaloo College, Bates secured a job working in the Jackson public schools. She had been teaching at the city's oldest black school, Smith Robertson, for almost four years when she submitted her petition to the Jackson school board asking that they quit "discriminating against Negro teachers and principals in the payment of salaries." The school board president briefly responded: "I know of no discrimination against the colored people in the Jackson Public Schools." Faced with this defiant stand on the part of white school leaders, Bates refused to back down and filed a lawsuit against the school district. Her principal declined to offer her a contract for the following year. Her husband, John, who taught at Jackson's Lanier High, also did not receive a renewal of his contract at the end of the year. In addition, the Bates's home was destroyed in a mysterious fire soon after Gladys filed her lawsuit. Another teacher, R. Jess Brown, joined the lawsuit in 1949, and he also did not receive an invitation to return to teach in the Jackson public schools. Even with the support of the national NAACP, the lawsuit failed. The local federal court dismissed the case in early 1950 when it ruled that although the unequal salaries between black and white teachers resulted from racial discrimination, the plaintiffs had not exhausted their administrative appeals before filing suit. In addition, the court found that the dismissal of Bates and Brown was not illegal, even though little evidence existed that the firings were motivated by anything but the lawsuit.[25]

The Bates lawsuit demonstrated how little leverage black teachers in the state had in pressing equalization claims. While some black teachers in Jackson supported Bates in her struggle, much of that support necessarily could not be expressed openly. According to Bates, some area "principals and teachers vied for first place as informers to the Superintendents, each trying to secure an audience to let 'the man' know that 'I'm not in that mess' "; other teachers merely avoided contact with Bates after she filed her suit. As Bates noted, "The old cry [was] 'I have too much to lose to become involved in anything of this nature.'" Such attitudes were clearly prudent, for those few teachers who refused to shun Bates soon found themselves without jobs in the Jackson public schools. When the school board tried to have the Bates case dismissed in 1949—on the grounds that Bates was no longer an employee of the district—the board delayed the renewal of teachers' contracts as long as possible to discourage any teachers who might consider joining Bates in her lawsuit. Against such pressure, only R. Jess Brown stepped forward to keep the lawsuit alive.[26]

The MATCS, which had secretly helped to initiate the legal action, made no public statement in support of the Jackson equalization effort, but the organization continued to promote the struggle behind the scenes. In fact, the MATCS hired Bates after she lost her teaching job, and it paid for Brown to attend law school at Texas Southern University when the school system fired him. Although state NAACP leaders believed that the Bates example would lead to the launching of equal pay suits in every county in the state, they overestimated the effect the exceptional courage of Bates and Brown would have on other black teachers and underestimated the enormous pressure local white school officials could put on black teachers and principals.[27] If an equal pay lawsuit in the state's only true urban area could be so easily crushed, the state's rural black teachers had little hope of standing up to demand equal salaries.

The Bates lawsuit did, however, jolt many whites into rededicating themselves to the cause of educational equalization, for although the court had dismissed Bates's suit, it did note that the inequality in teachers' salaries sprang from racial discrimination. By the end of 1948, newspapers around the state reported that more counties had begun to "equalize" teachers' salaries and "are building new schools for Negro children and also providing transportation for Negro children where it has not hitherto been given." When the legislature made additional appropriations for school construction in each of the two sessions of 1950 and 1952—for a total of $10 million between 1946 and 1952—state officials took greater care to ensure that blacks received their fair share of the state funds. In fact, the $2 million approved for school construction by the legislature in 1950 mandated that all the funds go to black schools. When some white legislators tried to direct at least half of the monies to white schools, Representative Curtis Swango of Panola County (later judge in the Emmett Till case) helped quash the movement by reminding legislators that "since 1946 we have appropriated $5,000,000 for school building improvements and mighty little of it has gone to Negroes." As the state moved to designate building funds specifically for black schools, the school construction program began to look more like an actual equalization program. By 1953, the state funds that had been spent on school construction since 1946 were almost evenly divided between black and white projects.[28]

More forceful state action after 1948 led to the eventual equal division of state building funds between the black and white school systems, but the state's building program ultimately failed to work as an equalization measure because of the continuing disparity in local funds spent on black and white schools. Most local boards of supervisors raised taxes during this period to cover the building of new schools, levies that frequently generated revenues beyond the amount necessary to match state building funds. However, few local governing bodies, elected almost solely by whites, dared to devote the largest portion of any local tax increases to support the betterment of black schools. As a result, between 1946 and 1953 counties and local school districts spent almost $30 million on white schools yet only $11 million on black ones. In some cases, the disparity in spending stemmed from the fact that local officials refused to use local funds to equip the new black schools properly. For example, when officials in Monroe County took advantage of the equalization program to build a new black school in the western part of the county, they provided school books and teachers, but according to area blacks, the black community still "had to buy the desk[s] and equipment to equip the building because the county didn't give us anything."[29] In the end, state building funds, by sparking an increase in local funds available for school construction, succeeded in creating a virtual boom in the building of white schools and classrooms, while only a much smaller effort aimed at improving black school plants.

The Bates lawsuit also put pressure on the state to revisit the issue of salary equalization. White politicians and teachers in the state generally did not favor a true salary equalization plan. With black teachers earning on average only 38 percent of what white teachers made in the 1948–49 school year, many whites worried that the state did not have the resources to raise black teachers' salaries up to the level of white teachers' salaries. Kirby Walker, the longtime superintendent of the Jackson public schools, recalled that "it just was not possible for the legislature to appropriate enough money and the school districts to get enough money to equalize compensation." If the state could not pay for the increase in black salaries, white teachers fretted that any equalization plan would lower white salaries "to level out the wage structure."[30]

With the actual equalization of teachers' salaries seemingly blocked because of the enormous cost, Governor Fielding Wright supported a plan that would provide some semblance of equalization while locking in or even worsening existing inequalities. In 1949, Wright advocated a program to "equalize" black and white teachers' salaries on the basis of education, experience, and the results of the National Teacher Examination (NTE). During the 1940s, other southern states had adopted the NTE as the basis of state salary scales. By using the NTE, Jim Crow governments could justify paying white teachers more than black teachers not because of racial discrimination but because of an "objective" and "scientific" measure, albeit one that ignored the history of years of inadequate training of black teachers.[31] Some white leaders who firmly believed in white supremacy saw testing as a panacea for avoiding the real costs of equalization. They incorrectly assumed that all whites would do better than all blacks on any test.[32]

In Mississippi, any salary scale pegged to test scores or educational qualifications or both would have led to a dramatic decline in the money received by the average black teacher. In 1945, less than 10 percent of black teachers possessed a bachelor's degree; over 23 percent did not even have a high school diploma. At the same time, almost half of white teachers had a college degree, while over 98 percent had completed high school. In addition, black teachers in the state had no access to local graduate education. For example, when N. R. Burger, a black principal in Hattiesburg, sought to obtain a master's degree in the early 1950s, he had to take a leave of absence without pay to earn one from Cornell. Fearing that deficiencies in the training of black teachers and the lack of opportunities to obtain higher degrees would naturally translate into lower test scores on the NTE, black teachers predictably and overwhelmingly rejected Wright's school pay plan. In a statewide vote held in the fall of 1949 at eight regional meetings, black teachers opposed the measure 4,579 to 208. But white teachers also rejected the governor's teacher pay proposal. Their statewide referendum, held during the same period at twenty local meetings, disavowed the initiative by a tally of 5,529 to 2,462. Many white teachers in the state were apparently not convinced that testing would necessarily preserve the prerogatives of white supremacy. Even the president of the all-white MEA, Zack Huggins, who supported the governor's plan, admitted that some white teachers would likely see their salaries reduced—especially those white teachers earning the most money—once the test results were obtained. White teachers suggested that Wright's plan be adopted without the testing component, but legislators, led by J. A. Thigpen of Bolivar County, remained committed to the use of the NTE as part of any state salary plan.[33]

When teachers and legislators failed to agree on a suitable salary proposal, the legislature decided to delay any salary equalization in favor of another round of general salary increases, although this time with specific monies designated for black teachers. In both 1950 and 1952, the legislature made a special appropriation to augment the salaries of black teachers; each county received a share of the funds based on its number of black teachers. These state funds would have gone a long way (though not all the way) toward closing the gap between white and black teachers' salaries, but many counties ignored the intent of the legislature and refused to pass along the extra monies to black teachers. Of the $2.24 million dispersed to the counties for the 1952–53 school year as part of the special allocation for black teachers' salaries, the counties probably spent less than half of this amount on its intended target.[34] A legislative committee in 1953 revealed that the state funds appropriated to improve black teachers' salaries had not always reached black educators, and after an investigation by the state attorney general, twenty-six counties had to return funds to the state treasury. Many local school districts were obviously opposed to placing more money in the hands of black teachers even if the state footed the bill. As Bolivar County superintendent A. H. Ramsey reasoned at the time, "our negro teachers are getting all they are worth." As a result of this local opposition to the state's special effort to improve black teachers' salaries, by the 1953–54 school year black teachers still earned on average only 56 percent of what their white counterparts received.[35]

While the state's post–World War II equalization program brought some small improvement in black school plants and black teachers' salaries, nothing in the state's equalization campaign addressed the consolidation of black schools. As late as 1951, the state still had over fourteen hundred one-room schools, almost all of them black schools.[36] Since white school consolidation had already largely been accomplished through the use of local funds, state leaders simply ignored this expensive yet basic improvement to black schools. Without a state mandate requiring consolidation of local black schools, when state funds for black education became more widely available after 1946, counties typically would only pledge local matching funds for projects that shored up the antiquated one-, two-, or three-teacher black schools rather than construct truly modern, consolidated facilities, which would have entailed even greater expenses. For example, almost 77 percent of the black school projects built with state funds in 1946 and early 1947 involved the construction of one-, two-, or three-teacher schools. As noted earlier, when school districts began to increase the monthly salaries for black and white teachers after 1946, one reason black teachers received a smaller share of the funds was because most still taught in unconsolidated, short-term schools.[37] The failure to provide for black school consolidation undermined the state's equalization effort, because unconsolidated schools meant substandard buildings, shorter school terms, inadequately trained and poorly paid teachers, and no provisions for transportation of students.

Overall, the state's equalization efforts between 1946 and 1952, underfunded, vaguely construed, and implemented by local officials more concerned with preserving white privilege than fending off some seemingly faraway threat to segregation, represented a hopeless attempt to make separate schools more equal. If nothing else, however, the equalization attempts of the late 1940s had generated a great deal of discussion among whites about the state's educational shortcomings, especially on the question of unequal facilities for blacks and whites. In one instance, white educators collaborated with their black counterparts to undertake the first serious study of the true costs of school equalization.

In the fall of 1950, three white education organizations—the state PTA, the State Department of Education, and the MEA—joined the MATCS to create the biracial Mississippi Citizens Council on Education (MCCE). Its mission was to investigate the widely discussed school equalization question. Among other actions, the MCCE tried to gauge public opinion by sending out twenty thousand questionnaires to black and white citizens around the state. The survey results demonstrated, among other things, that over 75 percent of the more than sixteen thousand respondents (many undoubtedly teachers and parents) believed the state should provide "equivalent school services and facilities" to black and white children. The MCCE's recommendations, presented to the governor and legislature before the opening of the 1952 session, called for a massive equalization of school facilities, teachers' salaries, and curriculum and instruction funds, as well as a major consolidation program. Total cost of these changes, exclusive of the building campaign, was estimated at $34 million annually. Building needs would require an initial outlay of another $144 million. These numbers were staggering, given the size of Mississippi's budget at the time. During the 1948–50 biennium, the entire budget for the state was only $99.1 million, of which $36.3 million was allocated for public school expenses.[38]

Legislative supporters of the MCCE introduced bills to enact the council's recommendations during the 1952 session. The program was delayed, however, when the legislature received a report about the widespread padding of school rolls. Every district in the state had apparently overestimated the number of educable children, perhaps in an effort to secure a larger share of the miserly biannual education budget. Statewide, the 1951 school census listed about 37 percent more school-age children than shown in the 1950 federal census; some counties, such as Clay and Warren, claimed almost twice as many children on their rolls as found by the census enumerators. The "padding" scandal not only caused the legislature to hesitate before appropriating additional millions to educate phantom children but also provided a convenient excuse to delay acting on the costly equalization program laid out by the biracial MCCE. Instead, the 1952 legislature passed another stopgap education bill, which continued to increase the funds spent on education but still without adequate regard to equalization, and it created the all-white Recess Education Study Committee, composed entirely of state legislators.[39]

The Recess Education Study Committee essentially duplicated the work of the MCCE, except for the canvassing of public opinion, and in the end adopted recommendations similar to the original MCCE report. Governor Hugh White called a special session of the Mississippi legislature to meet in the fall of 1953 to act on the committee's suggestions. When the legislature assembled in early November 1953, it adopted a sweeping array of educational reforms: completion of school consolidation; a single salary scale for all teachers, based on the type of certificate held; a Minimum Foundation Program of an eight-month term and a thirty-to-one student-teacher ratio; and annual credits toward a building fund based on a district's average daily attendance, with $12 per child granted for each district.[40]

The 1953 equalization plan, the first serious legislative proposal to end the inequalities in the state's segregated school system, initially remained an unfunded mandate, as legislators balked—during both the special session and the regular 1954 session held a few months later—at funding any of the acts other than the teacher salary measure. Lawmakers split on the advisability of sinking so much money in an equalization scheme when a federal court decision on the legality of the South's separate but equal arrangements seemed imminent. The argument that carried the day was best expressed by state representative Hilton Waits from Washington County in the Delta, who issued a minority report to the Recess Education Study Committee's report. Waits insisted that any equalization program should be delayed until the Supreme Court rendered its decision and also pointed out that the 1953 equalization program was "too ambitious" and too costly. Promising to improve on separate but equal was one thing, but Waits and many other whites, especially Delta leaders, cringed at the hefty price tag attached to a comprehensive equalization scheme. As Joe Wroten, perhaps the most "liberal" member of the legislature at the time, later observed, most legislators viewed the equalization program as "sort of a last gasp to try to maintain a segregated educational system" by putting more money into black education, but "I don't think they really meant to make it equal."[41]

Others saw the full funding of the 1953 educational program as a preemptive strike. Most members of the Recess Education Study Committee had reasoned that "the fact that Mississippi has made an honest attempt to remedy an inequitable situation may have a psychological influence upon the United States Supreme Court in its decision in the segregation cases." Others, including Governor Hugh White and George W. Owens of Pontotoc County, vice chairman of the Recess Education Study Committee and chairman of the Senate Education Committee, believed that the improvements in education were needed whether the Supreme Court required integration or not. Owens reasoned that if the Supreme Court did invalidate Jim Crow schools, "the only possibility of maintaining a segregated system in Mississippi is by persuading the Negro to attend of his own volition schools provided for him." Such persuasion would be easier if "adequate, respectable, and equal facilities are provided."[42]

While state leaders such as Owens often recognized that black support was necessary for the success of the state's equalization program (especially if the separate but equal doctrine was invalidated), blacks were rarely consulted, except briefly through the MCCE, about whether or how the state could build a better Jim Crow school system. When black leaders complained in 1948 about the unequal distribution of the 1946 school building funds and called for the creation of a biracial commission to oversee the process, Governor Wright initially agreed to adopt such a commission if the black members assured him that their objectives did not include overturning segregation. After all, maintaining segregation remained the rationale for the state's equalization campaign. In April 1949, however, Wright told a gathering of Mississippi teachers that he "was ready to make the appointments when it was learned to my amazement" that some of the blacks being considered for membership on the commission "did believe in the abolition of segregation and [it] would be their purpose to work to that end." Wright apparently never recovered from his discovery that leading blacks in the state did not wholeheartedly support segregation, as he appointed an all-white education advisory committee.[43] Doubts about black support for segregation led to a situation in which constructing a better form of segregation remained the sole prerogative of those who had long benefited from the inequalities of separate education. In such an atmosphere, the state's equalization program never had much chance of being funded fully or implemented fairly.

Even so, many black Mississippians endorsed the state's equalization efforts. From 1925 until 1950, blacks throughout the South, working primarily through the NAACP, had focused their efforts on trying to equalize educational spending rather than directly assaulting the separate but equal doctrine; after the NAACP shifted its tactics to challenge Jim Crow head on, many black southerners continued to embrace the equalization policy as the best method for improving black education.[44] Some had long accommodated themselves to the segregated world of Mississippi, and the state's post–World War II equalization attempts, however flawed, only bolstered the willingness of a number of black leaders to embrace an improved version of separate but equal. H. H. Humes, a Greenville minister and newspaper editor, claimed in 1949 that "a majority" of black Mississippians supported the equalization efforts and recognized that school integration "would make it complicated and difficult for the whites and the Negroes to exist here together without friction."[45] Many teachers also accepted the logic of the equalization strategy. W. Milan Davis, president of the MATCS in 1949, told Governor Wright that teachers wanted equalization of facilities and salaries; they considered segregation an "'old account—settled long ago.'"[46] After all, black teachers were employees of a state that had created Jim Crow schools, and now, with state promises to improve the institutions they had labored so hard to build and nurture, accommodation and compromise seemed preferable to resistance and confrontation. The obvious pride most blacks took in black schools, despite their inadequacies when compared to white educational facilities, also generated support among black parents for the state's equalization proposals.

Although educational equalization had many black allies in Mississippi—even some who were willing to pledge fealty to segregation in exchange for more funds for black education—Governor Wright and other white leaders were correct in recognizing that Jim Crow education also had its black opponents. By the early 1950s, a small but growing number of black Mississippians, especially those affiliated with the NAACP, recognized the failure of the state's equalization bid, sensed the national mood was shifting in opposition to the South's racial mores, and supported the NAACP's new strategy of a more direct assault on segregation. These individuals believed that the days of trying to accommodate to and improve on Jim Crow had passed and that a new era had dawned, even in Mississippi. These voices became most public in the months before the historic Supreme Court decision. At a meeting of the state's NAACP branches in November 1953 in Indianola, an assembly attended by "no teachers" according to one report, the group's president, the Reverend Amos O. Holmes of Amory, denounced those who would support the state's equalization efforts. Holmes claimed that NAACP leaders would "work toward the goal of full freedom, full integration, and full democracy for every Mississippian, Negro and white, and see to it that the vicious system of segregation is challenged until it is removed."[47]

Some Mississippi blacks associated with the NAACP, however, supported both the assault on segregation and the promised equalization funding already long delayed. For example, C. R. Darden, a photographer and NAACP leader in Meridian, in the fall of 1953 sent a formal complaint from a group of the city's blacks to the Meridian school board demanding immediate action on improving the local black schools: "Our children sometimes have two lessons daily, some days they are sent home at noon for no reason at all [*sic*]. . . . Now I am concerned about what is happening to our children while we are waiting for the decission [*sic*] of the Supreme Court. We do not know how long the decision may be, nor how long the officials will hang on to the administration that is depriving our children the full benefit of the limited facilities that we now have." The board refused to meet with Darden's group, and while the Supreme Court's decision was only months away, Darden's concerns that the current school administration might "hang on" for some time proved quite prescient.[48] Darden sensed that the struggle for better schools for the black children of Meridian and the rest of Mississippi would indeed be a long one, whatever the Supreme Court might decide. School integration would likely not happen overnight, and additional funds for black schools were needed immediately.

As state leaders contemplated in 1953 whether to undertake a sweeping attempt at educational equalization in a last-gasp hope of undermining an almost-certain decision by the Supreme Court attacking the separate but equal doctrine, more and more black Mississippians seemed prepared to abandon Jim Crow if they had the backing of the federal government. At its annual meeting in March 1953, the Mississippi Teachers Association (MTA) (formerly the MATCS) generally endorsed the stance of the association's president, J. D. Boyd, principal of the Utica Institute, who "called for further patience" with the state's equalization program. But by the fall of 1953, when Boyd organized a meeting of almost three hundred black leaders (including teachers and others) in Jackson to "crystallize opinion" on the upcoming legislative equalization plan of 1953, the conclave adopted a resolution that black Mississippians would only accede to Jim Crow if the Supreme Court upheld the practice. Apparently blindsided by the group's stance, Boyd rushed off a rebuttal to Governor Hugh White in which he claimed that the state's teachers endorsed the governor's special session "as a forward step in improving and providing equal educational opportunity for all children of the State."[49] His claims notwithstanding, even a growing number of teachers apparently seemed prepared to abandon segregated education if the courts ruled against the practice. With black opinion in the state divided on whether to trade the promise of educational equalization for a pledge of loyalty to segregation—even if the Supreme Court ruled against the practice—state legislators balked at funding a comprehensive equalization package.

Mississippi's push for school equalization in the decade before the *Brown* decision, never fully funded and never wholeheartedly endorsed by white Mississippians, proved largely ineffectual. Throughout the state, equalization efforts only slightly narrowed the wide chasm separating white and black education. The equalization project of the 1940s and 1950s had its most impressive impact on school districts with relatively small black populations. For instance, in Covington County, located in south Mississippi, a district where white students outnumbered black students almost two to one, the school equalization effort that began in 1946 had spurred the construction of three white schools and three black ones. Perhaps the most impressive school building in the county at the time of the *Brown* decision was the black Carver school in Collins, completed in 1954. Despite the improvements to the physical plant of Covington County's black schools, however, they still remained seriously understaffed compared to their white counterparts. While the white schools had a student-teacher ratio of twenty-five to one in 1955, in the black schools, each black teacher taught an average of thirty-five students.[50]

In school districts with larger black populations, the effects of the state's equalization program on black education were much less noticeable. In Benton County in northeast Mississippi, with a roughly equal white and black school population, whites had two schools in 1955, each accommodating first through twelfth graders. While these white school facilities were not perfect, for the most part they were modern facilities, not overcrowded, and staffed with enough teachers to handle the school population. In contrast, in 1955 Benton County had thirteen black schools. The one school that included a high school program, Old Salem (also a twelve-grade attendance center), was described by whites from the University of Mississippi who surveyed the district in 1955 as having "three buildings, none of which might be considered good." Of the other twelve black schools in the county, eight were one-teacher schools, two were two-teacher operations, and five were located in black churches. The white surveyors recommended abandonment of the entire black school plant in favor of a new school facility for all black children in the county. In addition, none of the black schools in Benton County, including Old Salem, had enough teachers to allow one teacher per grade. In the majority-black Delta, equalization had done so little that the effort to improve on separate but equal education in the late 1940s and early 1950s had probably gone largely unnoticed by most of the region's black parents. Tallahatchie County is a good example. At the time of the *Brown* decision, the county had thirteen white schools. Three of the buildings were in need of replacement; one, West Tallahatchie High School, was a brand-new $650,000 facility. Most of the other white schools had been constructed before World War II, but the thirteen white schools in the district were valued at over $1.5 million in 1954. The only real serious building need for whites was a new high school in the eastern part of the county. Tallahatchie County officials had also built at least three new black schools since 1946, but this new construction barely made a ripple in the glaring inadequacies of the county's black school system. In 1954, blacks in the county attended fifty-nine different schools. Most of the buildings were not owned by the county; all but six of the structures, including the three new schools, were judged in 1954 to be "in such condition as to be of no value at this time."[51]

In 1954, equalization seemingly became a moot point. The *Brown* decision declared segregated schools inherently unconstitutional and shifted constitutional presumption in favor of ending state-sanctioned segregation. Mississippi's political leaders, however, essentially ignored the decision; ten years would pass before the state took even the first step toward dismantling its system of dual schools. Private and state-sanctioned economic and physical intimidation forestalled any black attempts to desegregate Mississippi schools for a decade after *Brown*, while at the same time the state continued to move forward on its program of improving its separate black schools. But this second decade of equalization within segregation efforts proved as ineffectual as that of the post–World War II years and ultimately heightened black discontent with Jim Crow schools. Mississippi politicians refused to admit what the state's most perceptive observers could easily see: that equalization of two separate school systems would never succeed in a state that did not even have the resources to adequately fund one group of schools. Mississippi writer William Faulkner succinctly explained the folly of the state's equalization program in 1954: "Our present schools are not even good enough for white folks. So what do we do? Make them good enough, improve them to the best possible? No. We beat the bushes, rake and scrape to raise additional taxes to establish another system at best only equal to that one which is already not good enough, which therefore won't be good enough for Negroes either; we will have two identical systems neither of which is good enough for anybody. The question is not how foolish can people get, because apparently there is no limit to that. The question is, how foolish in simple dollars and cents, let alone in wasted men and women, can we afford to be?"[52]

CHAPTER THREE

TEN YEARS OF NOTHING BUT DELIBERATE SPEED

The Aftermath of Brown *in Mississippi*

O n the morning of July 30, 1954, between eighty-five and one hundred black leaders sat down with Governor Hugh White and his all-white Legal Education Advisory Committee (LEAC) to discuss the fate of school segregation in the wake of the momentous *Brown v. Board of Education* decision.[1] The origins of the meeting stemmed from Governor White's continuing effort to secure support for his as-yet unfunded school equalization within segregation program. After the *Brown* decision, a number of white leaders continued to champion White's 1953 equalization plan, but all agreed that before the state moved to expend large sums of money to improve black schools, they needed firm assurance from blacks that they favored the status quo of segregated schools.

Governor White moved to gauge black opinion in the state on this subject by holding a meeting in late June 1954 with two confirmed black supporters of the equalization drive, *Jackson (Miss.) Advocate* editor Percy Greene and Baptist minister and leader of the General Baptist State Convention, H. H. Humes, as well as six prominent black educators in the state: college presidents J. H. White, Jacob Reddix, and J. R. Otis; and three teachers, J. D. Boyd, N. R. Burger, and E. S. Bishop, all former presidents of the MTA. Governor White told the black group and a handful of white officials present that "he recognized the Negro citizens of Mississippi and their needs" and urged them to support his equalization within segregation program, which would necessarily include a disavowal of any desire to press for integrated schools. Although the black leaders did not explicitly renounce *Brown*, they did not suggest that the decision would necessarily undermine segregation either. They implied that a school system "that will satisfy both black and white without circumventing *Brown*" could be developed. The black leaders talked about local meetings of "responsible" blacks and whites to set up satisfactory school systems. With segregation no longer the law and with a "true program of equalization of schools" established, all-black schools in the state would be no more segregated than the all-black schools in the North or the West. For black educators who had witnessed the state's bumbling equalization efforts of the past decade, their most important demand was for assurances that blacks would have a voice in the planned equalization program. Of course, for the white officials listening to these proposals, nothing less than the maintenance of strictly segregated schools would be satisfactory, and while none of the black leaders shared white hatred for the May Supreme Court decision, they cautiously avoided any indication that they had an interest in pressing for Jim Crow's immediate demise. So both the white officials and the black leaders at the meeting essentially heard what they wanted to hear from the other side about how to organize schools in the post-*Brown* era. The meeting adjourned with an agreement to organize a larger conclave of black leaders the following month to discuss these matters further.[2]

Although Governor White and other state officials tried to ensure that the selection of the larger group of black leaders scheduled to meet in Jackson would merely be an expansion of the group of eight, white leaders ultimately decided to invite individuals who represented the range of black opinion in the state in the hopes of giving the meeting real legitimacy. Ultimately, at least one-fourth of those invited to attend the meeting were educators in the state's woefully inadequate black school system, people perceived as the best potential backers of the equalization within segregation program. Over half of the delegates hailed from the Mississippi Delta; school integration would mean black-majority schools in that area, and white officials were especially anxious to get a pledge of voluntary commitment to segregation from black leaders there. The group of eight suggested many of the invitees, and while the governor did not always know the opinions of these individuals on the issues at hand, he had to invite people whom he clearly knew opposed the equalization scheme and favored the beginning of school integration, such as Dr. E. J. Stringer, head of the state NAACP, and Dr. T. R. M. Howard, head of the Regional Council of Negro Leadership (RCNL).[3]

As black leaders in the state prepared to meet with the governor, they sought to present a united front. To that end, they assembled the night before the July 30 meeting at the Farish Street Baptist Church in Jackson to plot strategy. They quickly discovered that they were seriously divided. Some, especially the educators, endorsed the *Brown* decision but favored supporting the equalization within segregation program, probably in the similarly vague manner as the group of eight who had met with the governor a month earlier. Others, however, supported the NAACP's approach of pressing for school integration, now that the Supreme Court had ruled segregation illegal. After hours of heated debate, the two sides agreed on a compromise statement, to be read the following day by E. W. Banks, a Jackson undertaker. Although most left the church that evening willing to accept the so-called Jackson Declaration, some of the most conservative black leaders, including Rev. Humes, J. H. White, and Elks president Fred Miller, left the meeting still determined to back the governor. The divisions among black leaders, though papered over by the Jackson Declaration, almost sank the meeting with the governor. As previously agreed, the group of eight met with Governor White on the morning of July 30, an hour before the larger meeting was to begin. When the group reported that the black leaders were divided on their support of the governor's equalization strategy, "the Governor grew angry and almost called off the meeting."[4]

Cancellation at such a late hour, however, was not a real option, and the arranged confrontation began. The meeting started off calmly enough, with Governor White and other white officials explaining their plan, which called for black support of a program of voluntary segregation in exchange for funding the state's long-discussed but minimally implemented equalization program. After some brief comments by Speaker of the House Walter Sillers, E. W. Banks began to read the Jackson Declaration, which contained both a firm commitment to the *Brown* decision and a plan for a nominally integrated school system that in practice would remain largely segregated yet equalized.[5] The declaration stated that "we can do no other than to endorse and abide by the decision of May 17, 1954 of the Supreme Court of the United States" and noted the need "to remove as soon as possible from the lives of our children, both Negro and white, those severe penalties which they now suffer because of an inadequate and segregated system of education." The declaration, however, also noted that "the only solution to the school problem" was "to consolidate and integrate the present schools on all levels and then equalize and expand within the framework of consolidation and integration," with a "principal requirement" being "that each child must attend the school nearest his or her home." Such a process would mean that "the attendance in these schools will be largely white or largely colored, for the present at least, inasmuch as the residential areas are largely segregated." And the appointment of blacks to "all policy making Boards and Committees at all levels in matters of human relations" would ensure that these plans were carried out fairly.[6] While they probably underestimated the amount of integration that their neighborhood school plan would have led to in the state's rural districts, where housing patterns were not always strictly segregated, the black leaders in their declaration clearly de-emphasized widespread "mixing" of the races as long as equalization was rapidly carried out within a unified school system, with a single standard for distributing equalization funds overseen by both black and white leaders.

The speakers who followed Banks all generally elaborated on the principles laid out in the Jackson Declaration, though what part of the document was emphasized varied from speaker to speaker. T. R. M. Howard spoke first. He praised the *Brown* decision lavishly and castigated whites for "all the injustices that you have heaped upon the Negro in Mississippi," but even he did not demand immediate integration of the state's public schools, except for the state institutions of higher education. He believed that the details of how "the public school in Mississippi may be saved within the spirit of the Supreme Court's decision" should be left to a state biracial committee (twenty-five blacks to join the twenty-five-member LEAC). Howard also emphasized the desirability of an equalization program as long as one standard was used for all buildings and as long as the "school building program will be on the basis of need and not because the Negroes of the State have agreed to any type of segregation in our schools." Conservative black leaders, such as J. H. White, later criticized Howard's remarks as "out of place" and "a blow to the good-will of the people of the State," but White's comments at the meeting, as well as those of H. H. Humes, reiterated the substance of Howard's speech, though without the strident rhetoric. In fact, despite their lingering dislike of the Jackson Declaration, neither White nor Humes publicly repudiated the statement; instead, both men endorsed the substance of the proclamation, recognizing the Supreme Court's recent decision as the law of the land while also calling for an improvement in black schools and the creation of a biracial group to oversee future school developments. Only one of the blacks at the meeting made any sort of statement supporting segregation. J. W. Jones, the Jeanes supervisor for Union County and editor of a black newspaper, rose to speak in favor of preserving segregation, but he was soundly humbled by Ruby Lyells, who operated a truck store in Jackson, when she claimed that the attitudes of someone like Jones represented the best argument for the "damaging effect" of segregated education, a system that would lead "a Negro to accept himself as inferior."[7]

Governor White and the LEAC soon dismissed the black invitees and moved on to plans to resist the new Supreme Court ruling by any means necessary. Although the *Brown* decision seemingly transformed the education debate in Mississippi by outlawing the state's dual school system, white Mississippians, after the failure of the July 1954 meeting between Governor White and black leaders, made clear that no attempts to abandon the dual school system would be tolerated.[8] Instead, state leaders offered to move forward on Mississippi's program to enhance separate black schools. Black school officials and parents in the state welcomed the continued improvement of black education that additional state monies would bring. Many, however, also remained skeptical that any kind of equal funding would be forthcoming under a segregated system. A few black Mississippians pressed for adherence to the *Brown* decision, but they were rebuffed swiftly, decisively, and repeatedly. To block black attempts to desegregate Mississippi schools in the decade after *Brown*, white Mississippians resorted to private and state-sanctioned economic and, sometimes, physical intimidation of blacks. In essence, the strategy adopted by white Mississippians between 1954 and 1964 to avoid the mandate of the *Brown* decision involved both a continued devotion to the state's recently adopted, comprehensive equalization program as a viable alternative to desegregated schools and a determination to quash any efforts by black Mississippians to assert their new legal rights.

Even if black leaders at the July 1954 meeting did not demand immediate implementation of the *Brown* decision, their straightforward support of the decree, the blunt suggestions about the failures of separate but equal, and the bold talk of sharing power to determine the state's future educational course undoubtedly terrified Governor White and the LEAC. For these white leaders, if blacks did not support voluntary segregation, they must favor integration and, by extension, social equality. LEAC member R. M. Newton of Wiggins left the meeting thinking "there is no use cooperating with them. They want to be social equals in every way." Perhaps Newton was not listening when T. R. M. Howard, perhaps the most strident black speaker at the meeting, explicitly refuted this notion: "Your big fear, of course, is social equality. There is not a thinking Negro in Mississippi today that bothers about social equality, but we are mighty concerned about equality of educational opportunity."[9]

The black proposal for addressing *Brown* was actually somewhere between the two extremes of segregation, on the one hand, and integration and social equality, on the other, but white leaders essentially were incapable of hearing the black proposition. Ironically, had they been able to understand the middle ground blacks offered in their compromise proposal, whites might have been able to construct a unitary school system that entailed far less school desegregation than later ordered by the courts. Instead, immediately following the meeting with the black leaders, White and the LEAC called for a special session of the legislature to initiate steps to abolish the state's public schools if necessary to avoid integration. In the coming years, white Mississippians would commit themselves to a number of other draconian and wasteful measures to fight school desegregation.

In the aftermath of the failed assembly with the governor, blacks affiliated with the NAACP in the state cautiously resumed their attempt to implement the *Brown* decision, but local whites moved swiftly to discourage such efforts. In the Delta, the organization of anti-integration Citizens' Councils had already begun. In the summer of 1954, the state only had approximately thirty NAACP branches in even fewer counties, with a total membership of under twenty-five hundred, but this fledgling cadre made a valiant effort to indicate their desire that *Brown* be realized. In August, the Walthall NAACP branch submitted a school desegregation petition to the county school board; school officials responded by closing the county's black school for fourteen days and firing a school bus driver who signed the petition. In nearby Amite County, the white sheriff, a member of the white school board, and fifteen to twenty other whites barged into a local NAACP meeting at the black school, seizing the group's records and questioning those present about their motives for meeting. Undoubtedly convinced that the meeting revolved around challenging the existence of local Jim Crow schools, the school board member even offered the gathering a bribe, urging them "to take this money and put it into the school building." In Columbus, state NAACP president E. J. Stringer collected a number of signatures for a school desegregation petition, but he inadvertently lost the petition while making his rounds. When the document fell into the hands of local whites, Stringer received threatening phone calls and had his credit revoked. Not surprisingly, Stringer soon indicated that he did not want to be considered for a second term as state NAACP president. In other communities, mere rumors of a school desegregation attempt by blacks mobilized white resistance to integration. After stories circulated in Kemper County during the summer of 1954 that a group of prosperous, light-skinned African Americans would attempt to enroll their children in the all-white Lynville school, whites from all over Kemper (including the county sheriff) showed up at the school on opening day armed to the teeth to prevent an assault on segregated education that never materialized.[10]

White reprisals for these smallest of implementation efforts by the NAACP strengthened the hand of blacks in the state who favored pressing for equalization over integration. J. H. White, president of Mississippi Vocational College, noted in August that "the White people of Mississippi are not ready and the Negroes of Mississippi are not ready for many things that are being asked" by the NAACP. White urged NAACP leaders' support "in asking for adequate facilities and other things that our people need first and when you lay that foundation you have made a great contribution and many other problems will be solved in years to come." Such feelings had enough support in the state that T. R. M. Howard called a meeting of the RCNL for September 1954 "to release or cause to be released the pressure from the reactionaries." It is perhaps a measure of how much pressure had

increased over the summer on those in the state endorsing the *Brown* decision that the RCNL meeting of more than one thousand black leaders from
forty of the state's counties had to be held outdoors in a tent after both the
Mound Bayou school trustees and elders of the African Methodist Episcopal
(AME) church in the town refused to allow their buildings to be used as
a meeting site. When the meeting convened, the RCNL executive board
endorsed the *Brown* decision but satisfied those unwilling to press for
implementation by agreeing not to petition for school integration during
the 1954–55 school year. Howard claimed that the decision to hold off on the
school petitions was made in part to wait for the court's anticipated implementation decision, but mindful of the white retaliation that greeted the
halting implementation efforts already launched, Howard also observed
that "to petition school boards in Miss. at the present time is like going to
hunt a bear with a cap pistol." As the most outspoken black proponent of
Brown in the state, Howard especially felt the pressure applied by whites. In
fact, Howard soon left Mississippi to save his life. Two other outspoken
black leaders in the state, Rev. George Lee and Lamar Smith, were murdered
in 1955 for their civil rights activism by whites who embraced the call to
resist *Brown* absolutely.[11]

   While black Mississippians debated how best to take advantage of the
opportunities for change presented by the *Brown* decision, white leaders
moved forward with their plans to defy the ruling. Even before the court's
directive, the state legislature during its 1954 session had passed a pupil
assignment plan that required school boards to make "individual assignment" of students on the basis of a variety of vague criteria, thereby obscur-
ing the fact that the true basis of pupil assignment was race. After blacks
demonstrated their support for *Brown* at the July 1954 meeting, state leaders
pushed for an amendment to the state constitution to allow the legislature
to abolish the public schools if integration occurred, in favor of publicly
supported "private schools." Such an amendment had first been advanced
during the 1953 special session by Speaker of the House Walter Sillers, but
the legislation went down to defeat in the midst of uncertainty about the
outcome of the legal challenge to segregation. After the Supreme Court
handed down the *Brown* decision, the proposal gained new life. Following
Governor White's meeting with black leaders, the LEAC immediately

recommended that a special session be called to consider a school closure amendment. Once Mississippi whites had ratified this change to the constitution, the legislature could proceed with the equalization plans previously developed. The proposed school closure amendment breezed through the 1954 special session with only limited opposition, and key legislators promised to fund the equalization program at the scheduled special session of 1955 if Mississippi voters ratified the amendment.[12]

Many white political leaders thought they had found a real loophole in the *Brown* decision. As LEAC member Maurice Black remembered, "we said if they are not in the public schools, they can't be integrated. . . . [I]f they are private, privately operated and privately owned, why the *Brown* decision won't apply here." The details of how public schools could be transformed into publicly supported "private" schools remained necessarily vague, but proponents of the change sometimes talked about the creation of private school corporations, with the legislature making "donations" to the counties for "scholarship funds" to be used to underwrite the school expenses of "each educable child." Supporters of the school closure amendment, however, generally claimed that the details could be worked out as needed at a later date. They more often emphasized the necessity of the measure to demonstrate Mississippi's resolve to oppose school integration and to use as a weapon to hold over the heads of blacks who might press for integrated schools; promised that school closure would only be used as a "last resort" to resist integration; and in the odd logic of white supremacy, argued that the amendment would actually represent the best way to preserve the state's public school system.[13] The idea that the school closure amendment would be a club over the heads of potentially troublesome blacks seemed somewhat ridiculous to black Mississippians. Conservative educator J. D. Boyd noted that "except in a very few instances, the Negro people have no school system that should not have been abolished long ago. . . . It is your White school system built up over the years that in reality would suffer. When we face the facts of the situation, we know that the Negro is very skilled in the operation of private schools. He has had to raise most of the money for land, buildings, equipment, maintenance, and often part of the salary of the teacher."[14]

Even some whites in the state were not convinced of the amendment's necessity. White teachers were a group of particular concern to state politicians. A meeting of school administrators in the spring of 1954 had already indicated firm opposition to the amendment. Soon after the LEAC floated the school closure idea following the debacle with black leaders, rumors began to circulate that "the school folks were against this constitutional amendment." To head off this potential opposition, the LEAC called eight hundred school officials (teachers, superintendents, school board members, college education professors) from around the state to assemble in Jackson on August 12 to discuss the proposed amendment. At the assembly, an early "standing" vote revealed that about a third of the education officials remained decidedly opposed to the state's proposed school abolition plan. Most of the opposition came from the attendees from northeast Mississippi, south Mississippi, and Lauderdale County. At one point in the meeting, Otho Smith of Meridian proposed that the group listen to the LEAC's pitch but take no formal action, but his motion was tabled. Carl McQuagge, an education professor at Mississippi Southern College in Hattiesburg, then tried to adjourn the meeting, but that motion was ruled out of order.[15]

As the opposition forces struggled to disrupt the proceedings, Governor White, who was also on hand, gave the education folks an ultimatum, one only slightly more subtle than his demand two weeks earlier that black leaders embrace segregation. White told the educators that the LEAC needed to know the sentiment of the group and hinted that a failure to support the LEAC might doom the unfunded equalization program, which would help poor white schools as much as impoverished black ones. White's threat proved decisive. As Walter Sillers told Governor White a few days later, "as witnessed at the recent meeting of school people one of the strongest assets you have with which to enlighten some of those who otherwise would be wilfully [sic] blind to the disasterous [sic] consequences which will follow integration of the negros [sic] into our white schools is that no additional legislation can be enacted during your term of office . . . to supplement the now inadequate funds to operate the 1955 school sessions unless you call an extra-ordinary session of the Legislature for that purpose." After a few more individuals rose to speak at the meeting, many who now posed the choice as simply supporting the governor and the LEAC or backing "the Negroes," a voice vote was held in which a loud roar of support for the defenders of white supremacy was followed by only four who dared oppose the benevolent state officials.[16]

Despite the somewhat coerced show of unity in evidence at the conference, opposition to the school closure amendment did not disappear. In fact, a number of educators and politicians in south and northeast Mississippi created the Friends of Segregated Public Schools in October to try and build support against the amendment's ratification in the December 1954 election. As their name suggests, the group opposed school integration, but it castigated the school closure amendment as an unnecessary and perhaps dangerous tactic in the battle to preserve segregated education. Representative Joel Blass of Stone County, one of the leaders of the organization, noted that if the amendment represented a "last resort," as its supporters claimed, the amendment was uncalled for since the state had other "legal measures to maintain segregated schools" that might delay school mixing for as long as twenty years. Perhaps more important, members of the Friends group showed a traditional Hill distrust of Delta motives. They claimed that "in the present instance the bugaboo of integration is raised by those who would escape taxation through abolishing the public schools," specifically "the legislative leaders from the Delta and Black counties, the same people who have consistently opposed and stymied every attempt to increase appropriations for education." Since practically all whites generally agreed that the only effective alternative to integration was effective equalization of black and white education, the organization argued that whites in the black belt would face a difficult choice: raise local taxes substantially or improve black schools at the expense of white ones. Not wishing to endorse either option, black-belt whites would instead eagerly embrace the opportunity to create a publicly funded "private" school system for whites in order to "avoid the heavy burden of equalizing educational facilities in their counties for the two races." Since Delta tax receipts also helped fund largely white schools in the poorer Hill sections of the state, many in the Friends group and their supporters believed that the Delta would use the amendment as a way to prevent Delta wealth from supporting either local black education or public education for whites in the state's poorer districts.[17]

The fears that Delta whites saw the abolition of the public schools as a first rather than last resort were not entirely unfounded. Walter Sillers, the author of the school closure proposal, had a reputation, along with other Delta leaders, as someone who "really didn't care about educating the masses of people. . . . [T]he way to keep them satisfied with the low wages and with the status quo was not to let them get too well educated." Sillers never supported the idea of trying to get blacks to go along with voluntary segregation and believed from the beginning that private schools represented the only "lasting and permanent" answer to the threat posed by the *Brown* decision. In June 1954, Sillers consulted with Jackson attorney Pat Eager about the viability of using a private school plan to circumvent *Brown*. Eager informed Sillers that "such a scheme would be nothing more than a subterfuge," and the Supreme Court would see the plan as such "so long as the funds are provided from the public treasury." Eager also noted that "at all times we would have to honestly admit that the sole purpose was an effort to avoid abolition of segregation and to maintain segregation of the two races in the schools of Mississippi." But Sillers and other Mississippi officials tried for decades to mold a successful plan to create a publicly supported private school system without ever admitting their true motives. Though advised that publicly funded "private" schools would never survive a legal challenge, Sillers continued to advocate the solution as the state's only recourse for many years.[18] The idea that school integration could ultimately be avoided by the creation of some kind of publicly funded "private" school system continued to be explored by state officials as late as 1970.

In the end, the Friends of Segregated Public Education managed to convince many whites in the Hill counties of northeast Mississippi and in south Mississippi that the school abolition amendment was not a good idea, but the voters ultimately ratified the measure in the December 21 balloting by more than a two-to-one margin. The final tally, however, demonstrated that despite an almost unanimous endorsement of the amendment by Mississippi's entire state and national political leadership, many white Mississippians remained skeptical of the school closure idea. Although only fourteen of the state's eighty-two counties voted against the amendment (all in northeast or south Mississippi), almost 41,000 of the more than 132,000 votes cast opposed the measure. The average white Mississippian in general apparently did not view passage of the measure as the important necessity touted by state leaders. Although voter turnout was generally always lower for special elections, one might have expected that more than a third of the eligible voters would have ventured out to vote in an election designed to pass a measure billed by its proponents as "the only course left to maintain segregation."[19]

When the Supreme Court handed down *Brown II* on May 31, 1955, the ruling that outlined how the first *Brown* decision would be implemented, it announced that school desegregation should be accomplished "with all deliberate speed." Most white Mississippi leaders proclaimed the decision a victory, zeroing in on the word "deliberate." LEAC member Thomas J. Tubb noted that "we couldn't ask for anything better than to have our local, native Mississippi federal court judges consider suits in good faith and act accordingly on the 'as soon as feasible' element." Governor Hugh White envisioned a timetable that would delay school desegregation "for ten or more years." Attorney General J. P. Coleman recognized that the Court's implementation decision placed the burden firmly on the backs of black Mississippians to initiate the process of school desegregation: "the next move is up to those who wish to destroy segregation in the public schools, and we are thoroughly ready for anything they may wish to come up with." That move came six days after *Brown II*, when the Mississippi NAACP directed its branches to petition local school boards for desegregated schools; over the next three months, blacks in five communities submitted petitions. As Attorney General Coleman suggested, however, the state, along with local whites, stood ready and willing to crush the effort. The LEAC, which had been granted broad "court powers" by the legislature in January 1955, decisively declared in early June 1955 that "there will be no integration of the races in Mississippi and there will be no compromise on the matter."[20]

The Vicksburg chapter of the NAACP filed the first school desegregation petition on July 18, and the white response included both a studied avoidance of the document and an all-out effort to harass those who signed it. The Vicksburg petition, drafted with the help of the national NAACP office, took note of the *Brown* decisions and called on the school board "to take immediate concrete steps leading to early elimination of segregation in the public schools." When word of the petition reached Jackson, the state's chief law enforcement agent, Attorney General Coleman, canceled two stops in his campaign for governor (with the all-important Democratic Party primary less than three weeks away) and rushed to Vicksburg to declare the NAACP petition a "legal nullity." Coleman told the Vicksburg school board that "it will not be necessary . . . to consider this thing as a petition. At the very best, it is nothing more than a lame attempt at one." This legal opinion was perhaps shaped by Coleman's personal observation that the document would "accomplish nothing but increased friction between the races in Mississippi." The day after the petition was filed, the *Vicksburg Evening Post* published the names of the 140 signers, and within days a number of the petitioners asked to have their names removed from the document.[21]

In the next few weeks, petitions were also filed in Jackson, Natchez, Clarksdale, and Yazoo City. The school boards in these other cities, as in Vicksburg, responded with silence. Jackson school officials simply marked the petition signed by forty-two parents as "Received" and filed it away. As in Vicksburg, local papers in these other cities also published the names of the petition signers, resulting in harassment of the black parents and subsequent requests by many that their names be removed from the documents. In Clarksdale, where a vigorous NAACP campaign had resulted in a petition with 342 names, blacks who signed faced a variety of reprisals. As local NAACP leader Aaron Henry remembered, "if the whites saw your name on the list, you just caught hell." In Natchez, although "enthusiasm was high" within the black community as the local NAACP launched its school petition drive in mid-July, after the publication of the petition and its almost one hundred signers in the *Natchez Democrat*, three-fifths of the petitioners reconsidered their action. Requests poured into the offices of the newspaper and the school board asking that names be excised from the petition; many of the black parents claimed, not very convincingly, that they had misunderstood what they were signing. The methods used to persuade Natchez blacks that their petition action was misguided were obviously quite effective, for even the local NAACP president, David Bacon Jr., who worked for a white-owned business, renounced his endorsement of the document and quit the NAACP. The Jackson petition, by comparison, was a relative success; only seven of the forty-two signers later asked to have their names removed from the document.[22]

The most unrelenting persecution of black school petitioners, however, came in Yazoo City, the site of the last of the 1955 petitions. The virulence of the attacks on blacks there can be partly attributed to the fact that while the earlier school petitions had aided the recruitment efforts of local Citizens' Councils chapters, by the time the Yazoo City petition was filed the local Citizens' Council had already grown significantly. In fact, the Yazoo City Citizens' Council chapter paid for the newspaper ad listing the names and addresses of the fifty-three signers of the school petition as a "public service." The local chapter also coordinated the harassment of the signers. The president of one local bank called his customers on the list "and told them to come down and get their money out, that the bank did not want to do business with them any longer." James Wright, a plumber with primarily white customers, not only lost his patrons but also was "refused plumbing supplies by a wholesale house, and notified by his grocer that a loaf of bread would cost him a dollar." He soon left for Detroit. As the Citizens' Council applied pressure on the signers, fifty of the fifty-three asked that their names be removed from the school integration petition. Two of the three who did not had already left town. Many who did remove their names from the document also left, especially when the pressure continued even after they had recanted their activism. The Yazoo City NAACP branch, which had about two hundred members before submission of the petition, soon disappeared. The assault against this act of black activism was so thorough that the city remained almost unorganizable by the civil rights movement during the early 1960s.[23]

White Mississippians obviously believed implementation of the *Brown* decision with "all deliberate speed" meant something longer, something much longer in fact, than the "immediate concrete steps leading to early elimination of segregation in the public schools" proposed in the NAACP petitions. With the outbreak of black activism in the summer of 1955 quickly squelched, white leaders reiterated their stance of "never." In 1956, the Mississippi legislature passed a resolution of interposition, promising to interpose the sovereignty of the state of Mississippi between any federal court decision requiring desegregated schools and the local school districts called on to begin integration. To further "protect the sovereignty of the state," the legislature authorized the creation of the Mississippi State Sovereignty Commission (along with a $250,000 budget) to replace the LEAC as the watchdog group for preserving segregation. The official state position of absolute opposition to school desegregation reflected the beliefs of most white Mississippians, even if they remained divided on the best tactics to achieve this objective. White opposition ranged from those who merely did not want to change time-honored mores to those who seriously saw in school desegregation the apocalypse. A Natchez woman expressed the latter opinion in a poorly written 1956 letter to liberal Louisiana federal judge

J. Skelly Wright: "Many parents in the south (white) would keep their children out of school before they would have them exposed to Syhilis, Gonnoreah, & the other disease, that is so prevalent among Negros, . . . and if the Government tried to force the children to go to schools, I imagine we would hear of many mass murders and suicides, because so many people [would] rather see their children dead than live a lifetime of shame and degredation, which integration would cause."[24]

The call for massive resistance to *Brown* encouraged some whites to use economic intimidation and other threats, if necessary, to discourage any blacks who dared to endorse the decision, but white leaders also worked for what they saw as the only lasting solution to the school desegregation order: getting blacks to agree to a program of separate but (truly) equal schools. Armed with the ability to close the public schools if integration was forced on the state, legislators fulfilled their promise to pass the most ambitious equalization within segregation plan ever. Meeting in yet another special session in early 1955, the legislature approved a two-year $88 million education budget, which included an $11 million annual increase to cover the equalization of teachers' salaries, transportation, and administration—billed as a minimum foundation program—as well as a down payment on the $117 million needed for buildings and to complete the consolidation effort. This increase in education spending was financed largely by increases in the state sales and cigarette taxes. Although the new equalization plan adjusted the 1953 formula by adding an additional $3 for every black child in a district to the already-approved $12 per child granted to each district in the form of annual credits toward building funds, the legislation made no explicit requirement that these additional levies be spent on erecting black schools.[25]

In the post-*Brown* era, however, state officials took the equalization program much more seriously than they ever had. Even without a specific mandate that the new building funds approved by the legislature go toward the creation and improvement of black schools, a majority of the monies appropriated by the state in the late 1950s did fund black building projects. In the first two years of the program, more than two-thirds of the state funds allocated went to black school projects. Between 1955 and June 1957, the state approved 117 projects at a cost of almost $19 million; 79 projects (68 percent) were for black schools. Whites soon clamored for a larger share of the available funds, but the majority of the state monies continued to be directed toward black school ventures. For example, between July 1957 and the end of 1959, an additional 399 new building projects received state funds ($52 million), and 166 (55 percent) of these undertakings involved black schools. Noticeable improvements were also made in the area of equalizing black and white teachers' salaries, eliminating the unconsolidated black (and few remaining white) schools, and providing adequate school transportation to many more black students than ever before.[26] All over the state, one could see visible evidence of the efforts, long overdue, to improve black public education.

The equalization campaign gave white Mississippians a glimmer of hope that school segregation might be maintained. While some white conservatives in the state, such as House Speaker Walter Sillers and members of groups like the Citizens' Councils, groused about the huge sums being "lavished" on black education, many white leaders recognized the equalization effort as the only possible chance to preserve segregation. As Erle Johnston, public relations director for the Sovereignty Commission, argued in the early 1960s, "the only way we can retain our separate school system is through the cooperation of the colored race." That cooperation could only be gained by "an honest attempt to make certain that colored people have adequate facilities to which they are entitled." Johnston often reminded those critical of the large expenses associated with educational equalization that blacks had "the federal government and federal courts ready to support them," so it might be better "to give up an inch" than "to give up a mile."[27]

With additional funds being pumped into the state's black schools and with the viable options for blacks narrowed by the intimidation directed against those who did support implementation of the school integration order, most whites believed blacks would surely accept a better version of Jim Crow schools. Senator John Stennis suggested that local white leaders should give blacks in their community a simple "ultimatum." If blacks accepted segregated schools, whites would "help them get better schools." Ultimately, most whites convinced themselves that the vast majority of blacks in the state supported the equalization effort over the NAACP's attempt to bring about immediate school integration. The seeming absence of black demands for integrated schools for years after the summer of 1955 seemed to confirm these beliefs. In 1959, for example, the Sovereignty

Commission, ignoring the role it played in quieting black demands for school desegregation, concluded that "nothing has been more advantageous in keeping the negroes of Mississippi satisfied than the new schools which have been built for them." That same year Attorney General Joe Patterson told a subcommittee of the U.S. House of Representatives holding hearings on pending civil rights legislation that "the dual system of education in Mississippi is working to the complete satisfaction of both races. There is no strife, confusion or dissatisfaction. . . . Both races are working in complete harmony looking forward to a greater, bigger and better educational system in our state for the benefit of both races." The following year state education chief J. M. Tubb claimed that the lack of desegregation efforts by the state's blacks could be attributed to the fact "that Mississippi Negroes are more interested in education than integration—when given equal opportunities in their own improved and fully equipped schools." By the early 1960s, Mississippi officials claimed that the equalization program had allowed the state to provide a quality education to both races without integration.[28]

Although the equalization program brought some real improvement to black education, Mississippi's project to avoid school desegregation failed for two reasons: blacks in the state refused to endorse segregation voluntarily (even though they welcomed the additional funding), and the equalization program never succeeded in truly equalizing white and black education. After the *Brown* decision, white violence and intimidation dampened black enthusiasm for school desegregation. Nevertheless, even after the state had decisively quashed the NAACP school petition drive in the summer of 1955, a number of black Mississippians (including some teachers) in the late 1950s and early 1960s rejected equalization and continued to push for implementation of the *Brown* decision. When J. P. Coleman, the former state attorney general who was elected governor in 1955, claimed in 1958 that blacks were satisfied with the new schools recently built in the state, C. R. Darden of Meridian, president of the Mississippi State Conference of NAACP Branches, denied the truth of Coleman's statement by noting that "the Mississippi Negro knows that any schools constructed for Negroes are inferior." The Mississippi NAACP, led by state field secretary Medgar Evers, flatly rejected the state's "so-called 'equalization' program," as an effort "to construct inferior buildings with beautiful fronts, suppress our teachers,

and enslave the minds of Negro children." The organization vowed to continue the fight for school integration as "the one and only channel through
which equality in education, economics and political freedom may be
attained." The MTA also both publicly questioned the operation of the
equalization program and privately supported NAACP efforts to build support for school desegregation in the state. J. W. Grantham of Magee, who
served as MTA president during the 1956–57 academic year, regularly pointed
out the continuing inequalities of the state's equalization program in the
areas of teacher salaries, teacher training, and supervisory responsibilities
within the educational system. He also cleverly suggested that any "honest
approach to equalization" would recognize the right of black teachers to
vote and to belong to any organization they chose. In 1959, a Sovereignty
Commission informer reported that MTA officials, including Gladys Noel
Bates—who had gone to work for the organization after her unsuccessful
salary equalization lawsuit against the Jackson schools in the late 1940s—were
helping the national NAACP in a recruiting effort aimed at Mississippi's
black teachers.[29]

Black supporters of school desegregation in the late 1950s and early
1960s, however, had to negotiate a landscape full of obstacles. For one thing,
state officials kept close tabs on those communities suspected as potential
sites for school desegregation lawsuits. As the 1956 school year approached,
Governor Coleman asked Sovereignty Commission investigators to monitor those cities where school petitions had been filed in 1955; all was quiet,
according to the investigators. And the state quickly dealt with a number
of reported black efforts to press forward with school desegregation. The
Sovereignty Commission vigorously investigated numerous rumors of
planned school desegregation efforts around the state during these years
and, when necessary, provided local officials with information to undermine the attempts.[30]

Augmenting the work of state officials, local officials also sought to
discourage even the most minor activity that might challenge school segregation. For instance, in the late 1950s C. R. Darden waged an ongoing
but always contested struggle to force school officials to accede to *Brown*.
Darden, a lifelong resident of the Meridian area, worked as a photographer
in a studio in his home and as a salesman for a New York school jewelry
firm, so he had the independence necessary to challenge the local white

community on the school desegregation issue. In May 1958, school officials refused to allow Darden to attend a school board meeting at which the board was scheduled to discuss plans to build a new black school. The meeting had been announced in the local paper as the "regular" monthly meeting of the board, but when Darden appeared at the meeting, the school board attorney declared the gathering to be an "executive session" and therefore closed to spectators. The following May, Darden outfitted two of his boys and several other students involved with the local NAACP Youth Council with badges that read "U.S. Supreme Court Decision, May 17, 1954." When the students arrived at Harris High School, the school's principal, W. A. Reed Jr., told them to remove the "controversial" badges. When four of the boys, including Darden's two sons, refused, Reed suspended the students. Darden and the NAACP Meridian branch president, Robert Stanton, returned to the school the following day with the four boys to talk with Principal Reed. He refused to readmit the students. At some point during this visit, Darden took some pictures of the boys wearing their badges with the school in the background. When Darden returned to his house, the local police served him with an arrest warrant for "willfully disturbing a session of a public school" (an offense he was subsequently convicted of and fined $50) and confiscated his film, apparently to destroy the evidence of this "assault" on segregated education.[31]

Darden's experience in Meridian suggests another obstacle faced by those blacks who favored school integration: members of their own race who accepted Governor White's dichotomy of choices for blacks—that they could only support the state's equalization campaign if they opposed efforts to implement *Brown*. Medgar Evers believed that school principals such as Reed were the main obstacles to building support for school desegregation in the black community. Evers thought that the equalization program essentially "paid off" black principals so they would not challenge the racial status quo. As the head of local black schools, black principals did occupy a crucial position from which to shape the opinions and actions of black parents, teachers, and students. With many blacks supportive of or at least sympathetic to the state's efforts to replace the mandate of *Brown* with a promise of educational equalization within segregation, black activists seeking willing plaintiffs and local funds for school desegregation lawsuits had to proceed cautiously. When John Melchor, an NAACP leader in

Clarksdale, was trying to raise funds for a school desegregation lawsuit in 1955, he cautioned other supporters to "be careful about those men and women who seem to enjoy telling the opposite race what we are doing, otherwise we can, and may be, cut off before we achieve our goal."[32]

After the massive white assault on the 1955 NAACP school petition drive, blacks in many communities did indeed opt for the less controversial strategy of urging white leaders to upgrade black schools. Even while Melchor tried to raise funds for a school desegregation suit, another group of black parents in Clarksdale met with the all-white school board not to demand integration but to request improvement in black school conditions. In Hattiesburg, which had long possessed one of the better black school systems in the state, black parents never embraced the NAACP's position of aggressively demanding school desegregation. Weeks after *Brown II*, parents from two of the city's black schools, Eureka and Royal Street, met with the school board to complain about overcrowding and other shortcomings of their schools. School board member R. L. Morrison assured the parents that "building plans [have] just begun. We consider your children in our planning just like ours."[33] Having made their case, the black parents went home to wait for the requested changes.

It is perhaps not surprising that many blacks endorsed the state's equalization effort, and not only because support for implementing *Brown* seemed to be a certain dead end given the agitated state of white public opinion against any breach of the educational color line. Black Mississippians supported the equalization program for a number of reasons. To begin with, although whites often believed blacks favored school integration merely to achieve "social equality" (read miscegenation), many blacks often sought desegregated schools simply to force whites to provide adequate schools for black children. If no separate black schools existed, the thinking went, all schools would receive adequate funding. In the wake of the failed desegregation petition in Natchez, a black newspaper editor there sought to explain the grounds for the recent action by area blacks. He claimed that "the social intermingling of the two races in Adams County is definitely not desired by the vast majority of colored people." Rather, "equality of opportunity, equality at the ballot box, equality in a chance to live [as] human beings, equality of education to bring out the best in us, these are our age-old dreams, this is what America means to us." As far as this newspaperman was concerned, the recent attempt to desegregate the schools sprang from the failure of state and local officials to make "genuine and concrete efforts to provide for Negro children adequate school facilities." A northern reporter who interviewed blacks in Jackson in early 1956 found much the same attitudes. He discovered that while a small number of black parents favored pushing for integrated schools on principle, most wanted their children to remain in black schools, as long as improvements continued to be made. James Gooden, black supervisor of the city's black schools, perhaps expressed the sentiment of many of the city's black residents when he noted that while most forms of racial segregation were humiliating, school segregation was not necessarily a bad thing: "Let us bring up our children in our own schools. But don't make us get off the sidewalk to let you pass; don't make us take a back seat in a bus; don't make us sit in a separate waiting room."[34] For many black Mississippians, securing a better education for their children represented their most important objective. School desegregation offered a means to achieve that end, but if whites remained adamantly opposed to that solution and proffered more funds than ever before to support black education, perhaps supporting the state's equalization program remained the most realistic way to achieve the primary goal.

In addition, in the post-*Brown* years whites in many communities seemed more willing than in earlier years to heed black demands and even seek black input when spending equalization funds. For instance, while Hattiesburg had spent most of its construction funds on white schools during the equalization push of 1946–53, of the first five projects approved under the state's post-*Brown* equalization program in early 1956, three were for improvements to existing black schools, and the largest project was for the construction of a new black elementary–junior high school. When Scott County received a $315,000 state grant to build a black high school in Morton in the late 1950s, the school board consulted black educators and parents on how to proceed with the project, and a number of changes suggested by local blacks "were incorporated in the proposed plans."[35]

As in the days before *Brown*, a number of blacks also favored the state's equalization push of the late 1950s and early 1960s because, despite inadequate facilities, poorly trained teachers, and limited instructional supplies, black Mississippians treasured the educational institutions they had labored so hard to build and that they generally ran, since whites often had little interest in the day-to-day operation of black schools. Sovereignty Commission investigators did not need to exaggerate when they reported, on their travels across the state during this period, that blacks were "taking great pride" in their new school facilities. The very real improvements made to black educational institutions during this period were indeed greatly appreciated.[36] Not surprisingly, Mississippi's state officials sought to capitalize on any black expression of support for the equalization program as further proof that the state's black residents favored continued segregation. When Canton constructed a new and large black high school, Rogers High, area blacks expressed their appreciation to local officials; black educators even bought a full-page ad in the local paper communicating their thanks for the new school. Canton whites used these expressions of gratitude as the centerpiece of a publicity campaign to demonstrate to potential northern industrial concerns that "racial harmony" prevailed in a city that nevertheless maintained "equal but separate schools."[37]

While the state's business and political leaders tried to capitalize on every expression of black support for school equalization, most whites realized that the program's success rested on an often ambivalent base of black support. Consequently, white officials pressed blacks when they could to support the campaign. For instance, white officials made a special effort to ensure that all of the state's black public school teachers endorsed the program. As a group, black teachers were particularly vulnerable to white coercion. L. S. Alexander, the longtime executive secretary of the MTA (1956–68), claimed that some white superintendents instituted an elaborate system of payoffs in the black schools they oversaw. These white superintendents would allegedly only promote to positions such as principalships those blacks who would kick back part of their salary to the superintendent. In turn, the black principal, "knowing that he was paying out to the superintendent, demanded the same kind of thing of black teachers who were hired under him."[38] Even without such corruption, black educators knew they were state employees in a system controlled by whites; those who rocked the boat were not retained or rewarded by such a system.

As the state's equalization plans were being unveiled in 1955 and 1956, white politicians called on black teachers to approve continued voluntary segregation as part of the state's equalization venture. MTA president for the 1955–56 academic year, N. R. Burger of Hattiesburg, advised black teachers in February 1956 to take a "position of silence" on the question. Within months, however, the Mississippi legislature passed a measure requiring all teachers to sign an affidavit listing their organizational memberships. The law was primarily designed to uncover teachers who belonged to the NAACP and essentially operated as a loyalty oath designed to root out any potential educator opposition to the state's plan to bypass the *Brown* mandate through the creation of separate but now "truly" equal schools. The actual use of the disclosure forms varied from district to district. In some areas, especially south Mississippi, white superintendents had teachers complete the required affidavits but rarely used them as grounds for teacher dismissal, especially as long as these teachers did not openly endorse the NAACP and its school desegregation efforts. In other areas, such as the Delta, the disclosure requirement represented merely one more tool of intimidation available to white officials concerned about even the slightest signs of potential danger to the established racial order. For example, even before the use of the disclosure affidavits, school officials in several Delta counties had forced black teachers to remove their names from the voting rolls as a condition of having their teaching contracts renewed.[39]

The state also employed its segregation watchdog agency, the Sovereignty Commission, to help monitor the "loyalty" of black teachers. As commission investigators toured the state in the late 1950s and early 1960s looking for potential enemies of Mississippi's racial status quo, they regularly visited white school superintendents to inquire whether local black teachers remained loyal to the segregated school cause and uncontaminated by NAACP membership. Commission investigators also visited prominent black educators around the state to gauge where their sympathies lay. For example, in 1959 commission investigator Zack Van Landingham called on Stone County's Needham Jones, president of the South Mississippi Association of Negro Teachers in 1959, for a statement of support for the state's policy of maintaining school segregation. Jones at first was reportedly "very cool and suspicious." He may have been quite rightly fearful of talking about racial matters with any white man. Or he may have hesitated to express opinions that did not reflect the sentiments of the hundreds of black teachers he represented. For whatever reason, he soon told Van Landingham everything he wanted to hear: Jones opposed the NAACP, believing that "the interest of the negro lies along separate school lines" and that the state was making good progress in helping the state's black citizens.[40]

The commission even tried to foster the creation of a network of black educators sympathetic to the state's efforts to maintain segregated schools, a group that could keep the commission informed about potential school desegregation attempts. B. L. Bell, a black teacher from Cleveland who served as supervisor of black schools in Bolivar County and who opposed the entire concept of school desegregation, originally suggested the idea for such an organization to Governor Coleman in 1959. Bell had close ties to other conservative black leaders in the Delta, such as the recently deceased newspaper editor and Baptist leader H. H. Humes and the president of Mississippi Vocational College, J. H. White. The Sovereignty Commission put Bell on the payroll to implement his proposal, and though he did briefly assemble a group of Delta educators interested in the plan, his scheme for a larger statewide spy network of educators never materialized. The commission then employed Bell as an informer to attend and report on NAACP meetings around the state, but he proved ineffective in this capacity, as NAACP officials such as Aaron Henry soon recognized him as a Sovereignty Commission spy.[41]

With the state and local school officials closely monitoring their attitudes in the post-*Brown* years, black teachers generally avoided civil rights organizations and activities, or at least kept their involvement as quiet as possible. Few teachers could afford to play an active role in local NAACP chapters; in fact, the virtual absence of teachers from NAACP meetings was one reason B. L. Bell's presence at such gatherings struck NAACP leaders as odd. When the Clarksdale NAACP organized an economic boycott in 1961 to protest the failure of the local Chamber of Commerce to allow black school bands to march in the town's annual Christmas parade, local teachers supported the boycott but did so through a separate community organization organized by the NAACP to offer "an opportunity of expression for the Teachers without them having the fear of participating in an NAACP only sponsored affair." When civil rights groups began to operate in the state during the early 1960s, organizing voter registration campaigns and testing the segregation of public accommodations, teachers, whatever their true sentiments, generally could not openly endorse or engage in such activities. For example, Henry Kirksey, who in 1963 worked at MTA headquarters

and had a close relationship with Medgar Evers, produced a newsletter following Evers's assassination "asking the teachers that out of respect for this
man giving his life, that each of you should register to vote." MTA officials
deemed the publication so inflammatory that they fired Kirksey. When the
Congress of Racial Equality (CORE) tried to organize a school boycott at
the Camden school in Madison County in March 1964, the school's principal knew better than to let the group use the school's facilities for its organizing efforts, because granting such permission would, if known to local
white officials, likely cost him and other school employees their jobs.[42]

The fear felt by black teachers in the state was well-founded. Those
teachers who openly expressed support for school desegregation or who
became involved in civil rights activities did indeed lose their jobs. When
Robert Clark, who had a degree from Michigan State University and who
would in 1967 become the first black elected to the Mississippi legislature in
the twentieth century, publicly announced his support for school integration while teaching in the Humphreys County schools in 1959, he did not
receive a contract to return the following year. When he tried to secure a
teaching job in another Delta community the following year, he was told
that his "education philosophy from Michigan just wouldn't fit those kids
in the Delta." After Ernestine Talbert, who had been Medgar Evers's class-
mate at Alcorn A&M College, tried to register to vote in the southeast
Mississippi county of George in January 1962, the nearby Greene County
schools where she taught did not offer her a contract for the following year,
despite the fact that her principal recommended that she be rehired. Her
civil rights activity had become widely known after the U.S. Justice Department filed suit against the George County registrar in the spring of 1962 and
used an affidavit from Talbert as part of its evidence that local voting officials had systematically denied blacks the franchise. After her very public
support for the state's incipient civil rights movement, Talbert found that
no other school district in the state would offer her a job. As in the earlier
case of Gladys Noel Bates, the MTA came to Talbert's rescue by creating a
position for her within the organization's central office.[43]

Mississippi whites never managed to quiet all black opposition to the
equalization program, but they did mute most of the dissent through the
use of coercion and intimidation. Black Mississippians, of course, had
ample reason to reject the state's equalization campaign. For one thing,

segregated schools were now illegal. In addition, Mississippi's equalization program failed to deliver on its promises. Indeed, the state's project could not even guarantee equal expenditures on black and white education. The biggest flaw in the state's equalization campaign remained the same one that had plagued the equalization program of the late 1940s and early 1950s: the state had no requirements on how most local education funds were spent, beyond the local cash required to match state construction money. An unpublished State Department of Education report of 1962 found that statewide, the average school district spent $4 in local instruction funds on each white child for every $1 expended on each black child. In some districts, the gap was even wider, as table 4 demonstrates. Though the state was supposedly engaged in an effort to bring underfunded black schools at least to the level of the often poorly financed white schools, only 3 of the state's 151 school districts—Issaquena-Sharkey, Ocean Springs, and Itawamba

Table 4. Per Capita Local Education Funding, by Race, for Select Mississippi School Districts, 1962

School district	$ spent per white student	$ spent per black student
Benton County	59.42	15.63
Amite County	70.45	2.24
Canton	35.79	17.00
Clarksdale	146.06	25.07
Coahoma County	139.33	12.74
Coffeeville	68.95	6.55
Greenville	134.43	34.25
Grenada	79.00	27.38
Hattiesburg	115.96	61.69
Jackson	149.64	106.37
Meridian	116.58	63.11
Montgomery County	48.73	6.71
Sharkey-Issaquena	18.75	25.74
Tishomingo County	41.60	2.70
Tunica County	172.80	5.99
Statewide	81.86	21.77

Source: *New Orleans Times-Picayune* (1963) article citing information from an unpublished report by the Mississippi State Department of Education, American Friends Service Committee Archives, Philadelphia.

County—were spending more of their local school funds per black child than white in 1962.[44]

The unbalanced local funding of education canceled out much of the potential for actual parity in black and white schools promised by the state's equalization program. For example, despite the creation of a uniform teacher salary scale by the state legislature, school districts often distributed their local salary supplements only to white teachers, "a shrewd maneuver," according to state NAACP leader Aaron Henry, "to get around the *state law* that equalized teachers' salaries." Since local school districts spent fewer funds on outfitting black schools and hiring black teachers, over half of the state's 638 black schools in 1962 remained unaccredited by even the relatively lax state accrediting agency, primarily because of poor libraries and "abnormal teaching loads." At the black high school in Ruleville, for instance, the "library" in 1964 contained six incomplete sets of encyclopedias and a dictionary; a number of the classes there had more than sixty students, while two of the classes contained more than seventy-five children. Even the building of black schools after *Brown*, the one area the state could point to as a success in its equalization effort, did not always receive the same care as the construction of white school plants. W. B. Thompson, a white principal in Greenville during the late 1950s, later remembered that at the black school "accommodations were not as good, and buildings were not built with the same degree of aesthetic quality and those things."[45]

As in the pre-*Brown* years, the intransigence of local white officials frequently undermined state equalization efforts, even the seemingly straightforward building program. In most cases, local districts only applied for state building funds and undertook school construction after educational consultants had studied the district's needs and recommended changes. The consultants were generally quite candid about the actual costs of equalization. H. M. Ivy, a former school leader in Meridian whose firm conducted educational surveys in more than forty counties, recognized in 1955 that "the need for facilities for Negro pupils is appalling throughout the state," a situation that demanded that substantial funds be spent on upgrading black schools. Local white officials, however, typically looked for cheaper alternatives than those recommended by the consultants. For example, although a 1956 study of Benton County recommended that a new $500,000 school be built to accommodate all the black children of the county, local officials ultimately built a somewhat smaller school for $250,000. Two years after its construction in 1960, Benton County's black school, with a maximum capacity of 900 students, had almost 1,150 enrolled, leaving school officials scrambling for additional state funds to build "any number of rooms" at the school to relieve the overcrowding.[46]

In other locales, especially many rural areas and majority-black districts, white officials moved slowly to take advantage of the state equalization funds. Educational consultant Ivy believed that "the temper of most of our people is such that outside a few of our cities there is not much hope for bonds being voted" for black education. In the Delta county of Tunica, the all-white school board vacillated on whether even to develop an equalization program. In 1958, they first approved an equalization scheme but then later that year decided to postpone indefinitely "all plans for the construction of Negro Schools . . . due to the uncertainty now existing throughout the South with respect to public education." The county eventually did adopt an equalization plan and by 1962 had built two large schools for most of the county's black children but still had forty-two small, unconsolidated black schools dotting the local landscape, despite the state mandate to consolidate and upgrade all black schools. Rather than build any additional black schools, additions were made to the two new black schools, Dundee and Rosa Fort, which allowed the remaining unconsolidated schools to be closed in 1963.[47] Obviously, spending funds on improving black schools remained a low priority for people who had their doubts about the continuing viability of public education, as many whites did after *Brown*, especially in the black-majority areas of the state.

The consolidation program, a central part of the state's efforts to equalize black and white education during the late 1950s and early 1960s, was also problematic. Most of the remaining unconsolidated schools in the state by the late 1950s were black schools. In 1958, only 9 percent of white schools but 62 percent of black schools were one-, two-, or three-teacher schools. Whites, as they had in years past, continued to resist school consolidation at times and grew particularly vocal when the reorganization involved transforming previously white neighborhood schools into black facilities.[48]

For blacks, however, consolidation meant overall improvements in educational facilities and instruction, but the process also often served to highlight the long-standing inequities inherent in the dual school system.

For one thing, black parents had little input into the decisions made by state and local school officials to reorganize the state's black school systems. As a result, black school patrons were often faced with a process imposed on them without much warning or generally any consultation, a reorganization that eliminated important community establishments in black neighborhoods. At the same time, consolidation often meant the loss of assets actually owned by local black communities. During the years of Jim Crow, white authorities generally refused to use much tax revenue to construct black schoolhouses, which meant that many black schools had literally been built by black residents with community funds and labor. School consolidation involved taking all the black schools in the state—many that were part of the state school system in name only—and combining facilities to create a more modern school system. Consequently, in some cases the state's post-*Brown* school consolidation project involved state appropriation of school structures and land owned by black communities. In one Louisville school, blacks had long attended classes in a schoolhouse built by black parents on property deeded to the local black community many years earlier. As part of their school consolidation project, white school officials incorporated this black school into the new consolidated school system. As one resident simply noted, "the parents built it and when they put consolidated in the school program, we as a Colored race, we lost our school." Given the loss of assets and both control over and involvement with their local schools, some black parents were, not surprisingly, willing to forgo the extra state resources consolidation promised in order to preserve their local unconsolidated school. In 1957, the PTA of the all-black school in Hoy, just north of Laurel, told the state superintendent of education that "we just feal [*sic*] like they ought to give us just a little of the money we [are] due an[d] we would beg for [the] rest" if their school in Hoy could remain rather than be consolidated with a school in nearby Mount Olive.[49] Of course, black school patrons had long been accustomed to begging for money for their schools. Now the state proposed to make all those hard-acquired resources state property and in the process eliminate the limited black control over black education that typically prevailed in rural districts.

By the early 1960s, Mississippi's attempt to preserve its system of dual schools faced additional challenges. One came from an increasing, though still half-hearted, willingness of the federal government to enforce the *Brown* decision. The main leverage the federal government had always possessed to press southern states on the school desegregation issue was the federal dollars that flowed into state coffers. By fiscal year 1964, Mississippians paid over $300 million in taxes to the federal treasury but received over three times that amount back (more than $1.1 billion). Only a small portion of these federal funds, however, were earmarked for education in the late 1950s and early 1960s. In Mississippi, less than 2 percent of the state's education budget was financed with federal monies.[50] About twenty-five school districts in the state, however, received a disproportionate share of the federal aid to education that came to Mississippi by the early 1960s. Two laws passed in 1951 had provided construction funds and maintenance and operation monies for school districts in "federally impacted" areas, generally locales where federal military facilities had been established during World War II and after. By 1963, Biloxi, home to Keesler Air Force Base, had received more than $4.5 million from the federal government, over $2 million of which went to fund more than sixty construction projects in the city's schools. Federal funds also constituted more than 5 percent of the district's annual maintenance and operation funds.[51]

The executive branch only gradually accepted the notion of using the power of the purse strings to move southern states to accept the *Brown* decision. The Eisenhower administration consistently rejected arguments by the NAACP and others that agencies such as the Department of Health, Education, and Welfare (HEW) should withhold federal education funds from those states that failed to follow federal court decrees. The Kennedy administration also initially dismissed such reasoning. In the spring of 1961, the new president—worried about losing the support of white southern Democrats—helped defeat a Senate amendment to an education bill (proposed by Prescott Bush, father of George H. W. Bush) that would have withheld federal funds from those districts that had not made a "good faith" effort toward school desegregation. By the following year, however, the Kennedy administration had shifted course. The president's HEW secretary, Abraham Ribicoff, suggested in March 1962 that the administration would explore cutting off the federal-impact school funds from recalcitrant southern school districts and would consider the possibility of a school desegregation lawsuit against those districts, since the federal-impact legislation required that "suitable free public education" be made available to the children of all federal employees.[52]

In Mississippi, the targets of this federal initiative were the school districts in the Gulf Coast cities of Biloxi and Gulfport, which had received sizable sums under the federal-impact laws. The federal government at first hoped that a threat to cut off the federal funds would induce the local officials to desegregate their schools voluntarily. Biloxi superintendent R. D. Brown and his school board at first indicated a willingness to comply, but after meeting with Governor Ross Barnett, Brown told HEW representatives in late 1962 that "there was no possibility of the district agreeing to begin integration . . . anytime within the next two or three years on a voluntary basis." He noted that state law required the closing of any desegregated school, that teachers who taught in desegregated schools would lose their teaching certificates, and that the issue of school desegregation could not even be discussed in a public meeting without the entire board and the superintendent losing their jobs. When negotiations stalled, the Justice Department filed suit against the two school districts in January 1963, alleging that they had violated an "implied contract" made with the federal government when they accepted federal-impact monies and had violated the Fourteenth Amendment rights of the children of federal government employees. Both the local federal district court and the Fifth Circuit Court of Appeals rejected the government's arguments.[53]

The federal government's increasing support for civil rights had other ramifications in those Mississippi communities with a federal presence. In 1963, the Department of Defense issued an advisory that all military personnel be briefed about "school segregation practices" in their area. In August 1963, the commander of Keesler Air Force Base, Lewis H. Walker, notified his charges that the Department of Defense supported the constitutional right of all citizens to be assigned to public schools without regard to race. Walker also noted that schools in the Keesler area "operate a dual system of education in accordance with Mississippi law." He reminded all military personnel that if they felt "aggrieved by this assignment," they had a right to complain or "to sue for their children's constitutional rights," although any legal costs would have to be borne by the individuals involved, not the military. At least two black Keesler airmen did protest, though they never went so far as to file a lawsuit against the Biloxi public schools. When three black airmen at Columbus Air Base in east Mississippi notified that city's public schools in August 1963 that they intended to seek a transfer to the white schools for their children, city school officials initially announced that they would bar all of the almost nine hundred base children from the city's schools on the grounds that the base was outside the city limits and the city was no longer going to accept children outside the city's boundaries. For two weeks, the base children, white and black, had no access to any schools, but the air force and the Columbus public schools finally reached an agreement allowing the base children to return to the Columbus schools as long as "they adhere absolutely and strictly to Mississippi laws and regulations of the trustees," in other words, as long as no one tried to challenge the state's segregation laws. When one of the airmen nevertheless persisted in requesting a transfer for his children to the white schools of Columbus, the school board president enlisted the aid of Senator John Stennis, asking him to talk to the air force brass about having the "trouble-maker" transferred to another post.[54]

While the federal government's ability to force white Mississippians to accept the *Brown* mandate proved largely ineffectual in 1963, the federal approach remained potentially powerful. White Mississippians certainly recognized the danger the federal government's strategy posed to their way of life. By the early 1960s, various organizations around the state, such as the Mississippi Economic Council, the Delta Council, and the Mississippi Farm Bureau, urged the state to avoid accepting the small outlay of federal aid to education if such funds would imperil the maintenance of school segregation.[55] Within a few short years, however, federal funding for local education would increase dramatically (because of the Elementary and Secondary Education Act [ESEA] of 1965), providing much needed money for cash-starved Mississippi education and creating an even larger stick to move Mississippi from its position of "no school desegregation ever."

In addition to the threat to school segregation posed by an increasingly active federal government, Mississippi leaders had to contend with minor but annoying cracks in white support for the policy of resisting school desegregation through any means necessary. While practically all whites still favored segregated schools, some had seemingly come to see the wisdom of compromising on the state's position of "never." Some white leaders continued to perceive white teachers as a weak link in the effort to uphold segregation; suspicions about their loyalty to the cause of preserving segregated schools had persisted since Governor White's meeting with educators in August 1954. In the early 1960s, the Sovereignty Commission from time to time received reports about white teachers saying favorable things about the civil rights movement in their all-white classes or embracing the possibility that school integration might not mean the end of the world. Some people thought that a loyalty oath for white teachers was needed, where they would take a pledge to quit their jobs "if integration is forced upon our schools" or be fired if they refused to swear the oath. Other white defections from the massive resistance party line also emerged in the early 1960s. Following the violence that surrounded James Meredith's prolonged struggle to enroll at the University of Mississippi in 1962, the Mississippi Economic Council, an influential state business group, passed a resolution stating that while school segregation should continue to be preserved, resistance to the *Brown* decision should not include violence and, most important, should not include any closure of schools, a key part of the state's plan to prevent school integration from ever being implemented. Some local officials also floated plans to retreat from the stance of absolute resistance to school desegregation. In 1963, Mayor C. E. Schmidt of Ocean Springs on the Gulf Coast proposed to eliminate black and white schools in his town in favor of a school district with one set of zoning lines. Schmidt believed that because of racially segregated housing patterns in the town, the schools would remain largely segregated, though a few blacks would attend previously all-white schools. State attorney general Joe Patterson quickly reminded Schmidt that such an action remained clearly illegal under state law.[56]

Mississippi managed to maintain total segregation in its elementary and secondary schools for ten years after *Brown*. Claiming that school segregation had to be preserved, white Mississippians offered as an alternative to *Brown* a quixotic plan to make separate but truly equal schools a reality. Most black Mississippians welcomed the aid for black education. Those who remained convinced that black education could only be improved if the dual school system was destroyed had to face white Mississippians who used state-sanctioned and private economic intimidation, along with sporadic violent terror, to discourage them. Although the state poured millions into a school equalization program designed to upgrade black schools, the project never equalized funding between white and black education, and evidence of black activism on the school desegregation front continued to grow, despite the widespread intimidation of black supporters of racial change. Following the debacle at Ole Miss, even some whites in the state had seemingly lost their enthusiasm for the "absolutely never" cause. And the federal government finally seemed poised to force the state to follow the law. The Sovereignty Commission, as the state agency charged with preserving segregation, continued to try and put out all the little fires that threatened to undermine the state's sworn determination to evade the mandate of *Brown* completely. But change loomed on the horizon.

CHAPTER FOUR

THE CRACK IN THE WALL

School Desegregation Begins

O n August 31, 1964, with twenty federal marshals and local law enforcement officials on hand and a "backup emergency force" of eighteen hundred members of the Mississippi National Guard ready to be federalized, twenty-one of an expected twenty-three black students enrolled in four previously all-white elementary schools in Biloxi. The next day, though more trouble was expected in rural Leake County, the home of rabid segregationist and former governor Ross Barnett, a similar assemblage of state and federal forces prevented any harm to Debra Lewis as she became the first black student to attend the formerly all-white Carthage Attendance Center. Other black children had planned to join the desegregation attempt, but their parents backed down after a campaign of intimidation by local whites. In Jackson on September 14, Jean Fairfax, a member of the American Friends Service Committee (AFSC), a Quaker group involved in a number of peace and social justice causes around the world, observed that "history was made—most uneventfully," as thirty-nine black six-year-olds attended eight previously all-white schools. An effort by a group of white women, organized as the Mississippians for Public Education, encouraged white parents to stick with the public schools and ultimately had more success than the Jackson's Citizens' Council chapter's effort to create a system of white-only private schools.[1]

This first implementation of the *Brown* decision in the state, which occurred fast on the heels of the violent Freedom Summer of 1964, worried President Lyndon Johnson, among other observers, which explains the show of federal force that accompanied Mississippi's first school desegregation. The previous year, Alabama (a holdout since 1961) had resisted court orders to dismantle its dual school system with state plans to close the public schools and white violence against black parents. Federal intervention was required to enforce the court decrees in Alabama. In response, whites fled from the affected schools.[2] Despite the anxiety of Johnson and others, the initial school desegregation in Mississippi occurred with somewhat less drama, though not without problems.

Brown II effectively placed the burden of effecting school desegregation squarely on the backs of black parents. They would have to sue to force reluctant whites to implement the *Brown* mandate. So it is not surprising that the first school desegregation successes in Mississippi were undertaken by individuals and communities involved in the wider campaign to eliminate Jim Crow and disfranchisement in the American South. Mississippi segregationists could not keep the civil rights movement out of their state forever, despite sustained efforts to block it. A number of local black citizens, emboldened by the successes of civil rights activities in other southern states, decided to stand up to the violence and intimidation utilized by white Mississippians to defend the racial status quo. Often with help from national civil rights organizations, local black activists launched a variety of protests and demonstrations against Jim Crow and disfranchisement in the early 1960s. In Biloxi, Leake County, and Jackson, improving black education had been a priority that predated the civil rights movement. The state's equalization and consolidation program offered only the most recent proof of the inequalities of segregated education. As a consequence, an attempt to bring about school desegregation became part of the larger battle against segregation in these locales.

The first direct-action civil rights protest in Mississippi took place on the Gulf Coast in 1959 when Dr. Gilbert Mason and eight other citizens of Biloxi waded into the Gulf of Mexico from the city's all-white beach. In the spring of 1960, Mason, a Jackson native who had moved to Biloxi in 1955 to open a medical practice after earning his degree from Howard University Medical School, helped organize a branch of the NAACP in Biloxi. The group, led by its president, Mason, immediately organized two additional wade-ins that involved a small group of Gulf Coast blacks. The second wade-in sparked a violent reprisal from area whites. Local law enforcement officers looked on indifferently while eight blacks and two whites sustained injuries in the melee. Although the battle to desegregate Mississippi's beaches bogged down in a long legal dispute, unresolved until the early 1970s, Mason, his wife, Natalie, and other members of the Biloxi NAACP continued to fight on a number of civil rights fronts, including for the desegregation of the local public schools.[3]

Despite the violence surrounding the wade-in, Biloxi and rest of the Mississippi Gulf Coast were perhaps the one region in Mississippi where civil rights victories seemed possible. Heavily Catholic, with numerous second- and third-generation European immigrants, Biloxi was also home to Keesler Air Force Base, established during World War II and at one point during the conflict the largest air base in the world. Keesler brought both economic pros- perity and people from all over the United States to the Gulf Coast, and the facility provided jobs for blacks and whites during and after World War II. The air base also transformed Biloxi's outlook; according to one observer, the base helped to intensify Biloxi's cosmopolitan atmosphere and imbued the city with a "widened vision" of the world. In the early 1960s, the United Service Organizations (USO) at Keesler was an integrated organization, and the base also harbored blacks who were adamant about the need for a trans- formation of local race relations. Black airmen at the facility organized the Armed Forces Equality Committee, a group that considered the local NAACP branch to be overly cautious about pressing for change. In the end, although various moderating influences clearly existed in Biloxi, none of the white reli- gious, political, military, or business leaders in the city openly embraced the civil rights cause. In fact, they often seemed willfully oblivious to the injus- tices segregation inflicted on their black neighbors. Marge Curet, a former Democratic Party national committeewoman who actually accepted the need for school integration, nevertheless believed that "Biloxi Negroes have not had it too bad."[4]

Compared to the rest of Mississippi, Biloxi did have decent black schools, but gross inequities between white and black education continued to exist in the early 1960s. Natalie Mason waged an ongoing battle with Biloxi school officials during those years to address the obvious inequalities between the education her son received and that afforded white children. Among the various problems she encountered was the practice by the Biloxi school superintendent of instructing black teachers at Perkins Elementary School, where her son attended, to give their students a "C" for art, music, and gym, offerings available only at the white elementary schools. What Natalie Mason saw at her son's school was not unique. Biloxi's black high school offered only a fraction of the courses available to students at the white high school, and black students had to make do with substandard equipment in the classes that were available.[5]

Securing a better education for their son was the primary reason the Masons became advocates for school desegregation in Biloxi. But the background of the Masons, both in terms of their family and the organizations they belonged to, also led them to fight against segregated schools. Both came from families that had long contested the inequalities of African American life. Gilbert's family had a tradition of "fighting for freedom and liberty," and Natalie's father, a railroad brakeman, had been involved in a lawsuit in the 1940s to equalize employment opportunities. The Masons' religious and social life also convinced them that segregation was wrong. As Gilbert Mason later recalled, "All of the good teachers in the Bible, in the Boy Scouts, in Alpha Phi Alpha [African American fraternity], the wholeness of the Masons [fraternal organization] compelled us" to attack segregated schools. So Gilbert and Natalie Mason, along with a handful of other blacks in Biloxi, began petitioning the local school board for desegregated schools in 1960. Though many area blacks supported the cause, most of those who initially signed the petition, in addition to the Masons, held jobs at Keesler Air Force Base, positions that shielded them from white economic retaliation.[6] The Biloxi school district essentially ignored the parents' petitions for three years. After the failure of the federal government's federal-impact lawsuit against Mississippi Gulf Coast communities in early 1963—which the Biloxi petitioners believed did not adequately address the problem of school segregation in their city anyway—parents enlisted the aid of the NAACP's Legal Defense and Educational Fund to launch their own school desegregation suit.[7]

The civil rights movement came to Leake County in east-central Mississippi in the early 1960s when Mississippi's NAACP field secretary, Medgar Evers, helped the Hudson sisters, Winson and Dovie, organize an NAACP chapter in Harmony. Despite its rural setting in the heart of the state's historical Klan territory, Harmony was a logical community to support the movement: close-knit, all-black, and peopled by largely independent landowners. When

CORE launched a civil rights initiative in east-central Mississippi in the early 1960s, Harmony became a key project, one that focused on both voter registration and school desegregation.[8] Black residents in Harmony began to mobilize to fight for their civil rights largely because local school officials closed a black school and took the school property from the community as part of the county's school consolidation program. The Harmony school had been built in the 1920s, primarily with Rosenwald funds and community labor. It became the center of the community and was judged by local residents as "one of the best schools in the state." In 1961, school officials—despite warnings from local whites familiar with the Harmony community to "leave those darkies alone"—decided to close the Harmony school and move the children to a facility in Walnut Grove, more than ten miles away. At the same time, the state, as it often did when consolidating black schools, simply took the Harmony school property from the local community. According to Winson Hudson, "that's when we got real mad."[9]

The black residents of Harmony responded to this white decision that literally robbed them of a key community resource by filing a school desegregation lawsuit. Winson Hudson and others from the community first contacted Derrick Bell and Constance Motley, two civil rights attorneys with the NAACP's Legal Defense and Educational Fund in the state working on James Meredith's admission to the University of Mississippi. With the help of these attorneys and two local black lawyers, Jack Young and R. Jess Brown (Brown had been fired along with Gladys Noel Bates in the late 1940s for requesting equal salaries for black teachers in the Jackson public schools), fifty-two Harmony parents petitioned the local school board in early 1962 to desegregate Leake County schools. After a campaign of terror in which white vigilantes shot into the homes or businesses of many of the petitioners and a much-publicized attempt by black principal O. E. Jordan to urge the black parents to halt their efforts in the interest of preserving "good" race relations, all but about fifteen of the original group withdrew from the desegregation effort. As in Biloxi, a year after the parents submitted the original petition, the school board had never bothered to reply, so in March 1963 a group of black parents in Leake County filed a school desegregation lawsuit.[10]

In Jackson, Medgar Evers and others had worked on voter registration since the late 1950s. Then, in 1961, a group of Tougaloo College students associated with the NAACP Youth Council launched a number of direct-action protests against segregation. Although most older Jacksonians initially kept their distance from the students' highly visible direct-action campaign, in August 1962 nine parents (including Medgar Evers) petitioned the Jackson school board, asking that it "reorganize the schools on a non-segregated basis." While the parents' action was part of the emerging effort to end all forms of segregation in the city, Evers and the other black parents who signed the petition cited the failed equalization effort of the previous two decades as the primary motive behind their demand for school desegregation. The petitioners called for change because "we want equal school opportunities for our children," and they were clearly disillusioned by a long string of unfulfilled white promises to improve black education.[11]

The specific failures of school equalization in Jackson were numerous. Like most other districts in the state, Jackson continued to spend a disproportionate share of its local educational funds on white students. In 1959, 42 percent of Jackson's students were black. While the district spent almost 40 percent of the state's minimum foundation funds on black students, they reserved less than 30 percent of local district funds for black education. One consequence of this funding disparity was that student-faculty ratios remained significantly higher in the black schools. In 1963, Jackson's white elementary schools had a student-faculty ratio of 21.7:1, while the similar ratio in the city's black elementary schools stood at 31.5:1, slightly above the state-mandated Minimum Foundation Program requirement of 30:1. Although the district had a major building program between 1950 and 1965, securing six bond issues and building twenty-nine new schools, only nine of the buildings were for black pupils. As a consequence, the city's black schools remained significantly overcrowded. While the city's white high schools also suffered from some slight overcrowding, all of Jackson's black secondary school facilities housed many more students than originally intended when built; the city's three secondary schools for black students in the early 1960s, designed to accommodate 6,020 students, had an enrollment of 11,700. After the Jackson school board ignored their school desegregation petition, black parents filed a lawsuit in 1963, also with assistance from the NAACP Legal Defense and Educational Fund.[12]

The three school desegregation lawsuits in Biloxi, Jackson, and Leake County ultimately led to the state's first school desegregation with the opening of school in 1964, but not before Mississippi federal district judge Sidney Mize further delayed implementation of *Brown* on procedural grounds and not before white Mississippians received a hearing on their claim that black "inferiority" required continued educational segregation of the races. Mize, who was born in Mississippi in 1888 and had been named to the federal bench by Franklin Roosevelt, initially dismissed each of the three cases by claiming that segregation in Mississippi was voluntary and that the plaintiffs had failed to exhaust all possible administrative remedies. The latter conclusion blatantly ignored the fact that the school boards in all three locales had essentially shut down administrative channels by completely ignoring the pleas of black petitioners. On appeal, the Fifth Circuit Court of Appeals consolidated the cases, rejected Judge Mize's reasoning, issued a temporary injunction requiring the defendant school boards to submit desegregation plans in July 1964, and sent the matter back to Mize for a trial on the "merits" of the lawsuits.[13]

At the trial in Mize's court during May 1964, the defendants presented a series of witnesses designed to prove their claim that "there are such differences and disparities" between blacks and whites "that the establishment and maintenance of separate specially adapted schools granting equal opportunity for development of the differing capacities and abilities of the children of the two groups is most advantageous to all." The defendants' witnesses, described by Jean Fairfax of the AFSC as "a most distressing parade of segregationists and professional racists," included "seven distinguished scientists" (in the estimation of Judge Mize), as well as Congressman John Bell Williams, who testified how school desegregation in the District of Columbia had destroyed the school system there. Jackson school superintendent Kirby Walker also testified how the district's school records "proved" the "inferiority" of black students; Walker concluded that it would be "educationally unsound and unfair" to mix the two races in school as long as these intellectual differences continued to exist. One of the most notable defense witnesses was James Gooden, the recently retired but longtime black supervisor of black schools in the Jackson district. In his testimony, Gooden endorsed the idea of separate black and white schools, though for different reasons than the white witnesses. Like many black educators of his generation, Gooden recognized the very concrete benefits segregated black education had brought to his community. The educator, however, proceeded to undermine the

entire defense argument by concluding his testimony "with a ringing affirm-
ation that Negroes are not inferior."[14]

In his decision of early July, Judge Mize endorsed the defendants' positions
by finding "that White and Negro pupils of public school age have substantially different educational aptitudes and learning patterns which are innate
in character." As a result, Mize found "mixing of races injurious to both races"
and segregated schools "beneficial to members of both races." Mize even
urged a "complete reconsideration of the decision" in *Brown*, but recognizing
he had no authority to review or overrule a U.S. Supreme Court case, he also
was forced to make the Fifth Circuit's preliminary injunction against the
defendant school boards permanent. The boards presented plans that called
for the desegregation of one grade a year (thereby delaying complete school
desegregation another twelve years), starting with first grade. For the 1964–65
school year, parents of first graders in the three districts would have "freedom
of choice" in what school in the district to send their children. Even though
the plaintiffs objected to the school boards' desegregation plans, especially
the fact that under the first-grade only approach most of the plaintiffs' children would not be allowed to enter white schools, Judge Mize approved the
defendants' blueprints and agreed to look at speeding up the desegregation
timetable in 1965.[15]

In addition to the three lawsuits consolidated by the Fifth Circuit for adju-
dication by Judge Mize, there was another Mississippi school desegregation
lawsuit in the Delta town of Clarksdale that received less notice in 1964 because
it resulted in no desegregation. Clarksdale was the home of Aaron Henry, state
president of the NAACP since 1959; he had led a grassroots, direct-action campaign against all forms of segregation in Clarksdale, beginning in the early
1960s. Part of this effort, of course, included a challenge to school segregation,
and Henry's daughter, Rebecca, became the lead plaintiff in the lawsuit eventually filed against the Clarksdale public schools. The Clarksdale action initially proceeded much like the other school desegregation efforts. Henry and
twenty other black parents filed a school desegregation petition with the
Clarksdale board of school trustees in September 1963. After receiving no satisfactory response from the trustees, seventeen of the parents filed a lawsuit; as
in the other three locales, fear of white retaliation prevented other black
parents from joining the action. Federal district court judge Claude Clayton
heard the case, and his ruling in 1964 actually seemed to require more school

desegregation than anything Judge Mize approved for the other three loca-
tions. Clayton accepted a geographic zoning plan submitted by the defendant
school board that would divide the town into school zones on a supposedly
nonracial basis; in addition, the plan would apply to first graders in August
1964 and second graders in January 1965, a timetable for desegregation more
accelerated than any other accepted in the state up to that time.[16]

Despite the seeming progressiveness of the Clarksdale plan, it was actually a clever and effective tactic designed by Clarksdale school board attorney
Semmes Luckett and others to preserve segregated schools. Both the Sunflower River and the Illinois Central Railroad split Clarksdale in half north
to south, with blacks mainly congregated on the south side of town and
whites on the north. The geographic zones proposed by the school board
(and approved by Judge Clayton) generally followed these "natural" boundaries, creating "nonracial" school zones that actually reproduced the town's
mostly neat pattern of residential segregation. For those instances where
housing patterns diverged from the typical pattern, other mechanisms
existed to bolster continued segregation. In July 1964, as the school board
developed its desegregation plan, the Clarksdale City Council de-annexed a
black neighborhood north of the river, thereby eliminating a sizable group
of black children located in a school zone primarily populated by whites.
A gerrymandering of zone lines ("an irregularly drawn boundary," in the
words of the Fifth Circuit Court of Appeals) initially isolated a white neighborhood south of the railroad tracks from the black areas surrounding it,
though the district court eliminated this obviously unusual zone in 1965. As
for the fifty or sixty white children who lived in parts of other zones in the
southern part of the city, their parents placed them in private educational
institutions to avoid sending them to majority-black public schools. In the
end, segregated education remained intact in Clarksdale when school began
in September 1964 and for many years thereafter. While the Fifth Circuit
pondered the legality of Clarksdale's geographic zone scheme, eventually
requiring modification of the plan in 1969, Clarksdale schools remained
almost totally segregated. In 1967, three years into the operation of the plan,
only two of the district's three thousand black students had attended a previously all-white school in the town.[17]

While geographic zoning became an effective tactic of evading school
desegregation for Clarksdale, this approach would not work in most of

Mississippi. Few urban areas and none of the state's rural areas had the necessary orderly residential segregation to recommend geographic zoning as the best way to preserve school segregation. For example, while Jackson had a number of clearly delineated white suburbs and even one black one that had been incorporated into the city limits since 1949, the older core of the city was characterized by a checkerboard pattern of black and white residential housing areas. Geographic zoning, even in many of Mississippi's urban areas, would have led to significant school desegregation or would have required easily challenged gerrymandering.[18]

As the desegregation lawsuits made their way through the courts in the spring and summer of 1964, the state of Mississippi moved to lessen the blow of the seemingly inevitable school desegregation. Governor Paul B. Johnson Jr. called the Mississippi legislature into special session in late June 1964. Over the next several weeks, the lawmakers approved a number of measures to blunt the impact of any school desegregation the courts might require, including an act allowing for the separation of students by sex and a law to provide a $185 tuition grant to any student attending a nonsectarian private school (with a complementary measure that allowed boards of supervisors to place levies on "all taxable property" to aid children attending private schools).[19]

The proposal by the Mississippi legislature to address the coming of school desegregation by allowing the segregation of students by sex sought to address the gender-based fears prevalent among whites about the "horrors" of school integration. One Newton parent expressed these worries about school mixing simply by noting that "I have four children, three little girls." He explained to the governor that "these are the reasons I'm asking you not to give an inch—please!" Since whites believed that blacks favored integration primarily because miscegenation was their ultimate design, a program of sex segregation seemingly offered a way to stop the integration furor in its tracks. A Cleveland man reasoned that if there was a separation of the sexes in desegregated schools, "there would be fewer negroes ready to integrate and I think [it] would keep down a lot of blood shed." Some whites were so consumed with sexual fantasies about the outcome of school desegregation that they were ready to endorse the sex segregation of all school-children—even if it led to more school desegregation—rather than allow token school desegregation to place any black boys next to white girls. For instance, Mavis Hollingsworth laid out an elaborate sex segregation desegregation plan to the governor that encompassed all grades for her hometown of Terry; she believed the scheme "would be far better for our children in the long run than to integrate one grade at a time, as this ordinarily means at primary levels where the little ones are too young to realize the significance of close association with both sexes of the negro race." The significance of such biracial contact was quite decisive to Hollingsworth, who believed that her plan represented perhaps the best opportunity to "save our white race from extinction."[20] Given the small numbers of blacks the courts were slated to allow to attend the white schools in 1964, few whites were ready to endorse plans that promised to lead to more school desegregation than absolutely required, but the sex segregation mechanism would later reemerge as a way to deal with the perceived evils of school mixing once school desegregation moved beyond the initial incremental stage.

The legislature's other major proposal during its 1964 special session, the tuition grant law, represented a more practical way to remove from harm's way the relatively small numbers of whites affected by school desegregation. The tuition-grant law revived a decade-long dream of white lawmakers to somehow find a way around *Brown* through a system of publicly funded yet "private" schools for whites only. Many white Mississippians agreed with their state legislators that such a seemingly contradictory entity could actually be created. The system H. E. Pass of Water Valley envisioned, like the similarly vague plans put forward by more educated legislators, removed the state very little from the equation; Pass suggested "a change of segregated schools to a Apointed Agency by governer Ratified By State Legeslators to be collect dues from all property owners and parrents that has children of 6 years of Age to have privet schools and the State and U.S. Government to be Free from Schools in our State. . . . The apointed company to controll all schools and children under a state law and State to assist in orginizing the company for the porpose of haveing private segregated schools." Despite widespread white support for Governor Johnson's tuition-grant plan, there were a number of white dissenters who raised a variety of arguments against the strategy. The bill, as originally proposed, would have included all private schools, but a huge outcry that the legislation would violate the separation of church and state led to an extended debate in the special session and eventually convinced lawmakers to recommend the grants only for students of nonsectarian schools. Others objected to the governor's plan because it did not provide enough funds to help poorer whites. Henry Edwards of Schlater thought "there are lots of us that are not able to make up the difference so there wont [sic] be but one choice for the working people and that will be public intergraged [sic] school or no school at all." Still others agreed with the rationale behind the private school plan but correctly thought such an effort would never withstand legal challenges.[21]

The tuition-grant law, however, was passed and did help a number of white Mississippians secure a segregated private education, though there was no immediate, massive abandonment of the public schools. Before 1964, there were only three nonsectarian private schools in the entire state, one in Jackson and two in Harrison County on the Gulf Coast. With the beginning of school desegregation that fall, three more private schools opened. Two were in Jackson, one supported by the Citizens' Council, which warned the town's residents about the dangers of even token school desegregation and suggested that private schools run by the Council were the only answer. The group acknowledged that Jackson had a good school system, but the Council reasoned that "you cannot expect them to maintain the same level of excellence after they integrate." In Leake County, the Association for the Preservation of the White Race provided financial assistance for the creation of Leake Academy, which in 1964–65 had only a first grade with twenty-three students. During the 1964–65 school year, 525 students statewide received over $80,000 from the tuition-grant fund.[22]

As long as school desegregation remained a token enterprise, however, many white Mississippians argued against abandoning the state's substantial investment in the public schools. As newspaper editor J. Oliver Emmerich pointed out in 1965, Mississippi had spent $600 million in the two decades since World War II to upgrade its public schools; the state could hardly afford a similar investment to create a system of private schools. As school desegregation began in most of the state's school districts in 1965 and 1966, however, some began to call for segregated private schools, especially in the Delta, where school integration would ultimately mean black-majority schools. For example, the effort to establish a private school in Greenville was in part spearheaded by Curtis Walters, who launched his campaign after two of his children attended a desegregated school in the fall of 1966. When a teacher seated his second-grade daughter between two black boys at the school, his

fears of miscegenation convinced him of the absolute necessity of private segregated schools. Walters believed that "the black-mans secret goal (in this
communist inspired civil rights movement) is interracial marriage. Now he
knows, he can not change you and I, we are adults, we are set in our ways and
beliefs, and never under any cercumstance [sic] would you or I marry a negro.
But he also knows, that if he can mix the little children in the schools and
make the teachers teach them to love each other, it will inevitably lead them
into interracial marriage." Walters argued that the private schools could prevent such a scenario and represented the only way to organize education, "if
you want your Grandchildren to grow up all white and decent."[23]

In addition to worries about miscegenation, promoters of the private
school model stressed that "quality" education for whites could not be
obtained in a desegregated school. Of course, "quality" had a specific meaning in this context. An independent study done in 1965 of the state's educational system judged both the black and white systems as the weakest in the
entire South, with the white system in the state actually weaker in some measures than the black systems in other southern states. But for many whites,
"quality" schools were first and foremost one-race schools. When whites in
Meridian, working through the Lauderdale County Citizens' Council, created
Jefferson Davis Academy for the 1965–66 school year, they promoted the
institution as "[a] private school. Organized by parents and benefactors who
want children to have freedom of association and superior education." While
the school ensured that the white children who attended did not have to associate with blacks, the education offered there included, for the first three years
of its existence, teachers instructing multiple grades of children.[24]

Such thinking led whites in some areas to abandon the public schools en
masse at the first hint of even token school desegregation. After a court order
required freedom-of-choice desegregation for the first four grades of the
Holmes County schools in 1965, almost all of the more than 400 white children slated to go to four of the county's elementary schools boycotted the
public schools after almost 200 black children registered for the same classes.
The mayor of Durant, C. H. Blanton, where one of the elementary schools
was located, pleaded with white citizens to keep their children at Durant Elementary after 48 black children arrived to attend the first four grades, but of
the 165 white children scheduled to attend Durant, only 5 remained. Blanton,
for his moderate stance, received hate mail from the Klan, which also burned

a cross at his home and torched his dry-cleaning business, a fire that caused substantial damage to the enterprise. No white children came to attend the first four grades at the other three elementary schools desegregated. Several private schools were hastily organized and opened in the county within a few weeks to educate the white defectors from the public schools, although some white parents simply kept their children home, a viable option in Mississippi, which did not have a compulsory school law at the time. Over the following year, some of the white parents discontinued the boycott of the public schools and returned their children to the public system; however, most white parents in Holmes County still adamantly refused to accept even minimal school desegregation and left the public schools for good.[25]

Although the number of private schools grew with the spread of token school desegregation, as did the number of white students who received aid from the state to attend those private schools under the tuition-grant program passed in 1964, the vast majority of white Mississippians did not follow the example of whites in Holmes County during the freedom-of-choice era. Most whites remained in public schools. In the 1965–66 school year, 1,730 white children received public funds for tuition to thirty-three private schools; by the 1966–67 session, that number had grown to almost 3,000 students at the same thirty-three schools. Even with state support, the private school movement by 1967 had attracted only a distinct minority of the state's school population, approximately 1 percent of the state's white school children.[26]

While the state of Mississippi worked during the summer of 1964 to construct a segregated educational haven in publicly funded private schools for white students who might be affected by court-ordered desegregation, black youth throughout the state were being mobilized as part of the civil rights movement's Freedom Summer project. From the earliest days of the movement in Mississippi, black boys and girls had responded to the call for nonviolent, direct-action protests, sometimes after prodding, though rarely public support, from their teachers. During Freedom Summer, many more of the young were recruited to the movement, when summer volunteers set up Freedom Schools around the state. Even before Freedom Summer began, CORE had helped organize a boycott of the black schools in Canton during the spring of 1964. In March, over 70 percent of Canton's thirty-five hundred black children boycotted the schools for two days to protest the substandard education available to blacks in the city. Students at all-black Rogers High School—touted in the late 1940s by the state as a symbol of successful separate but equal education—offered a laundry list of their school's deficiencies: secondhand books and typewriters; inadequate laboratory supplies, library, and shop; no physical education or foreign language classes; insufficient first aid equipment; overcrowded classes; overloaded and broken-down school buses; no lockers; and a building badly in need of repairs. The students' demand that a member of the school board meet with them to explain "what the board is going to do about these conditions" was ignored. When the students returned to school after their protest, many were expelled by the principal for taking part in the action. CORE activists argued that the only way to improve the quality of the black schools was to integrate the white and black school systems, but at the time, of course, the only way to achieve school integration was for a group of parents to file a lawsuit and wait several years for the courts to rule on the complaint.[27]

Freedom Summer, especially the Freedom Schools organized as part of the campaign, sparked many black students in Mississippi to become active in the civil rights movement and demand a host of changes, including an end to the dual school system that continued to provide them with a substandard education. The Freedom Schools were first proposed by Student Nonviolent Coordinating Committee (SNCC) member Charles Cobb, who envisioned that the schools would both supplement the underfunded black schools of Mississippi with innovative curriculum and teaching and build a future generation of local civil rights activists. Although SNCC activists at the time thought that the Freedom Schools did not always fulfill the lofty political objectives many had hoped for, in retrospect the Freedom Schools were one of the real success stories of Freedom Summer. Forty-one schools were established in nineteen communities, often in local black churches, and more than two thousand students attended these schools. Hattiesburg had the largest operation, with five schools instructing almost seven hundred children and, at night, additional numbers of adults. The Freedom Schools had a profound effect on many of the black students who attended. Many gained a new appreciation for their own culture because of the unprecedented courses in black history and literature. For others, the Freedom Schools opened their eyes to the injustices Mississippi perpetuated against black people and introduced them to what Charles Payne has called "the organizing tradition." One student described the experience as "coming out of darkness." Glenda Funchess, a fourth grader in 1964 who attended a Freedom School at Mt. Zion Baptist Church in Hattiesburg, remembers that the school "raised our consciousness about what our rights were." As a result of Freedom Summer, she decided that she would become a civil rights attorney, a goal she achieved twenty years later. The Freedom Schools also facilitated SNCC's effort to organize the Mississippi Student Union, which brought Mississippi students from around the state together under an umbrella organization.[28]

The mobilization of black students during Freedom Summer opened the floodgates of protest against segregated education. Not content to wait for court action, black students in a number of communities, sometimes aided by their parents or other black adults, turned to direct-action protest in the summer and early fall of 1964 in an attempt to force compliance with the *Brown* decision. On August 3, in Shaw (where, as in many Mississippi communities, black schools were already under way so that students could be dismissed at harvest time to pick cotton), fifteen hundred students at the all-black McEvans High School began a boycott of the school cafeteria after the principal expelled three white summer volunteers who came to eat with the students. Within hours, the students decided to expand the cafeteria boycott into a general boycott of Shaw's black schools because of the many inadequacies of black education and the failure of black administrators and parents to demand any changes. The following day, local white officials called in a heavily armed contingent from the Bolivar County sheriff's department to shut down Shaw's black elementary and high schools, which remained closed for almost two months.[29]

Black youth took action in other locales as well. In Jackson, twenty black students unsuccessfully tried to expand the first-grade only desegregation ordered by the federal courts in 1964 by attempting to register at a number of all-white junior high and high schools in the city. In Meridian, several local black ministers and parents, including the mother of James Chaney, who along with Michael Schwerner and Andrew Goodman had been murdered by the Klan at the beginning of Freedom Summer, were turned away by school officials in two separate attempts to register black children in several of the city's white schools. In Marks, four black high school students, accompanied by one parent and two civil rights workers, were allowed to register at the white school on the first day of classes. To avoid any possible hint of school integration, white students were herded into the auditorium during the time the black students were actually in the school. School officials told the black applicants that the superintendent had to give final approval to the transfer. A week later, the superintendent refused to grant the request on the rather bizarre grounds that the black students were ahead of the white ones because the black students had already been attending school for two months because of the split schedule arrangement for black students who had to pick cotton. In Canton, nineteen black high school students renewed their complaints from the previous spring about the deficient education available in the black Canton schools by requesting a transfer to the all-white Canton High School. The superintendent accepted the transfer requests and told the students they would be notified of the disposition of their request; when no response came by the first day of school, the students returned to the school with their parents to enroll, even though some of them had been threatened by employers or local law enforcement officials. All the black Canton students were denied admission to Canton High.[30]

In addition to these struggles by black students, there were other isolated outbreaks of black activism surrounding the schools in the fall of 1964. A black parent in Summit in southwest Mississippi unsuccessfully tried to enroll her daughter in the town's all-white elementary school; the mother was told to leave the state if she knew what was good for her. Parents in McComb, Moss Point, and Greenwood launched brief boycotts of black schools in these towns during September to protest the inadequate conditions of black education.[31]

Despite these various attempts around the state to force white school officials to desegregate the schools, only the first grades in Biloxi, Jackson, and Leake County had been ordered by the courts to desegregate. In these locales, civil rights activists had worked throughout the summer to recruit black parents who would actually challenge the educational color line once the legal hurdles had been cleared. Taking the lead in the effort to ensure that school desegregation would actually occur in Mississippi was the AFSC. which initially came to Mississippi in late 1962 in the wake of the riots surrounding the admission of James Meredith to the University of Mississippi. Involved in a number of efforts, including helping black farmers in the Delta who had been displaced by the changes in agriculture and promoting interracial and inter-faith communication within Mississippi, the AFSC also became the main civil rights organization in the state focused on finding black parents who would allow their children to become "school desegregation pioneers."[32]

In Jackson, AFSC workers Jean Fairfax and Dana Johnson conducted a citywide census of black families living close to white schools and then recruited black women (including several of the plaintiffs whose children would not be able to desegregate the schools because of the first-grade-only plan) to call on these families personally or hold "house parties" to discuss school desegregation. Fairfax spoke to a number of black professional groups, from beauticians to insurance agents, during the summer of 1964 to build support for school desegregation in Jackson. She also proved influential in getting the support of black ministers for the school desegregation campaign. A number of ministers helped make house calls on families with first-grade children, and in August thirty-two ministers signed a declaration—drafted by Fairfax and Rev. Charles Jones and widely distributed in the black community—encouraging black parents of first graders to send their children to previously all-white schools. AFSC members, along with other civil rights activists, also worked in Leake County to identify black students who might attend the white schools there. In Biloxi, although it offered to help local activists recruit school desegregation participants, the AFSC found that Mason had already set up a program to recruit and prepare potential school desegregation parents and students for the upcoming assault on segregated schools.[33]

The AFSC also provided support for the efforts of white moderates in Mississippi who did not necessarily support school integration but who saw the inevitability of school desegregation and sought to avoid the massive white flight or violence, or both, that had accompanied the token desegregation of public schools in places like Prince Edward County, Virginia; Little Rock, Arkansas; and Alabama. The major white moderate group that arose in the months before Mississippi's first public school desegregation was the Mississippians for Public Education (MPE), a group of middle- and upper-class white women. Although the presence of "pure, virtuous" white women had often been claimed by white men as a primary reason for racial segregation, and the protection of such "gentle flowers" had been offered as the primary rationale for much of the racial violence directed at black men since the end of slavery, some southern white women, such as those who joined the Association of Southern Women for the Prevention of Lynching, had always spoken out against racial oppression.[34]

In the wake of the violence at the University of Mississippi surrounding the admission of James Meredith, a group of about 150 Jackson women (mostly upper and middle class) met throughout 1963 to discuss the implications of the Ole Miss riot and the apparently inevitable school desegregation that would soon hit the public schools. Pressured by white segregationists (in other words, the entire white establishment), the group ceased their meetings, but a core group of five women—Pat Derian, Winifred Falls, Elaine Crystal, Mary Ann Henderson, and Joan Geiger—continued to gather and discuss the impending crisis. Significantly, all of the women were married to men who were economically independent, except for Henderson, whose husband was a Millsaps College professor. When the Fifth Circuit issued its orders in the three school desegregation cases in the spring of 1964, the women realized they needed to take some kind of concrete action to encourage compliance with the court directives. They turned to the AFSC for assistance. The organization provided a young white woman, Constance Curry, to serve as the staff for what became the MPE; a North Carolina native, Curry had previously worked for SNCC in Georgia. With a skeletal staff in place, the MPE decided, soon after the state legislature proposed its tuition-grant plan for private schools, to launch a public campaign to support the preservation of public education. During July 1964, the MPE held its first public meeting in Jackson and also bought full-page ads in the two Jackson newspapers denouncing the effort of Mississippi's state leaders to provide public funding for private education as a way to resist the recent school desegregation orders.[35]

Members of the Jackson MPE, along with Curry, fanned out across the state to organize other local chapters. MPE groups were formed in several Mississippi towns, including Tupelo, Greenville, Meridian, Pelahatchie, Vicksburg, Biloxi, Oxford, and Clarksdale, although an effort to organize a chapter in rural Leake County failed. The white women who joined the MPE around the state did so for a number of reasons. Some were profoundly affected by the racial brutality occurring within their state; others saw a contradiction between racial segregation and their own religious training. The MPE cautiously avoided taking a firm stand in support of school integration. Rather, it urged compliance with court orders as the best way to keep the public schools open and avoid violence. The women of the MPE pointed out that the destruction of Mississippi's public schools through programs like the state's private-tuition voucher plan would harm the children of Mississippi and would also damage the state's economy and national image. While the MPE publicly encouraged support for compliance with the school desegregation mandates, it also counted on its members to use more traditional and personal forms of persuasion with individual men—their husbands. As Winifred Green (formerly Winifred Falls) remembered, the organization tried "to attract large numbers of white women across the state of Mississippi to, if in no other way, stand up in the bedroom and say to their husbands, 'We won't have this. We are not going to be Prince Edward County, Virginia, and we're not going to be Little Rock, Arkansas.' "[36]

Segregationists attacked the women of the MPE on the grounds that only some sort of gender and class dysfunction could have led them to break ranks and support a violation of the color line. One segregationist publication claimed the MPE was composed of "a few 'neglected' neurotic women" or women who had become dissatisfied with their traditional roles as wives and mothers. At the same time, despite their opposition to private schools, the MPE women were labeled members of the wealthy class who could afford private education and would ultimately avail themselves of this mechanism to avoid school desegregation: "These people care not a tinkers damn for what happens to our little children in a negro dominated school. . . . [T]he rich can live above the stench of integration but we will have to live with it."[37] Although they were vilified, the women of the MPE, along with the AFSC workers, played a crucial role in the relatively peaceful transition to desegregated schools in Mississippi. When schools in Jackson, Biloxi, and Leake County opened on a desegregated basis in the summer of 1964, there was no violence. Black demands supported by the federal courts had finally cracked the wall of school segregation. The efforts of the AFSC had helped recruit and prepare blacks for school desegregation, and the work of the MPE had helped build support for desegregated public schools (although on a limited basis) among whites.

The events surrounding the start of Mississippi's school desegregation, despite the apparent calm, revealed the limits of the negotiated legal remedy allowed by the courts and suggested that much remained to be done before Mississippi's dual school system would truly be eliminated. Much of the problem lay in the fact that the desegregation plans adopted in the three districts and approved by Judge Mize clearly fell short of dismantling dual education. Their primary objective was to comply with the law in the most minimal way possible. For example, although the Jackson plan claimed that "the maintenance of separate schools for the Negro and white children . . . shall be completely ended with respect to the first grade," parents in Jackson who had questions about the desegregation of first-grade children were instructed to call their respective white or black administrative office.[38] The method of desegregating schools proposed by the white defendants and approved by Judge Mize, known as freedom of choice, would become the dominant mechanism for desegregating Mississippi schools for the next six years. The technique would continue to serve white Mississippians as an effective tactic of delay, even after the federal courts outlawed the blatant stalling of grade-a-year desegregation.

Despite the sustained effort by committed black parents in Biloxi, Jackson, and Leake County, the fight yielded small results: token desegregation of one grade at a handful of schools. Other protests that erupted around the state as school began in the fall of 1964, which certainly made it difficult for whites to claim that blacks were satisfied with the educational status quo, resulted in no school desegregation. Yet even as the four Mississippi lawsuits reached their conclusions and as the demands of other black parents and students for school desegregation were ignored during the summer and fall of 1964, the federal government was becoming increasingly active in enforcing the *Brown* decision. Soon every school district in the state would have to accede to at least token desegregation, though the elimination of the state's dual school system would not be accomplished for six more years.

CHAPTER FIVE

FREEDOM OF CHOICE FOR WHITES

Massive Resistance by Another Name

From 1964 to 1969, Mississippi's school districts desegregated their schools through the mechanism known as freedom of choice. Under freedom-of-choice plans, students were supposedly allowed to go to any school in a district. Though this type of school desegregation conjured up images that suggested the epitome of the American way, white Mississippians sought to mold the freedom-of-choice method into a bulwark for preserving their dual school system. Indeed, segregationists in Mississippi and other southern states believed they had found a way to satisfy the requirements of the *Brown* decision while still preserving largely segregated schools. Much like the earlier equalization strategy, which was still promoted as a way to forestall school integration well into the late 1960s, freedom-of-choice desegregation was viewed by Mississippi segregationists as a way to bend their devotion to racial segregation just enough to satisfy federal laws and black demands while preserving as much of their dual school system as possible. In other words, as school desegregation finally began in Mississippi, massive resistance to the *Brown* mandate remained alive and well in the state.

The strategy of embracing freedom of choice as a delaying tactic became quite apparent as white officials in Mississippi squared off with a federal government that began, in 1964, to take a more active role in trying to force compliance with the legal requirement for desegregated education. The Civil

Rights Act of 1964 marked the end of a decade-long policy of limited action by the federal government in pressing the Deep South on school segregation. The landmark legislation gave the executive branch additional powers to effect school desegregation in the region. President John F. Kennedy realized as early as the summer of 1963 that while the federal courts had done a good job of "directing the desegregation of schools on the local level," the use of court action "cannot be left solely to those who may not have the economic resources to carry the legal action or who may be subject to harassment." This understanding lay at the heart of Title IV of the Civil Rights Act of 1964, which authorized the U.S. attorney general to initiate school desegregation lawsuits after receiving a complaint. Given the history of white hostility to any black support for school integration in Mississippi, however, this method of bolstering federal support for school desegregation offered little chance to change the racial status quo, since it still required blacks to step forward and demand change. A more promising section of the Civil Rights Act of 1964 for advancing school desegregation in the state was Title VI, a controversial and unprecedented federal enforcement measure that barred racial discrimination in any "program or activity receiving Federal financial assistance" and authorized a cutoff of federal funds to violators, subject to guidelines established by federal agencies and approved by the president.[1]

Title VI became particularly important in the mid-1960s because of the passage of another piece of unprecedented federal legislation, the ESEA of 1965, which initially provided $1.3 billion to fund a variety of elementary and secondary schooling costs, including the development of programs to aid low-income students. Before the passage of ESEA, despite spending a sizable part of its tax monies on public education, Mississippi lagged behind the rest of the nation in key measures of educational health. In 1964, the state had both the lowest average teacher salary and the lowest spending per pupil. Within a few short years, ESEA funding became a significant part of the Mississippi public education budget. By 1967, $38 million of the state's $200 million education outlay came from federal sources, most from ESEA monies. No other state had almost a fifth of its public education bill paid for by the federal government.[2]

Because of the money involved and the basic poverty of Mississippi's public education system, the state could hardly afford a Title VI federal fund stoppage, a fact recognized by at least some white Mississippians. For instance, the Ripley Junior Chamber of Commerce told the local school board that "we are in no way promoting integration but realize that we have no other choice if we are to continue to make the necessary progress of educating our young people. We feel that if we are to improve the image of Mississippi, education is our basic means," and good education could not be accomplished without federal aid.[3] Most white Mississippians, however, thought that no amount of federal assistance justified abandoning dual education. One Vicksburg woman urged state leaders to "have the courage to stand by the principles of the Constitution and lead the nation in telling the Federal government we have no use for their 'aid' to our education, that we would prefer, as a free people, to take our tax money and educate ourselves." Mrs. J. B. Dakin of Cleveland agreed, noting that "our school system would not be worth a single thing if it were integrated."[4]

Mississippi school districts, along with others across the South, received their first "instructions" on how to comply with Title VI in January 1965, basically a requirement that at least some type of desegregation plan be submitted to HEW. Despite grumbling about having to accede to any federal mandates for school desegregation, most Mississippi school districts did submit desegregation plans, primarily utilizing freedom of choice as the method of desegregation and generally designed to limit desegregation as much and for as long as possible. A group of seventy Mississippi school superintendents told Commissioner of Education Francis Keppel in April 1965 that the only acceptable desegregation timetable was the grade-a-year plan implemented the previous fall in Jackson, Biloxi, and Leake County. As the plans came into the HEW Office of Education from around the South, federal officials realized that most of them were "fraudulent" or "unacceptable." Federal school officials also recognized, as they sought to negotiate with local school districts, that local education leaders were "holding back on making any commitments until they determine whether the Office of Education means business." Indeed, Mississippi school officials claimed they had been advised by state political leaders that the most effective response to HEW compliance requirements was to "drag our feet." With white southerners paying nothing more than lip service to the original Title VI instructions, HEW tried to break the "impasse" by issuing in April 1965 specific guidelines on what was required for Title VI compliance. These guidelines, drawing on the requirements laid out in recent federal court decisions on school desegregation, called for a "good faith" start toward school integration by desegregating four grades during the upcoming school year (two grades would be permitted in "exceptional cases"), the completion of desegregation by the fall of 1967, and a beginning on faculty desegregation. In many ways, HEW realized that the guidelines were "a bluff." The agency did not have the staff to enforce the guidelines should the South choose to evade them en masse. Even with a larger staff, agency officials recognized that mass noncompliance would not lead to a wholesale cutoff of federal funds to southern school districts, a politically untenable move.[5]

Operating from this position of weakness, HEW frequently chose to compromise on the guidelines to encourage compliance. Mississippi, a state with a powerful congressional delegation and the last southern state to resist even token school desegregation, received special handling. When the guidelines were first issued, about a third of Mississippi school districts initially resolved to do nothing to try to comply. As late as mid-August 1965, 53 of the state's 151 school districts still had not submitted any desegregation plans to HEW. To encourage at least a start of school desegregation, HEW frequently allowed many Mississippi school districts a reprieve from the full guidelines. For one thing, federal officials granted a number of Mississippi districts filing desegregation plans the two-grade exception. Most districts cited the excuse of overcrowding as grounds for moving slower than the guidelines required, but some school districts, such as Western Line Consolidated in the Delta town of Glen Allan, received a two-grade exception after school officials lodged the rather unexceptional complaint that a faster desegregation pace "might frighten the white children out of school." Most districts around the state were also allowed to forgo faculty desegregation for another year. HEW accepted other plans that it knew were seriously flawed. For instance, the plan submitted for the West Tallahatchie school district called for freedom-of-choice desegregation for all twelve grades, but the plan also indicated that school officials would take no action to publicize the plan or notify parents of the plan's provisions. Overall, the desegregation plans submitted to federal education officials generally proclaimed the existence of a unitary school system for the affected grades, while such plans in fact maintained separate black and white school systems. SNCC activists in the state could point to ample evidence when they charged that HEW was "more concerned about facilitating the flow of federal funds to racist school boards than in insuring equal educational opportunities for all."[6]

Even with the federal government going out of its way to allow Mississippi to do less than any other southern state to comply with Title VI, twelve school districts eventually did forfeit federal funds in the fall of 1965 rather than submit a desegregation plan. A number of these school districts raised local taxes to replace the shortfall. For example, the Amite County school board in southwest Mississippi decided to increase the local school tax from twenty to twenty-eight mills, the maximum allowed under Mississippi law, because it believed that "the majority of the citizens and taxpayers of this county and patrons of this school district object to this board executing an agreement of compliance with the Civil Rights Act of 1964." Any increase in local millage above twenty-five required voter approval, and the citizens of the county validated the understanding of the school board by voting almost two-to-one to raise local taxes significantly to avoid even token school desegregation.[7]

Even though most Mississippi school districts in 1965 technically satisfied the HEW Title VI compliance guidelines, either by voluntarily submitting a desegregation plan to the agency or going under a court order, the freedom-of-choice plans used to conform to the federal government's requirements led to only a few black children entering the white schools, which reflected an ideal scenario in the minds of white Mississippians. As one Canton woman later recalled, "we had freedom of choice[,] meaning we had two or three blacks in the school with our children. But that was not good enough for the Federal government." Mississippi officials were essentially ready to consider the matter of school desegregation closed once a school district had agreed to any freedom-of-choice plan. Senator John Stennis told President Johnson in the fall of 1965 "that any reasonable plan submitted by local school officials should be approved"; after all, Stennis believed school leaders had already "stuck their necks out quite a distance in going along with the desegregation plans." This approach, however, clearly did not comply with the *Brown* mandate. The 1965 guidelines allowed Mississippi school districts to do little more than proclaim freedom of choice in their districts while maintaining dual school systems, even though that practice had been declared unconstitutional by the U.S. Supreme Court a decade earlier.[8]

HEW officials recognized the problems with freedom-of-choice desegregation as conceived by the white South even before classes began in the fall of 1965, and they moved to strengthen the Title VI compliance guidelines. The free-choice mechanism was retained, but the new guidelines, which were issued in March 1966, established that a freedom-of-choice plan would be judged acceptable by the federal government only if it actually accomplished school desegregation. The 1966 guidelines promised to further school desegregation and the abolition of the South's dual school system through three mechanisms. First, any freedom-of-choice desegregation plan that did not lead to a doubling or tripling of transfers across racial lines would not be deemed satisfactory and would be subject to review by HEW's Office of Education. Second, any plan had to lead to "substantial progress" in the desegregation of both schools and teachers. Finally, the guidelines required that any plan provide for the "closing of small, inadequate schools for Negro students when they are inferior."[9] The last requirement posed particular difficulties for Mississippi. Despite two decades of official efforts by the state to pump money into the underfunded black schools, the institutions that educated the mass of the state's black youth remained "inferior" in any number of measures when compared with the state's white schools.

Douglas Cater, an Alabama native and Johnson White House aide who worked with HEW on education and health policy, predicted that the new requirements would be "a shock to many Southerners who believe that a continued dual school system is permissible so long as the students choose to keep it that way." White officialdom in Mississippi was indeed appalled, and public officials issued universal condemnations of the new school desegregation guidelines. Mississippi attorney general Joe Patterson railed against "ruthless politicians" who "use [federal dollars] as a weapon over the heads of the public schools of this nation, and seek to use the public school system of this country as a weapon of political expediency to further their political philosophy and sociological ideas." He believed the new guidelines showed "the government more interested in desegregation than education and could wreck the Mississippi school system." Governor Paul B. Johnson Jr. publicly urged Mississippi school boards to resist federal compliance efforts; he called them "a brazen attempt of the Health, Education and Welfare Department to gain absolute control over education." Senators John Stennis and James Eastland joined sixteen other southern U.S. senators in complaining to President Johnson that the new guidelines were unfair and went beyond the requirements of the 1964 Civil Rights Act by requiring targets for achieving "racial balance" in southern school districts. White school officials in Mississippi believed that the new guidelines would lead to massive white resistance if school desegregation proceeded beyond the token levels agreed to for the 1965–66 school year. The educators asked that in the current "cataclysmic period of transition," federal officials not ask for additional school desegregation, which would "place upon us tasks and burdens heavier than we who are seeking to make progress in good faith can reasonably bear."[10]

Although many in HEW considered the new 1966 guidelines still to be a conservative approach to encouraging the end of school desegregation in the South, the outcry from white southerners led the agency to backtrack on the new guidelines almost immediately. Soon after the 1966 guidelines were issued, civil rights attorneys in Mississippi, such as Henry Aronson of the NAACP's Legal Defense and Educational Fund, expressed fears that HEW would "cut a deal" with Mississippi officials to relax the new school desegregation requirements. When the regional Title VI director, Benjamin Hunton, met with representatives of Mississippi school districts in early April 1966, he did promise to make special allowances for the state. Hunton indicated that HEW would back off from the 1966 revised guidelines with regard to faculty desegregation and possibly in other ways as well. Aaron Henry, who attended this meeting as a representative of Mississippi's NAACP, thought the negotiations meant that "the expectations of Negroes for substantial progress in the area of school desegregation in Mississippi were badly shattered." President Johnson, for his part, affirmed his support for the new guidelines but soon realized that Congress, led by powerful southern members, would encourage noncompliance. Johnson told the southern senators who complained about the guidelines that the new rules "accept freedom of choice" and were not designed "to achieve racial balance." Rather, the president believed the guidelines were "designed to assist school authorities in administering freedom of choice plans to make sure that the choice is, in fact, free." Southern representatives and senators—and their northern allies, already beginning to fear how stricter federal enforcement might affect the fate of their own de facto segregated educational systems—were not impressed by Johnson's assurances. That summer, the House of Representatives approved an amendment that prevented HEW from requiring the "assignment of students to public schools in order to overcome racial imbalance"; the same legislative body almost approved a measure sponsored by Mississippi representative Jamie Whitten that would have required HEW to allow segregation to remain in southern schools as long as districts had freedom of choice in their school systems.[11]

The kind of logic embodied in the Whitten amendment accurately reflected the thinking of white Mississippians—and white southerners in other states—who essentially envisioned freedom of choice as a means to limit rather than promote school desegregation, to preserve as much of the dual educational arrangement as possible.

The federal government's push in 1965 and 1966 to utilize the Civil Rights Act of 1964 to force compliance with the *Brown* decision met with only limited success. Faced with widespread opposition from white southerners, federal officials remained unsure if they could press southern state officials much further. Douglas Cater told President Johnson that "this year's tightening of the guidelines goes about as far as the Federal Government can go in trying to cut off avenues of evasion." In addition, with the majority of southern school districts failing to comply with the new guidelines in the fall of 1966, HEW simply did not have the resources to go after all the offenders. Indeed, HEW's preliminary review of performance reports from over seventeen hundred southern school districts in August 1966 revealed that two-thirds fell below the guideline standards in terms of student and faculty desegregation. But HEW only had the ability to pursue sanctions immediately against fewer than fifty of the worst districts, threatening them with a cutoff of federal funds pending an enforcement hearing. Another two hundred districts received a "letter of serious warning," which meant their cases would be reviewed before the end of the 1966–67 school year. The remaining eight hundred districts not in compliance merely received a letter telling them that they were not in compliance, but these districts were not "subject to immediate review."[12]

During the 1966–67 school year, the agency initiated enforcement proceedings against only fifteen Mississippi districts. Most of the other noncompliant districts submitted school desegregation plans that were seriously flawed but escaped censure. For example, West Tallahatchie's compliance documents included a statement that echoed Judge Mize's interpretation of *Brown* in his ruling on the state's first school desegregation lawsuits: the West Tallahatchie school district agreed to follow the *Brown* decision "to the effect that the 14th Amendment does not command integration of the races in the school, and that voluntary segregation is legally permissible." Under such a plan, segregation, though not voluntary for many black residents, certainly persisted. In 1966, only 2 of the district's 2,045 black children attended a previously all-white school. The authors of the Lauderdale County plan correctly concluded that the federal guidelines might not be rigidly enforced, so they included the following statement in their compliance documents: "this Board does not obligate itself to strictly comply with each provision of the guidelines." And it did not. In 1966, only 35 of the district's 2,219 black students crossed over to the white schools. Lauderdale County, like many other Mississippi school districts, filed a freedom-of-choice school desegregation plan because it had to, but these districts had no intention of abandoning their dual school systems. In fact, in Lauderdale County during 1966, the district's official stationery proudly itemized the district's schools on its envelopes—by race.[13]

Although HEW's 1966 compliance guidelines did little to advance the cause of school desegregation, white Mississippi officials, along with other southern leaders and increasing numbers of northern allies, fought between 1966 and 1969 to have what they perceived as the potentially onerous HEW regulations overturned and in general to roll back the efforts of federal education bureaucrats to force southern states to do much beyond a declaration that they no longer had dual school systems.[14] White leaders, under duress, had announced that blacks could have freedom of choice in selecting schools for their children and claimed that the dual school system was no more. When the federal government attempted to force Mississippi and other southern states to prove that freedom-of-choice desegregation was actually working by requiring some real evidence of school desegregation, white leaders in the South continued to resist federal authority and cried foul. They zeroed in on what Douglas Cater explained to President Johnson in May 1966 as the essential paradox inherent in Title VI enforcement of school desegregation: the Civil Rights Act of 1964 "excludes 'racial balance' as the objective to be achieved by the Act. Yet it is difficult to find any other measurement which indicates whether discrimination exists in a school system."[15] However, hearing white leaders in a state like Mississippi, which had resisted school desegregation at every turn—not to mention the Civil Rights Act of 1964—claim that the federal government was violating the Civil Rights Act of 1964 by requiring the state's school districts to assign students on the basis of race to achieve "racial balance" struck an odd-sounding chord. Resistance to school desegregation in Mississippi apparently now included, as part of the arsenal, seeking protection under the cloak of civil rights legislation for the state's long-standing practice of operating a racially discriminatory dual school system.

Congressional attacks on HEW limited the agency's effectiveness, as it struggled for several years to fight off threats to its funding by legislators hostile to all federal efforts to demand compliance with the *Brown* decision and the Civil Rights Act of 1964. The federal courts, however, validated HEW's 1966 guidelines, confirmed the agency's position that freedom of choice could only be considered an effective mechanism for school desegregation if the technique actually led to biracial education, and soon moved beyond that position to invalidate freedom of choice as a method for achieving school desegregation.[16] In March 1967, the Fifth Circuit Court of Appeals, in an Alabama case, *United States v. Jefferson County Board of Education*, ruled that HEW's 1966 guidelines were constitutional. In his opinion, Judge John Minor Wisdom also questioned the efficacy of freedom of choice as a method to desegregate the schools; he noted that freedom-of-choice school desegregation plans are "better suited than any other to preserve the essentials of the dual school system while giving paper compliance with the duty to desegregate." The following year, the Supreme Court explicitly ratified Judge Wisdom's verdict on freedom of choice. The High Court's ruling in *Green v. County School Board of New Kent County, Virginia* also noted that freedom of choice had basically been used to maintain segregation and ordered southern school districts to come up with plans that actually led to school desegregation.[17]

By 1968, freedom of choice as a method for resisting school desegregation seemed to be on its last legs. The federal courts in *Jefferson* and *Green* had identified the practice as the delaying tactic it was. Former head of the U.S. Justice Department's Civil Rights Division Burke Marshall told an interviewer in the fall of 1968 that "the official legal caste system, segregation in schools and all of that business, has basically been eliminated. I don't mean it doesn't still exist, but it doesn't exist officially . . . it's no longer considered a viable constitutionally protected system of state government. . . . So we changed that, and I think that change has basically been accepted. And that just doesn't happen to be very much of the problem any more."[18] Anyone familiar with Mississippi's long resistance to the *Brown* decision, however, might have suspected that the problems with school desegregation in the state were far from over simply because of a couple of federal court rulings. White Mississippians ultimately still believed that they might be able to preserve their segregated school system.

Despite the legal decisions attacking freedom of choice, and despite the claims of many white Mississippians that they were being persecuted by federal bureaucrats, the state continued to receive special handling from HEW. The agency allowed a number of Mississippi school districts to maintain the freedom-of-choice practice for an extra year or two, especially districts that had construction needs that precluded effective school integration or districts that had a majority-black student population. Other districts, however, received HEW permission to continue to utilize freedom of choice for seemingly little cause other than a desire to postpone the elimination of their dual school systems. For instance, the Gulfport school district received authorization from the Office of Civil Rights to continue freedom of choice for both the 1968–69 and 1969–70 school years. The district had no construction needs, and blacks made up only 22 percent of the student population. The primary reason for the extension of freedom of choice in Gulfport was apparently "community resistance." Since neighboring Biloxi continued to utilize freedom of choice as part of a court order, HEW officials acceded to the claims of Gulfport officials that "community political pressures" would hamper any other method of school desegregation. The Southern Regional Council, an Atlanta-based organization working throughout the South on racial issues, reported on the Gulfport situation and noted, "If the same reasoning were applied throughout the South, the pace of desegregation would be dictated by the degree of resistance it encountered."[19] In short, the standard HEW applied to Gulfport placed school desegregation back firmly in the age of "all deliberate speed."

At the same time, federal judges in Mississippi essentially ignored the rulings of higher courts and accepted claims by state officials that freedom of choice represented the only way to achieve school desegregation in Mississippi. In the summer of 1968, Judge William C. Keady, a Greenville native sitting on the federal bench in the northern judicial district of Mississippi, approved a freedom-of-choice desegregation plan for the Marshall County and Holly Springs school districts precisely because such a plan would lead to less desegregation than the alternatives. In the case, *Anthony v. Marshall County Board of Education*—in which the Mississippi State Sovereignty Commission paid the attorneys' fees for the defendant school board— Judge Keady rejected both geographic zoning and school pairing plans because they "would result in immediate and almost complete integration," which would lead to massive white flight from the public schools. Keady also favored token desegregation over more substantial integration because "the presence of Negro students in schools attended by whites would 'necessarily lower' the quality of education." Keady disliked what he called the Fifth Circuit's "doctrinaire approach of mandating biracial education in all twelve grades of public school systems"; he favored preserving freedom of choice at least for the elementary schools. Not surprisingly, the Fifth Circuit overruled Keady's decision in April 1969.[20]

A similar effort to preserve freedom of choice by Mississippi federal judges unfolded in the state's southern federal judicial district during 1968 and ultimately led to a second, and more strident, rebuke of freedom of choice by the U.S. Supreme Court. Following the *Green* decision, the U.S. Department of Justice challenged school desegregation court orders in twenty-five Mississippi school districts that utilized freedom of choice. The extent of school desegregation in these districts ranged from minimal to none. No white student had ever gone to a black school in any of the districts; only one district had seen more than 10 percent of its black students cross over to the white schools (Enterprise, at 16 percent); and both Lincoln and Neshoba counties had experienced no school desegregation under the freedom-of-choice arrangements. Although the desegregation rate in Hinds County was only 3 percent for the 1968–69 school year, county superintendent J. D. Aldridge claimed that "*all* vestiges of [the] dual system are gone!" When the Justice Department took the lagging school districts to trial, the defendant school boards presented expert witnesses, including a professor emeritus of psychology from Columbia University, who testified to the mental deficiencies of blacks, while also submitting testimony that further desegregation would lead to massive white flight and the "ruin" of their school systems. A three-judge panel of Mississippians, Harold Cox, Walter Nixon, and Dan Russell Jr., ruled in favor of the defendants in the case, *United States v. Hinds County School Board.*[21]

Although an appeal of this case to the Fifth Circuit seemed assured of success, white Mississippians hoped they might receive a reprieve from the new Republican president, Richard Nixon, elected the previous fall. Indeed, Nixon had employed a "southern strategy" during his 1968 campaign, designed to attract whites fleeing from the Democratic Party, increasingly associated in the white mind as the party of civil rights. As part of this strategy, the California

Republican had indicated his support for freedom-of-choice school desegregation and blasted the courts and HEW for their mandates that the process move beyond this remedy. In his inaugural address, the new president had also pledged that he would not seek additional civil rights legislation. As a result, white Mississippians believed that the long "nightmare" of civil rights might finally be over. As Mel Leventhal of the NAACP's Legal Defense and Educational Fund noted in early 1969, many white Mississippians viewed Nixon as a modern-day Rutherford B. Hayes, someone who would take office and "end the modern reconstruction," much as Hayes had overseen the Northern retreat from the post–Civil War Reconstruction of the South.[22]

Mississippi education and political leaders wasted no time clamoring for a retreat on school desegregation following Nixon's inauguration. Gycelle Tynes, superintendent of the Clarksdale public schools, complained in May 1969 to Representative William Colmer about the dire consequences that would result—especially in the black-majority Delta—from the recent court decisions outlawing freedom of choice: "The Fifth Circuit Court of Appeals continues to torture the Fourteenth Amendment and to mock the intent and clear language of the Civil Rights Act of 1964. Some of the decisions or orders read like the language of madmen or LSD addicts. . . . Charles Sumner and Thaddeus Stevens never displayed greater vindictiveness than Judge Wisdom and some of his cohorts. . . . Public schools for most white pupils in this state are facing termination. Many will not open next September." Likewise, state senator and Cleveland lawyer William B. Alexander urged Representative Sonny Montgomery to do something to "curb the U.S. Supreme Court and the Fifth Circuit Court of Appeals." Without such action, Alexander reasoned that "the public school system in about half the counties of Mississippi will be dead, insofar as white people are concerned."[23]

In early 1969, Senator Stennis began lobbying Nixon administration officials, including HEW Secretary Robert Finch, Attorney General John Mitchell, and other senior Nixon advisers, for changes in federal school desegregation policies; all promised that a more moderate set of school desegregation guidelines would be forthcoming soon. In May 1969, Clarke Reed, leader of the Mississippi Republican Party, asked Harry Dent, a special adviser to President Nixon on the South, to delay a government appeal of the *Hinds County School Board* decision to the Fifth Circuit in the hope that if the case could be "dragged out" until two vacant seats on the circuit were filled by Nixon appointees, then "the tone and direction of the courts on the school question" could be changed. Dent relayed Reed's request to Attorney General Mitchell, noting that any help for the Mississippi school districts "would be good from a political standpoint." But the appeals process was already in motion.[24] Unable to stop a review of the south Mississippi school case, Mississippi leaders hoped the promised new guidelines might provide some relief. In late June, Senator Stennis personally visited President Nixon to press for the long-promised, more moderate rules. Although Nixon assured the Mississippi senator that their issuance was imminent, they did not materialize until July 3, the same day the Fifth Circuit issued its ruling in the *Hinds County School Board* case. The ruling called for the twenty-five districts to desegregate their schools completely by September 1969.[25]

The new guidelines reflected Nixon's ambivalence on the school desegregation issue. Clearly, Nixon was no ardent segregationist. His civil rights credentials dated back to at least the 1960 presidential campaign, when a number of civil rights leaders had endorsed his candidacy because of his support for a strong civil rights platform, and the president had no intention of allowing the South to retain segregated schools at this late date. At the same time, his recent political victory at least in part rested on the success of his southern strategy, so he sought to compromise on the pace of school desegregation where possible.[26] The new guidelines, issued jointly by HEW and the Justice Department, affirmed the federal government's commitment to ending the South's dual school system but fudged on the fall 1969 deadline for accomplishing this task that had been set by the Johnson administration and upheld by the federal courts. The guidelines required that all school districts come up with a plan that would eventually eliminate dual schools, but rather than impose a strict deadline for fall 1969, a number of school districts were allowed a "limited delay," including black-majority districts, districts with construction needs, and any other district where full integration would cause "educational and administrative problems." At the same time, the guidelines announced that, when possible, the Justice Department, rather than HEW, would oversee compliance with the new guidelines. This change pleased many white southerners, who often agreed with the assessment of Harry Dent that the people at HEW were basically "left of center–zealots."[27]

Although the new Nixon administration guidelines offered the possibility of a "limited delay" in completing school integration, many white

Mississippians were not satisfied, for Nixon had not engineered the complete retreat they had anticipated or ensured that freedom-of-choice desegregation could be preserved. A week after the Nixon administration made the new guidelines public, the Justice Department filed suit against the Coffeeville public schools, which had managed by the summer of 1969 to desegregate only three of its eleven hundred black students. Senator Eastland responded by claiming that the "Republicans had promised this was not going to happen" and by predicting that the Coffeeville suit was just the opening act on a "rash of actions by the governement [*sic*] which would push our schools over the brink of choas [*sic*]." Eastland surmised that, much like the previous Democratic administrations, "the Republican[s] are seeking to promote integration at all costs." Charles Jacobs of Brookhaven, like many other white Mississippians, asked, "What can posibly [*sic*] be wrong or unfair in the Freedom of Choice plan?" Without this mechanism, Jacobs argued, Mississippi would be "forced to submit to the ruination of our school systems." A notable exception to such attitudes came from school officials in a group of twenty-two school districts, almost all located in areas with large white majorities, which voluntarily gave up on freedom-of-choice desegregation and adopted plans for fall 1969 that essentially eliminated their dual school systems.[28]

The vast majority of Mississippi school districts, however, continued the fight to preserve segregated schools. In the black-majority districts of Mississippi, whites scrambled to find some kind of way to forestall school integration as freedom of choice receded as a viable option. In the days after the Fifth Circuit's July 3 ruling in the *Hinds County School Board* case, white administrators in six black-majority districts in and around the Delta proposed to the federal district courts (and were granted) plans designed to assign students based on the results of intelligence tests, with the "smartest" students attending the white schools and the less talented going to the black schools. Though educators continue to debate the merits of ability grouping, few have ever suggested that students of differing skill levels should be placed in separate buildings. School boards embraced the plans because their notions of black inferiority convinced them that these schemes would greatly limit the extent of school desegregation, though even some local education officials familiar with intelligence tests had pointed out that the plans would not necessarily preserve racial segregation. Such plans ultimately did fail to achieve their purpose. Many black parents (and some white parents) refused to have their children subjected to such tests. In Coahoma County, Aaron Henry and the local branch of the NAACP led a successful boycott that essentially halted the testing. When actually carried out, the testing ultimately led to more desegregation than whites anticipated. In Tunica County, for instance, which had perhaps the most underfunded black schools in the state, more than 10 percent of the black students taking the intelligence test scored high enough to receive assignment to the white school, while the scores of a third of the white students landed them in previously all-black schools. Ultimately, the plan led to a situation where black pupils would have represented just over half the students in the first four grades at formerly all-white Tunica Elementary, the only grades scheduled to be desegregated under the Tunica school board's proposed but clearly unacceptable three-stage intelligence plan, itself another tactic for postponing full school integration for three years.[29]

White parents in the school districts involved in the *Hinds County School Board* case were perhaps the most alarmed in the state during the summer of 1969. Many of these districts had been among the most vociferous in resisting even the token desegregation of freedom-of-choice arrangements, and the new guidelines, as Senator Stennis had feared, had been promulgated too late to spare them from the Fifth Circuit's firm September 1969 deadline for complete school integration. The intensity of impending dread among white parents in these areas reveals that many white Mississippians, as late as the summer of 1969, did not so much want to preserve freedom of choice as they wanted to preserve segregated schools. As HEW worked with local school officials in the affected districts to develop desegregation plans that would result in complete school integration in the weeks after the Fifth Circuit issued its ruling, Senator Stennis received bags of mail from white parents in these areas, all of it with pretty much the same message (in fact, many of the letters were simply form letters signed by the individual parents): help preserve segregated schools by maintaining the freedom-of-choice arrangements. Mrs. R. R. Vance of Lauderdale County told Senator Stennis that "our hope for a better school system and a separate but equal education for all our children both black and white, are [*sic*] in your hands." She noted that such a result could be accomplished by the preservation of freedom of choice. Mr. and Mrs. Rudolph Harrison, also of Lauderdale County, believed that the proposed HEW plan for completely integrating their school district would be a disaster. They thought that the entire effort was "Communist inspired from beginning to end to promote marriage between the Negro and White races in order to weaken the high standards of education we now have, our morals, and every phase of our way of life." They urged Senator Stennis to do what he could "to keep our schools segregated." Mrs. Lavon Wade of Quitman asked the senator to help save "our *White schools of Mississippi.*" She felt that the end of freedom of choice meant that "our entire school system as well as the future of our children is at stake and is about to be destroyed," and she could not believe that the new school desegregation plan for the Quitman district might mean "[m]aybe even putting our white children in negro schools in negro communities."[30]

With so many white folks back home clearly agitated, Senator Stennis decided to throw around his considerable political weight in Washington to seek at least a temporary delay for white parents facing the imminent demise of segregated schools. At the time, Stennis, chair of the Senate Armed Services Committee, was leading the fight for a controversial military authorization bill proposed by the Nixon administration. The senator informed the president in an August 12 letter that he might have to turn over leadership of the committee to fellow Democrat Stuart Symington, an opponent of the pending military legislation, while Stennis went home to Mississippi "to try to protect my own people" from the "calamity" of the impending school integration mandated by the Fifth Circuit. Stennis also announced that he would introduce legislation requiring HEW to enforce equally in the North and the South what he called the "harsh and unreasonable" school desegregation guidelines. The Mississippi senator believed that once guideline enforcement began in the North, "a public outcry will result and we in Mississippi and the South will gain the relief." These maneuvers by Stennis came after HEW had filed school desegregation plans for the affected school districts but before the hearings on the plans had been held, expected by almost all observers to be a pro forma approval of the HEW-crafted plans.[31]

The pressure applied by Senator Stennis on the Nixon administration apparently changed matters considerably. Just over a week after Stennis's private letter to the president and his public declarations to seek new legislation to force more school desegregation enforcement in the North, HEW secretary Robert Finch told the federal district judges overseeing the south Mississippi cases that the agency, although it had already submitted school desegregation plans to the federal district court, needed more time to develop adequate plans and asked for a delay on the hearings until December 1969. In other words, the federal government switched sides and joined the defendant school boards of *Hinds County School Board* in seeking delayed implementation of the Fifth Circuit's July 3 ruling. The request for a delay was gladly granted by the district court, and although the Fifth Circuit questioned why the federal government's request for more time came so late in the process, the appeals court also allowed the delay. Not surprisingly, the postponement convinced whites in the affected districts that school integration might yet be thwarted. In Leake County, whites reportedly began plotting new delaying tactics. The matter, however, did not disappear just because the Nixon administration caved in when faced with southern pressure. The NAACP's Legal Defense and Educational Fund stepped forward to take up the cause of the black plaintiffs and appealed the case to the Supreme Court, now styled *Beatrice Alexander v. Holmes County Board of Education.*[32]

In addition to fighting the federal government's efforts to force the state to comply with the *Brown* decision and the Civil Rights Act of 1964, white officials in Mississippi also continued to support the state's "separate but equal" school building project. Such efforts further belied the claims by white Mississippians that they had eliminated dual school systems in favor of unitary systems where everyone had the right to choose to go to any school they desired. During the freedom-of-choice years, from 1964 to 1969, Mississippi's equalization project, begun in the years after World War II, continued. In fact, one of the by-products of the black effort to desegregate Mississippi schools during the freedom-of-choice years was that the state of Mississippi made its most serious effort to improve black schools in the entire history of the equalization program. Additional black schools were consolidated, black and white teachers' salaries were further equalized, the school term for almost all black children was extended to nine months, and the state continued with its separate building program. The state's Educational Finance Commission (EFC), created in 1953 to disburse funds in Mississippi's school equalization program, continued until 1966 to disburse funds for "white" and "Negro" building projects. Even after this date, however, the commission refused to consider whether school building projects it funded would promote or help end the dual school system, and many proposals were clearly designed to bolster segregation. For example, in 1968 the commission approved a grant of $275,000 to create a countywide high school in Quitman County in place of the county's four predominantly white high schools in Sledge, Crowder, Marks, and Lambert, which together in 1968–69 had twenty-four black students. The only other high school in the county, Quitman County High School, constructed in 1958 with an EFC grant, had 963 students during the same year—all of whom were black. The 1968 grant would have fulfilled the equalization plan proposed in a county survey done in 1957, which recommended two countywide high schools, one black and one white. When local blacks objected to the EFC grant on the grounds that it sought to maintain segregation and initiated a suit against local school officials, the school board abandoned its plans for a white countywide high school and forfeited the approved state funds.[33]

As late as 1966, the federal district courts in the state also continued to encourage equalization as a means to limit substantial school desegregation. For example, although the federal court in Mississippi's southern district ruled in 1966 that Noxubee County schools could no longer operate on a segregated basis, the judge also ordered further equalization of the county's schools. Noxubee County in 1966 still had four hundred black children attending nine unconsolidated one-, two-, or three-teacher schools, and the court's ruling called for upgrades to these nine schools. In fact, the judge, in a verbal statement to school officials after his official ruling "abolishing" segregated schools in the county, threatened to order the immediate transferal of the four hundred black children "to the white attendance centers in the county" unless something was done at once to improve the nine unconsolidated black schools.[34]

While black Mississippians often applauded the state's effort to develop better black schools, the program continued to fail to achieve its goal of creating a separate and equal school system for black Mississippians. As in previous years, failure of the equalization effort remained certain as long as whites had all the power and made all the decisions. Throughout the 1960s, political power over the schools remained firmly in white hands in almost every school district in the state. As Obie Clark, an NAACP leader in Meridian, noted, the all-white school board there, as late as 1969, "were pledging their resources to the white schools, and we were getting what was left over."[35] Black exclusion from all levels of decision making about educational policy in Mississippi also allowed white officials in the state to tap into the increasing federal dollars available to elementary and secondary education during the second half of the 1960s to promote the state's "separate but equal" spending program. It is important to understand that after 1964, school districts could only receive federal funds once they had begun the process of school desegregation; indeed, the battle over Title VI compliance revolved around questions about how to ensure that southern states such as Mississippi would take at least the minimum steps necessary toward school integration before they could acquire the federal funds available under the ESEA. As has been demonstrated, most Mississippi districts submitted plans to federal officials that claimed to disestablish the dual school system but in actual operation barely tolerated token school desegregation. After 1965, the amount of federal funds available to the states for public education increased dramatically. Indeed, the Title I funds available through the ESEA, designed to augment educational spending in the nation's poor districts, made Mississippi eligible for a bundle of cash. In the first two years of the program, which began in 1965, the state received over $60 million. By 1969, Title I funds represented anywhere from 10 to 30 percent of the budgets in 115 of the state's school districts.[36]

The federal education funds Mississippi received in the late 1960s, however, were not used to help disadvantaged children in a unitary school system. Those school districts that did seek these funds frequently used them to pay for the basic expenses of black public education or to assist segregated private schools in the state, in other words, to maintain the dual system of education. In a few instances, federal education funds were used to assist the creation of or to furnish private segregated academies. An Office of Economic Opportunity (OEO) investigator in 1966 discovered that a group of young men enrolled in a federally funded vocational education program, instead of learning the basics of auto mechanics, were helping build a local Citizens' Council school, Central Holmes Academy, in Lexington. Another public school district apparently used Title I monies to buy a color television for a nearby segregated academy. Occasionally, Title I funds were used to assist all-white schools (Aberdeen) or the district administration (Shelby and Cleveland, where the funds were used to build offices for the school superintendents). In 1969, after blacks in Holly Springs and Marshall County lodged a complaint about the use of Title I monies, the OEO launched an extensive investigation. The inquiry found that the most common misuse of Title I funds was to pay not for new programs but for regular expenses at the black schools, for things such as "painting classrooms, furnishing offices, and buying band uniforms," items covered in the regular budget for the white schools. Benton County was fairly typical. Title I funds there were used to install a heating system at the county's only black school, Old Salem; to transform the school's band room to a classroom; to install eight mobile classrooms adjacent to Old Salem; to pay the salary of the school's "janitor-nightwatchman"; and to add a playground and about sixty new desks to the school. Thus, school officials in Benton County, and other locales where the OEO discovered similar practices, found a way to tap into federal funds for education while preserving segregated schools. Such an outcome was facilitated because, despite OEO regulations requiring community input on the use of Title I funds, black residents were generally never consulted about how the funds might be spent.[37]

Title I funds were also commonly misused to hire black teachers to bring the teacher-student ratio in black schools more in line with class size in the white schools. At King's Elementary School, an all-black school in Yazoo County, five of the fifteen teachers in the 1968–69 school year were paid with Title I funds. The student-teacher ratio was a comfortable twenty-six to one, but without the Title I teachers, the ratio would have been an unwieldy forty to one. Overall, the Yazoo County schools used federal Title I money to narrow, but not close completely, the gap between the amount of money spent on white and black children in the district. Even with all of the district's Title I money going to the all-black schools, the system still spent just $310 per pupil in the black schools, while providing almost $319 to every student in the traditionally all-white schools. The Coahoma County school district engaged in the same practice, using state and county funds to pay white teachers and Title I funds to finance the salaries of many black instructors. By the 1968–69 term, federal funds had finally allowed the county to hire enough teachers at the black schools to almost reduce the teacher-student ratio to the level in the white schools. When Coahoma County had its Title I funds suspended in February 1969, however, the county's equalization efforts came to an abrupt halt. The district fired thirty-five teachers, twenty-seven teachers' aides, and three janitors who were paid with federal funds from the black schools, and the teacher-student ratio in the county's black schools mushroomed back to its previous excessive level.[38]

Mississippi's use of Title I monies to "equalize" black education clearly demonstrated the bankruptcy of the state's long-standing program to try and make "separate but equal" a reality. Essentially, Mississippi had never committed to an equitable distribution of state and especially local funds. When new federal funds became available in the late 1960s, state and local education officials viewed the funds as extra resources that could be spent on upgrading black education without undermining the unshakeable conviction that Mississippi taxpayers' monies should be used primarily for schooling the white youth of the state. The revelation about Mississippi's misuse of Title I funds led the Lawyers Constitutional Defense Committee, a civil rights organization working in Mississippi, Louisiana, and Alabama during the 1960s, to consider filing an equalization lawsuit against the state in the fall of 1969. As Armand Derfner, one of the group's lawyers, noted, while Mississippi leaders might offer excuses for the delays in school segregation, such as the need to give whites a chance to adjust to dramatic social change, those excuses "do not apply to equalizing expenditures. There is no social adjustment required to stop misappropriating funds (for that is what it is when money supposed to be spent equally on black and white schools is in fact poured heavily into the white schools)."[39]

The proposed school desegregation suit was designed to explode the myth of Mississippi's equalization program, to "stop the school officials from claiming that they are interested just in preserving social customs and that they really want to provide good education for both black and white children." Derfner believed that a lawsuit that exposed the state's educational spending would demonstrate that "school officials have systematically kept money out of the black schools while pouring it into white schools; in this way they are little better than common criminals, except that the amount of money they have misappropriated has been enormous."[40] Though the group never filed the lawsuit, the proposed indictment was a strong one. The very fact that Mississippi still even continued to try to equalize black and white education well into the late 1960s clearly conveyed the state's continuing devotion to the dual school system and undermined official white Mississippi's claim that freedom-of-choice school desegregation had satisfied the mandate of *Brown*.

In the end, white Mississippians favored the freedom-of-choice school desegregation blueprint primarily because it proved an exceedingly effective

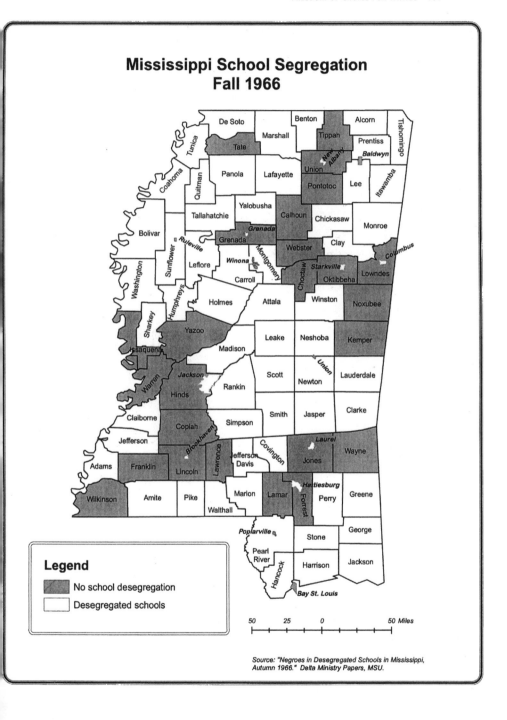

Mississippi School Segregation
Fall 1966

Legend

No school desegregation

Desegregated schools

50   25   0   50 Miles

Source: "Negroes in Desegregated Schools in Mississippi,
Autumn 1966." Delta Ministry Papers, MSU.

method for delaying meaningful school desegregation for another half decade. In 1965, the first widespread year of freedom-of-choice school desegregation in Mississippi, fewer than 1,000 black students (less than 0.5 percent of total black enrollment) moved into previously all-white schools. As the school year opened in the fall of 1966, few black children broke the educational color barrier in the state. Only 7,200 of the state's almost 296,000 black students (2.4 percent) attended previously all-white schools, while 54 of the state's 148 districts maintained strictly segregated schools (see map 2). Two years later, still less than 7 percent of the state's black children attended classes with whites. The progress of faculty desegregation during the freedom-of-choice era was even more dismal. As late as the 1968–69 school year, forty-two of Mississippi's school districts (28 percent) had not attempted any faculty desegregation; another thirty-four districts (23 percent) had transferred fewer than five instructors across racial lines.[41] In actual operation, freedom of choice was just another effective manifestation of massive resistance.

CHAPTER SIX

FREEDOM OF CHOICE FOR BLACKS

"Very Little Choice and No Freedom at All"

O rbra Harrington Porter was one of thousands of Mississippi school desegregation pioneers during the freedom-of-choice era. Born in Jackson in 1953, she grew up in a close-knit community where her parents were actively involved in church, civic groups, and, by the late 1950s, the city's civil rights movement. Her mother did clerical work for Medgar Evers; her father, J. B. Harrington, worked as a truck driver. Fearing he might lose his job, J. B. did not join the front lines of the movement during the early 1960s, but he was active in the movement. He had been a registered voter in Jackson since 1952 and also provided transportation for civil rights participants, "hauling people to the poll, hauling them to the picketing line, going getting food for them, carrying them back home." In 1966, during the second year of Jackson's freedom-of-choice school desegregation plan, Orbra and one other black girl chose to attend previously all-white Hardy Junior High School. The other girl's mother was a maid, and soon after school began this woman's employer threatened to fire her if she did not remove her daughter from the "white" school. So, within days of the new school year, Orbra found herself as the only black student among the more than one thousand students attending Hardy Junior High.[1]

Orbra's experience at Hardy proved difficult. The students generally ignored her. Some of the teachers offered limited support, while others told her, "Don't say nothing to me and I ain't going to say nothing to you." The people who really watched out for the young girl were the school's black janitors and cooks, who always made sure to greet her and let her know that they were available if she needed any assistance. Orbra was not allowed to participate in extracurricular activities. She came to welcome the dismissal bell, when she could flee from the hostile environment. The next year, Orbra moved to Murrah High School, which during the 1967–68 school year had eight black students. There, she encountered many of the same problems. Many of the white students continued to ignore or harass their black classmates, although some tried to befriend Orbra and the other black students, perhaps because by 1967 the whites at Murrah had encountered blacks in their classes for a couple of years. The ban on black participation in extracurricular activities, however, continued at Murrah. When Orbra and several other black girls attended a school-sponsored dance at a local country club, officials of the club "told us that it was a private club and we were not welcome there and we had to go home. And they sent us home."[2]

Although Orbra missed her neighborhood black school, and many of her friends questioned her choice, she quickly discovered why going to a previously all-white school was so important. At Murrah, located in one of Jackson's wealthiest white neighborhoods and consequently one of the best schools in the Jackson system, Orbra had new textbooks, not the hand-me-down versions common at the black schools she had attended. Her teachers were well educated and offered a challenging learning environment; her English instructor, for instance, also taught at Belhaven College, a private school in the city. The curriculum at Murrah offered a full range of college prep courses, many unavailable at the black schools. The white parents of the neighborhood regularly provided money for any unmet needs at the school, something impossible for the black community to accomplish on the same scale. Orbra underwent the heartache and hassle of choosing to attend a white school simply because she wanted "to get the best education that I can get," and that education was in Jackson's white schools.[3]

The freedom-of-choice arrangement that stood at the center of almost all school desegregation in Mississippi from 1964 to 1969 posed a daunting obstacle to the efforts of black Mississippians to end the state's system of dual education. Given the history of segregated education, a desegregation mechanism such as freedom of choice, which allowed whites to preserve dual schools while placing the onus on black parents, children, and teachers to eliminate the practice, had little chance of being implemented fairly. Freedom-of-choice school desegregation saddled blacks with the burden of having to choose affirmatively to topple a segregated educational structure dearly supported by whites. The freedom-of-choice strategy for achieving school desegregation also presupposed that people actually had the freedom to choose. In Mississippi, and in much of the rest of the South during the 1960s, most black people did not. Winifred Green, who worked with the AFSC, recalled the remark of one black parent in the Delta who succinctly calculated the problem with freedom-of-choice school desegregation for the mass of black Mississippians: "Very little choice and no freedom at all."[4]

As the federal government and white Mississippians wrangled over the boundaries of school desegregation during the 1964–65 academic year, black protest continued to build, with direct-action campaigns focusing on schools launched in a number of locales, including Indianola, Valley View, Moss Point, Clay County, Amite County, Pike County, Issaquena County, Sharkey County, and Benton County.[5] A closer look at the protests in Issaquena, Sharkey, and Benton counties highlights the nature of black protest and the concerns of black students and teachers as white Mississippians scrambled to limit desegregation in a world fast shifting beneath their feet.

In January 1965, local members of the Mississippi Student Union, an organization of high school students launched by civil rights activists during Freedom Summer, distributed SNCC pins to black high school students in Issaquena and Sharkey counties. The students from these two counties attended the same school near Rolling Fork in Sharkey County, Henry Weathers High School. Some of the students wore the pins to school, which were emblazoned with the letters "SNCC" and showed a black hand and a white hand embracing. When a disagreement between two students broke out over the pins on a Friday afternoon, the principal, O. E. Jordan, noticed the pins for the first time and told the students they should not wear them. This admonition, however, only spurred the students to find more of their peers who would sport the button on Monday morning. Jordan, a respected black educator who was a past president of the MTA, was a man who worked his whole life to improve black education, but he had no desire to challenge the white power structure. Three years earlier, he had publicly pleaded with blacks in Harmony to drop their path-breaking school desegregation lawsuit in the interest of preserving "good" race relations in Leake County. When almost two hundred students arrived on Monday wearing the SNCC pins, Jordan took down their names and huddled with white school officials about how to proceed; they decided to suspend the offending students. At a mass meeting on Wednesday night, black students and parents came together to discuss the escalating situation. At first, "the parents dominated the meeting," with some criticizing the school and the principal while others defended the principal's actions. The students, however, had already decided that the protest should be expanded to include a boycott of the school. Their argument carried the day. Most of the parents signed a pledge to keep their children out of school and agreed to try and negotiate the matter with the school authorities. When approximately forty parents met with the white superintendent the next day, he reiterated the school board's stance that the students could not return to school wearing the pins; he also reminded the parents "about the new baseball diamond, and the new additions to the school." The parents' request for a meeting with the all-white school board was denied.[6]

Local whites remained convinced that outside agitators had roused the students to action, despite the overwhelming evidence that the movement had been organized entirely by local black students and, with some prodding from their children, local black parents. Initially, about eleven hundred students participated in the boycott of both the high school and the elementary school in the district, and about three hundred students remained out of school for the remainder of the year. SNCC workers did come in after the boycott was under way to set up a number of Freedom Schools in the two counties. But the boycott raised awareness in the local black community about the need for school desegregation. In March, over three hundred parents signed petitions delivered to the school board demanding school desegregation in the district. The school board had no intention of making such a move. It ignored the documents submitted by local blacks and also refused to submit any school desegregation compliance materials to HEW. On April 1, Unita Blackwell—who had become a SNCC field worker in 1964 and was a member of the Mississippi Freedom Democratic Party—and other black parents filed a lawsuit against the Issaquena-Sharkey Consolidated School District. According to Blackwell, the suit was filed not because the community wanted racial integration but rather because of the continuing inequalities in local black education and the lack of control blacks had over their children's education, a fact made transparent during the SNCC pin controversy. Though there had been gradual improvement of the district's black schools, parents remained convinced that the school board had not "fix[ed] our schools as well as you have the white schools." The effort by the white school leaders to coerce Principal Jordan into stamping out all evidence of civil rights activity in his school only highlighted how little power black residents had over their school. As Blackwell noted, "the school board had a black principal that they was controlling and told him to tell children to do this and that."[7]

In Benton County, there were three schools in 1964, two for whites (Ashland and Hickory Flat) and one for blacks (Old Salem). The northeast Mississippi county at the time was a relatively poor agricultural area; in fact, until 1965 both the white and black schools operated on a split session—a common practice among black schools in the Delta—in which school would begin in midsummer to allow the children to be dismissed for a month or more to help with the annual fall harvest. As elsewhere in Mississippi, inequality between the white and black schools existed in Benton County, though the disparity here was not as great as in some other areas. Old Salem was the most modern of the three schools, having been remodeled as part of the state's equalization program in 1959. Curricular offerings at the white and black schools were almost identical, and the amount of operating funds spent per black student trailed that disbursed to educate each white student by only about fifty cents. Much like every other black school district, however, whites handled all the decision making about education in the county, which led many black residents to believe that the remaining gap between white and black education would never be rectified. In 1963, a number of black residents in Benton County, including some teachers, became involved in the effort under way in Mississippi to secure voting rights for black citizens. During Freedom Summer, civil rights workers from nearby Rust College in Holly Springs came to the county, expanding the reach of the civil rights campaign.[8] As the movement grew, the inequalities in the county's school system came under attack.

The organizational heart of the Benton County movement was the Benton County Citizens Club, established before the arrival of the summer volunteers. As part of the drive for equal rights, Citizens Club members began in 1964 to hold meetings with the principal of Old Salem, W. B. "Woody" Foster, clamoring for upgrades to the school's educational program. Foster had little interest in pressing the white power structure for change, so in January 1965 Citizens Club members Loyal Thompson, Walter Reaves, and Rebecca Doris petitioned the Benton County school board for a number of changes, including improvements to Old Salem, the most immediate being the establishment of a school library. The black leaders also asked that Principal Foster be removed at the end of the school year. The school board agreed to "take the presented problems under advisement." Foster had become a target of the Citizens Club not only because of his unwillingness to lobby the school board aggressively for more resources for the black school but also because of his perceived hostility to the local civil rights movement. Teachers who supported civil rights faced reprisals from Foster. For example, Genevera Reaves, a teacher at Old Salem, had long been active in the civil rights movement, along with her husband, Henry. Most notably, the Reaves had for several years been leaders of a clandestine NAACP chapter in the county. In early 1963, the Reaves's civil rights activities became well known, leading Foster to recommend that Genevera's contract not be renewed for the 1963–64 school year. Community anger toward Foster only intensified later in January 1965 when he initiated the arrest of a white SNCC activist, Aviva Futorian, who dared to attend a basketball game at Old Salem. On February 1, another Citizens Club delegation, led by Walter Reaves (the Reaves's nephew), returned to the school board with a report on the "bad conditions" at Old Salem and with a petition signed by more than three hundred people asking for the dismissal of Foster and four Old Salem teachers, including Foster's wife. Board members agreed to consider the group's demands, and they met with Citizens Club members several times in early March. At the last of these meetings, on March 8, the school board and its lawyers indicated that they would agree to the group's demands if Benton County blacks agreed to "stay out of the white schools and the white cafes." When the black activists refused this "deal," the board adjourned the meeting without addressing the Citizens Club's demands. The next day, after a three-hour discussion, the Citizens Club voted 257 to 2 to boycott Old Salem. The boycott began the following day, with 90 percent of the school's twelve hundred students staying out of the school. Students from Rust College came in and set up five Freedom Schools in the county.[9]

Faced with the loss of state funds because of declining enrollment, Benton County school officials relented at the end of March, agreeing to the Citizens

Club's demands. But the school board tried to punish those who had led the school boycott. A number of school bus drivers who supported the boycott, including Loyal Thompson, were fired, presumably because they refused to run empty buses to Old Salem during the boycott. In addition to not renewing the contracts of Foster and the four Old Salem teachers deemed unfit by the Citizens Club, the school board released six teachers who had supported the Benton County movement. The school's attorneys also supported, and perhaps encouraged, Foster's libel lawsuit against the Citizens Club. During the school fight, the club's newspaper, the *Benton County Freedom Train*, had called Foster, at various times, a "puppet," a "dummy," and an "Uncle Tom." Although a local judge ruled in favor of Foster and awarded him $60,000, the Mississippi Supreme Court later overturned the verdict.[10]

As in Issaquena and Sharkey counties, much of the black anger that sparked the boycott in Benton County centered around the continued inequities in black education compared to white schooling and the lack of control blacks had over the education of their children. Benton County blacks, like those in Issaquena and Sharkey counties, believed that the only way to solve this problem was through the elimination of the state's dual educational system. In February 1965, while waiting for the school board to respond to its petition on the conditions at Old Salem, the Citizens Club began preparing petitions asking for school desegregation. At the same time, faced with pressure from the federal government, Benton County school officials, a week before the boycott of Old Salem began, filed their first desegregation plan, one that could have been exhibit A for HEW's case for more stringent Title VI compliance guidelines. The Benton County scheme called for a freedom-of-choice plan for the twelfth grade for both the 1965–66 and 1966–67 school years. Thereafter, freedom of choice would be used to desegregate one additional grade a year, leading to a fully desegregated system with the commencement of the 1977–78 academic term. In May 1965, however, more than forty black families filed suit against the Benton County school board, expressing their dissatisfaction "with the continued operation of our public schools on a segregated basis" and requesting desegregated schools. That summer, the federal courts ordered a four-grade-a-year free-choice plan for Benton County, beginning with the 1965–66 school term.[11]

Black parents and black children continued to push for school integration because they wanted a better education. Despite more than two decades of official but half-hearted efforts to improve black schools, they were—with some notable exceptions—still lacking in resources compared to their white counterparts throughout the state.[12] Dr. Matthew Page, a black Greenville physician, favored school integration simply "[b]ecause I am convinced that if there are white students in all schools, there won't be some schools that are inadequately staffed, some schools with inadequate facilities, and there won't be schools that are considerably subpar." Loyal Thompson, whose son was one of the school desegregation pioneers in Benton County, expressed the same sentiments more colloquially. He told the white lawyer who suggested that black children could get a sufficient education in the black schools that "one thing I know, if I'm at the same table with you, you eat steak, I'll eat some too, so that's why I carried him on up there [to the previously all-white school]." Mary Blackmon, one of two black students to desegregate Canton High School in the fall of 1965, recalled years later her motivation for seeking admission to the white schools; she noted that she did not "feel like I had to be with a certain group of people; that was not the point. The point was that we didn't feel like our schools were equal. We didn't feel like we got equal equipment, or textbooks, or anything." Lou Emma Shipp, a member of the Carroll County Freedom Democratic Party, perhaps summed up the attitude of many black Mississippians who lived in the vast majority of school districts where separate would always remain unequal: "We don't want to go to school with whites, but we just want a good education because we are tired of going to no-good schools; [for example] Vaiden Negro High doesn't have a library, and what good is that type of school, no business education, no music, no chemistry, only the common books, learning such as algebra, physics, education, English, and biology. We have no extra curricular activities like the white school[;] if we had equal schools, we wouldn't care to go to school with whites."[13]

For some black Mississippians, especially those veterans of the voting rights and public accommodation desegregation struggles, school desegregation also remained a basic issue of freedom, a crippling vestige of a Jim Crow South increasingly disappearing in every other obvious way. Indeed, a 1966 study of school desegregation in the state found that 60 percent of those blacks who sent their children to the white schools under the freedom-of-choice plans, like Orbra Harrington Porter's parents, were in some way involved with a civil rights group. In Greenville, Dr. Page noted in 1966 that "we got 135 Negro children in formerly all-white schools by having five or six organizations working at it night and day." Tellingly, he observed that "at Leland, 10 miles away, where there was no organization, there is no integration." In some cases, agitation for school desegregation increased awareness about other remaining civil rights issues. In Holmes County, the local movement's voter registration drive following passage of the Voting Rights Act of 1965 received a boost after people unsuccessfully tried to register their children in the white schools. This rejection "started them thinking," according to one movement activist, and led many to register to vote.[14]

A number of civil rights organizations were active in Mississippi in the school desegregation struggle, including the Delta Ministry, the Mississippi Freedom Democratic Party, the Mississippi Council on Human Relations, and SNCC. The most active organizations on the school desegregation front, however, were the AFSC and the NAACP Legal Defense and Educational Fund. As early as the fall of 1964, the two organizations had sponsored a leadership training institute on school desegregation at Farish Street Baptist Church in Jackson, where attendees from around the state were given information on how to bring school desegregation to their communities. In 1965, the two groups cosponsored a school desegregation task force to inform black families "of their rights and to provide assistance to local communities" seeking to desegregate schools under the freedom-of-choice school desegregation plans. In the summer of 1965, the two agencies had twenty fieldworkers, and in preparation for the first widespread free-choice school year, the task force put out three thousand school desegregation kits; distributed eighty-five thousand copies of the brochure "A Message to Parents About Desegregated Schools"; and talked to thousands of black families in over one hundred school districts, many of whom ultimately registered in the white schools that fall.[15]

Though black Mississippians had good reasons to press forward with school desegregation, freedom-of-choice desegregation placed heavy burdens on black parents and students, a fact that had become readily apparent beginning with the initial desegregation efforts of 1964. Black parents who chose to take advantage of the federal court's ruling and send their children to the previously all-white schools were harassed and intimidated by whites. In Jackson, middle-class blacks, especially schoolteachers and others dependent on white employers, often refused to step forward for reasons of simple self-preservation. Jackson school superintendent Kirby Walker made it clear to his black teachers that they should not be on the front lines of the desegregation battle. While the threats blacks faced in urban areas, such as Jackson and Biloxi, were often very real but subtle, the harassment black parents faced in a rural area like Leake County was more direct and blunt.[16]

After the Leake County school board issued its school desegregation plan in early August 1964, at least nine parents chose to send their children to the previously all-white Carthage Attendance Center. They soon received "threats and harassments" from white employers and merchants. Just days before the opening of school, the nine families remained committed to school desegregation, but the pressure applied by whites increased; the black parents contemplating the desegregation attempt were all threatened with the loss of jobs or credit. By the morning of September 1, only one black family resolved to go ahead with the desegregation attempt. A. J. Lewis, an army veteran who worked at a local sawmill, decided to proceed with the decision to send his daughter, Debra, to Carthage Attendance Center, in part because of a promise he had made to Medgar Evers before his assassination. While state and federal officials made sure Debra Lewis entered the Carthage elementary school without incident, the threats of what would happen to those who dared to cross the educational color line, which had scared off all other Leake County blacks, were realized by the Lewises. The day after his daughter began school, Lewis lost his job at the sawmill. In the following months, local merchants refused to do business with the family, their house was firebombed twice, and finally, the black policeman from whom the Lewises rented and who lived next door evicted the family from their home.[17]

To help the Lewises survive, a number of people and organizations around the United States contributed money, and the NAACP placed A. J. Lewis on its staff briefly to provide the family with an income. Debra faced her own set of trials at her new elementary school. Her teachers required her to sit in the back of class, made her go through the cafeteria line last and sit at a lunch table by herself, and gave her the oldest schoolbooks available. Despite all the hassles, the Lewises believed Debra was receiving a better education than she ever could have in Leake County's all-black schools; half a year after Debra's heroic efforts, her mother, Minnie, weighing all the pluses and minuses, noted that "I think I would do it all over again if I had to."[18]

By the following year, most Mississippi school districts had some type of freedom-of-choice school desegregation plan in place, yet few black children made the move to the white schools. White Mississippians attributed this abysmal record simply to the fact that blacks did not choose to go to the white schools. To some extent, this assessment was correct. Many black parents did not want to send their children to a school where they would feel unwelcome, and black children, like all children, did not often relish the thought of leaving their friends behind to attend a school where they would not know anyone. Oftentimes, one of the first grades slated for freedom-of-choice desegregation was the twelfth grade. White segregationists correctly recognized that few twelfth graders would volunteer to leave their schools in their senior year. As Orbra Harrington Porter noted, "That's your crown and glory, your senior year."[19]

Of course, most whites had become so certain of the organic nature of racial segregation that they naturally assumed that given a choice, blacks would always choose their "own" schools, no matter how substandard they might be. In fact, many whites initially believed that the freedom-of choice mechanism would further delay the abolition of the dual school system simply because blacks would always choose to remain in their separate black schools. Whites were often genuinely surprised when blacks they knew chose to send their children to white schools, because the prevailing notion among white southerners was that "the South's Negroes does [sic] not want to MIX any more than the whites." As school began in the fall of 1966, a Vicksburg woman was flabbergasted; she could not believe that local blacks were choosing white schools. She asked, "Why would these people want to abandon their schools and their teachers?" She recognized that the blacks who challenged the educational color line were sometimes "the better class [of] negro children," but she attributed black activism primarily to "the lowest type," probably people getting "paid for doing it." At the same time, she believed that blacks who sent their children to white schools were simply rude people who were violating the politeness so central to southern social relations. Having heard from an elderly school superintendent the old false claim that blacks contributed little of the public funds that built black schools, the Vicksburg woman asked: "How much do they pay in State taxes? No one begrudges the help they were given but it is strictly a slap in the face to see them turn against us in so many ways."[20]

Prior to 1969, only two school districts in Mississippi, Long Beach Separate Municipal School District and the George County School District, voluntarily integrated their schools. Before integration, Long Beach actually had no black schools; the seventy black children in the district were bused to neighboring Pass Christian. After black parents in Long Beach petitioned the local school board in August 1964 to integrate the schools, the board agreed to undertake the move but asked for a year to prepare for the transition. During the 1964–65 school year, the school board and the superintendent talked to numerous groups—including city officials, civic organizations, church groups, faculty, students, and PTA groups—"explaining what is and must be done." The superintendent always emphasized that "the Negro children will be treated officially as students, not of a peculiar kind but as children going to school to learn with neither 'red carpet' or [sic] discrimination treatment." In September 1965, without incident, ninety-five black children began attending all grades at three of Long Beach's four schools (one of the district's two elementary schools remained all-white), along with the district's twenty-one hundred white students. In George County in south Mississippi, which had one black school and an almost six-to-one white majority in the public schools, the school board initially approved a freedom-of-choice plan, beginning with the second semester of the 1965–66 academic year. Before the beginning of school in the fall of 1968, however, the board decided to close the black school and integrate the 475 black children and eighteen black teachers into the district's white schools.[21]

Every other school district in the state waited for individual black parents to take the affirmative step of requesting that their children attend the previously all-white schools. The response of white Mississippians, once they quickly recovered from their astonishment that any blacks would actually choose white schools, was often to intimidate and harass those black parents who exercised their "free choice." This intimidation was most prevalent during the first two years of freedom-of-choice desegregation, the 1965–66 and 1966–67 school years. A 1966 study of school desegregation by Kenneth Dean, director of the Mississippi Council on Human Relations, found that black parents who chose the white schools faced numerous types of pressure: 28 percent were coerced or fired by their employers; 7 percent lost their housing; 20 percent lost their credit at the local bank; 5 percent lost their welfare benefits; and 47 percent received threatening phone calls, had crosses burned on their lawns, or were "victims of physical intimidation."[22]

The method of intimidation ranged from the merely disrespectful to the decidedly deadly. In Vicksburg, blacks registering their children at the white schools had to use the back door, a typical requirement of Jim Crow arrangements throughout the South but certainly not a strong indication that freedom of choice represented an end to dual schools. When twenty-five blacks enrolled at previously all-white Enterprise High, they were met by a man "armed with a shotgun" who "threatened to 'clean out' the Negroes." The armed white man was arrested, but only because he pointed the gun at an FBI agent observing school desegregation in the town. One of the two families that chose to desegregate the schools in Aberdeen in 1965 had thirty-two shots fired into their home. Likewise, the one family that desegregated the Chickasaw County schools in 1966 had shots fired through their living-room window on the first day of school. Everyone from employers to school officials to law enforcement officials stepped in to counsel blacks who had made the "wrong" choice. In Rankin County, the owner of a timber firm that employed several of the black parents who had selected one of the white schools in 1965 sent a man out to "pressure" the parents into withdrawing from the white schools. When black parents went to register at the all-white Goodman School in Holmes County, the school principal asked them whether the black school was still offering classes. He also reminded the parents that "any time they wanted to transfer children to the colored school, they would be free to do so." After a group of black parents in Covington County finally gathered up enough courage to sign freedom-of-choice forms choosing white schools in January 1967, an unknown black man, who said he had been sent by the sheriff, W. B. Canfield, told the black parents to fill out new forms choosing the black schools.[23]

Whites also sought to play on black fears, internalized after years of life under the rule of white supremacy, that their children could not compete intellectually with local white children. To be sure, black students who transferred to previously all-white schools did at times struggle academically, primarily because of the inadequate education they had received over the years compared to their white counterparts. At the same time, many of the free-choice pioneers represented the "cream" of the black student population, and they undoubtedly had more academic potential than the collection of academically underachieving white students that could be found in any school district. The sudden embrace of some form of admission testing after 1965 by a number of school districts had less to do with ascertaining intellectual ability and more to do with subverting black choice. In some cases, merely initiating a test as part of the school desegregation process scared off potential black transfers. In Canton, movement leaders had lined up sixty to sixty-five students to attend the white schools in 1965, but after school officials announced a standardized test requirement for all new students in the white schools, only four black children showed up to take the exam. When blacks did submit to testing, they had little assurance from white officials that their children would be judged fairly. In the South Pike County school district, one hundred black students applied for transfer in 1965. School officials had them take a test, and the entire group was then reassigned to the black schools. In Leake County, after four black high school seniors remained in the white high school despite being harassed and intimidated, as were their parents, school officials announced a week after classes began that the black students had to take a placement test since they transferred from an unaccredited school. Three of the students were told they would be placed in the seventh grade. The other teen was deemed eligible for only sixth-grade work, although he had passed both the eighth and ninth grades at a U.S. Air Force school in Alaska. All four students, not wishing to delay their graduation by five or six years, returned to the black high school in the county.[24]

The extent of white intimidation of blacks parents and children who chose white schools varied from district to district across the state of Mississippi. Some of the worst harassment occurred in the group of school districts in south and east Mississippi, where no school desegregation occurred in the first two years of the freedom-of-choice program (see map 2). Most of these districts had a white majority, and most were rural; in fact, some of the more urban areas in the same regions, such as Brookhaven, Hattiesburg, Laurel, Starkville, and Columbus, accepted token school desegregation and did not resort to threatening blacks who exercised their "free choice." Although Brookhaven schools admitted five black students in 1966, with the city police even providing protection for the black students, the situation was quite different in the rest of Lincoln County. Indeed, one black parent in the county system had apparently chosen a white school for 1966, but after "visits" from the principal of the black school and a local constable, she rescinded her choice.[25]

Although every freedom-of-choice plan required that all parents receive a "choice form," in 1966 many black parents in Lincoln County likely never even saw the forms. A nineteen-year-veteran black teacher in the county,

Luvella Markham, was fired for reportedly refusing "to obey orders, allegedly from the superintendent," to fill out the choice forms—complete with forged parents' signatures—and select one of the county's black schools. Such action was perhaps justified in the county superintendent's mind by his belief, which he relayed to HEW officials, that "Nigras can't read publications anyway." In addition, reports circulated in 1966 that the Klan had thrown "messages" into the yards of area blacks suspected of thinking about choosing a white school, and even the white superintendent feared that "my home would be burned if I made assignments" of black students to white schools. In such an atmosphere, it is not surprising that in the Lincoln County schools, freedom of choice produced no desegregation by the beginning of the 1968–69 school year.[26]

Whites carried out a similar initiative to subvert black "free choice" in other rural, white-majority school districts. In Poplarville, the small county seat of Pearl River County in south Mississippi where Mack Charles Parker had been lynched in 1959 with the help of county leaders, there were more than three times as many white students as black. Although the only black school in the district had been recently built, it was seriously overcrowded, with classes in 1966 being held in the gym, the auditorium, and the cafeteria; at least two of the white schools had room for scores of additional children. At the same time, the black high school curriculum contained at least ten fewer offerings than what was available at white Poplarville High School. Seeking access to a better education, eight students in 1965 indicated their desire to go to the white Poplarville schools. One family that made this choice faced economic sanctions and had a cross burned on their lawn. Another mother was visited by a member of local law enforcement and encouraged to change her choice. The families who had chosen white schools were eventually called to a meeting where they were threatened by local white leaders and then "given an opportunity to exercise new choices," which they all did, "choosing" to return to the black school. Not surprisingly, no blacks "chose" to go to the white Poplarville schools for the 1966–67 school year either. In northeast Mississippi, in Pontotoc County, where white students outnumbered black children by a two-to-one margin, black students sought admission to the white schools in both 1965 and 1966, but they were "scared away both times by hostile reactions from the white community." In one incident, someone removed an outdoor toilet from a black church and placed it in the middle of the town emblazoned with the words "Nigger, go home." School officials claimed they were powerless to stop the harassment of black parents.[27]

Places like Lincoln County, Poplarville, Pontotoc County, and many of the other white-majority, rural school districts in the state did not have strong civil rights movements, which is one reason that white intimidation was so effective in deterring blacks in these locales from successfully achieving even token school desegregation. In other areas of the state where black citizens had already mobilized to fight for racial change on other fronts, white intimidation also ran rampant in 1965 and 1966 but only succeeded in reducing, not eliminating, black efforts to choose white schools for their children. In the Issaquena-Sharkey Consolidated School District, for example, the beginning of freedom-of-choice school desegregation in the fall of 1965 merely escalated the confrontation between the races over local education. The federal courts had ordered that the Issaquena-Sharkey school district submit a desegregation plan that offered freedom of choice for grades one, two, three, and twelve during the 1965–66 school year. When registration opened in early August (school was to begin on September 2), almost two hundred black children in these grades applied for the white schools. The white campaign to discourage this exercise of black "free choice" began immediately. Black parents who went to register their children at the white schools had to wait until all whites had registered. Some black students who had been suspended the previous year were denied registration because they had not been cleared by school officials; others were not allowed to enroll until their guardians paid a newly required nonresident tuition fee.[28]

The requirement that the children whose parents were not residents of a school district pay tuition was the brainchild of the Mississippi legislature, enacted as law during a 1965 special session. Though unstated, white lawmakers, who had undoubtedly noticed the mobility of the state's poor black population, presumably concocted the measure to place another stumbling block in the path of blacks considering choosing the white schools. While advocates of the measure cited the law as sensible fiscal responsibility, the nonresident tuition legislation sought to save Mississippi taxpayers a few dollars by targeting the children of black parents, many from the Delta, who had left the state—or just the immediate neighborhood—to seek work because the mechanization of the agricultural economy had displaced them. They often left their children behind temporarily with grandparents or other relatives. The tuition measure ultimately affected seven thousand of the state's children, 85 percent of whom were black. When civil rights attorneys threatened the state with a lawsuit over the tuition measure, lawmakers quickly caved in, repealing the law in April 1966, but during the 1965–66 school year the nonresident tuition requirement became another weapon in the white arsenal of intimidation, as evidenced by events in school districts such as Issaquena-Sharkey.[29]

The black parents in this school district who did manage to register their children in the white schools had to face an enraged white populace. The night after the first registration session, the Klan held a large rally in Rolling Fork. In the days that followed, at least eight blacks who had exercised their free choice had crosses burned on their lawns, a black church associated with the movement was burned, and numerous black parents who worked on area plantations were evicted from their homes. When this drive to circumvent black choice left many of the black parents undeterred, local whites tried to "reason" with their black workers and neighbors. In late August, L. T. Wade, a plantation owner and county supervisor, organized a meeting with the local Mississippi Freedom Democratic Party, appealing to the group for a "slow-down" in school desegregation. Wade and other whites warned that if so many blacks chose to go to the district's white schools, whites would have to set up a private school for their children.[30]

When the Issaquena-Sharkey schools opened on September 2, seventy-eight black children entered the previously all-white schools. White intimidation had scared away about half of the original black enrollees, and the campaign of coercion against those families of the black students who had entered the white schools continued. Whites fired black employees, evicted black tenants from their homes, burned crosses on the lawns of black families with children in the white schools, and shot into black homes, in one case wounding a black mother who had dared to send her child to a white school. Later that fall, a thirteen-year-old girl who had failed in her attempt to attend the previously all-white school was blinded in one eye after someone fired a shotgun into her house. Some of the intimidation was truly relentless and petty. One black tenant family evicted from their plantation home secured an abandoned dwelling at the end of a long road on the property of a local black farmer. In order to keep up the pressure on the family, a group of whites spent the better part of a night digging a ditch across the isolated road. Most black parents courageously kept their children in the black schools despite the threats, though some understandably submitted. Ruby Barnes registered her two daughters in the white school. A week later she and her father were evicted from the plantation home where they had lived since 1951. When the two girls nevertheless started to attend the white school, a plantation owner promised Ruby's father a job if only he was not involved in "this school mess." Ruby and her father refused to be intimidated. They struggled to make ends meet, but the girls continued at the previously all-white school. Walter Collier Jr. was one of the black parents who had a cross burned on his lawn when he registered his two children at the white school in Anguilla. The local cotton mill where he worked fired him for his action. Once school began, three more crosses were burned at the Collier home. Though unable to find work, he kept his children in the white schools. Civil rights groups, such as the NAACP Legal Defense and Educational Fund, stepped in to provide financial support to many of these unsung heroes of the school desegregation effort.[31]

The violent riot in Grenada in September 1966 represented merely the most visible aspect of a more widespread campaign of white intimidation in that community. Approximately three hundred black children in Grenada had originally registered to attend the white schools in the fall of 1966, though only about half that number actually attempted to enter the schools on September 12. While some of those who failed to attend were scared off by the white mobs operating around the white Grenada schools on opening day, many others had already renounced their first choice because of the white threats that followed registration, an unwritten but seemingly standard part of most Mississippi freedom-of-choice school desegregation plans. In the days before school was scheduled to begin, a local white radio station announced that a list of black parents who had registered their children for the all-white schools was being distributed to area employers, a list presumably compiled by local school officials. As a result, numerous black parents in Grenada were threatened with dismissal by their employers. Cooper Davis, who ran a salvage business, told his black employee, Chester Stewart, that he did not like it "worth a damn" that Stewart had registered his children in the white schools. Stewart relented, told Davis the matter was not that important to him, and agreed to fill out new choice forms, returning his children to the city's black schools. Black parents in Grenada who resisted the initial wave of pressure frequently only delayed the timing of the reprisals. On the day that

Richard Sigh's leg was broken in the Grenada riot, his father received a pink slip from his employer. Many of the other black parents who sent their children to the Grenada white schools also soon lost their jobs.[32]

The white intimidation of black parents exercising their freedom of school choice occurred less frequently by the beginning of the 1967–68 school year but still continued on a more sporadic basis.[33] The damage, however, had already been done, and the need for white intimidation had diminished. Two years of widespread harassment of black parents had clearly demonstrated that whites were willing to use threats and sometimes violence to preserve school segregation. As a result, many black parents in the state were convinced to forgo subjecting themselves and their children to abuse for the abstract principle of integration and the uncertain benefits of desegregated schools. Only those black parents most dedicated to challenging the dual school system bothered with what essentially amounted to forcing their way, unwanted, into the previously all-white schools. For the most part, the white intimidation campaign succeeded. By 1968, whites could claim without too much prevarication that school desegregation had not proceeded further because only a small number of blacks chose to go to white schools. Unstated was the role white action played in diminishing black activism.

While black parents who chose white schools for their children often made monumental sacrifices, those on the front lines of the school desegregation struggle during the free-choice era were, of course, the black children themselves. Black parents played a key role in urging their children to leave familiar surroundings, classmates, and teachers to go to a white school, but others also influenced the decision, including church leaders, friends, and civil rights workers. Many of the students, especially the older children, were personally motivated to seek a better education and to play a part in helping to dismantle the dual school system. Bernadien Norwood, one of the first black students to attend Murrah High in Jackson during the 1965–66 term, agreed to be a school desegregation pioneer because she wanted "to find out the real difference between the white and Negro school." Melba Chambliss, who helped desegregate previously all-white Provine High in Jackson that same year, stepped forward because she "felt it was a necessity for someone to adhere to the federal laws of school integration, so that our race could start to be exposed to the better educational facilities." Orbra Porter simply wanted to show people that black students were not dumb.[34]

The treatment accorded the black students who entered the previous all-white schools under the freedom-of-choice arrangements varied from school to school. Some students reported few problems. Delores Orey, who had three children among the twenty-seven black students desegregating Poindexter Elementary in Jackson in the fall of 1966, reported that her children "had no harassment problems, no classroom problems re work, are doing well, have made friends and are visited by white neighborhood children." Unfortunately, the experience of the Orey children was not typical. More often, black children breaking the color barrier at white schools faced harassment from their classmates and, less often, their teachers; these problems were most acute during the first year or two after a school desegregated. The vast majority of the school desegregation trailblazers had objects thrown at them or were subjected to derogatory verbal slurs in their new schools. For instance, white children in the Lauderdale County high school greeted the black children who entered their school in 1965 by cursing them, calling them names, and throwing rocks at them. Johnnie Faye Inge recalled the various forms of abuse she endured as one of five young black women who integrated previously all-white Meridian High School in 1965: "Constantly being thrown spitballs [at]. Constantly walking through [the] hall surrounded by white men, and the guys were a lot worse than the girls. Constantly being called, 'nigger.' Constantly being made fun of. I remember going up a flight of stairs, and the stairs were crowded. . . . And somebody coming up behind me grabbing my hips, and I really felt violated." When harassed, black students generally refrained from retaliating, a strategy they were often instructed in by their elders. After Anthony Harris, along with four other black children, desegregated a white junior high in Hattiesburg, a white child spat on him, but Harris just kept on walking to class. His parents, and those of his black classmates, had cautioned restraint, "to prove to the bigots in the community that Black and White kids could go to school together. If we had responded to violence with violence the bigots would have felt vindicated and the schools would have remained segregated."[35]

White teachers at times acted little better than white children. For example, at the Durant Elementary School in Holmes County, where the beginning of school desegregation in 1965 caused most, but not all, whites to flee from the first four grades of the county's elementary schools, the all-white faculty almost completely ignored their black pupils, interacting with them only periodically, primarily to spray them with deodorant. A second-grade teacher at the previously all-white Iuka Elementary School in northeast Mississippi reportedly dealt with her new black students in the 1965–66 school year by segregating them within her classroom and by hurling racial epithets at the young black children.[36]

In other situations, black students encountered benign neglect or even fair treatment from their white teachers. Mary Blackmon, one of two girls to desegregate Canton High in 1965, remembered that her white teachers "didn't say a lot to me, but they weren't mean, or they didn't say anything negative, and I felt they graded me fairly." In some cases, treatment from white teachers toward the new black students stood in marked contrast to the reaction of white students. For instance, the black high schoolers who went to previously all-white schools in Jackson in 1965 faced harassment from their white classmates, but the black students found the vast majority of the white teachers they encountered to be "helpful and interested" in them. While Johnnie Faye Inge encountered verbal and physical harassment from her white classmates at Meridian High in 1965, those incidents occurred outside the classroom, "[b]ecause, in all my classes, I had teachers who didn't tolerate, who would not allow students to pick on us."[37]

Black students who desegregated the previously all-white schools did not necessarily even leave segregation behind when they transferred to the white schools. Students at the newly desegregated schools were sometimes segregated by race in the classroom, during lunch, and even on the playground. Black students were frequently denied the opportunity to participate in extracurricular activities at the previously all-white schools. Orbra Porter, for instance, wanted to be in the choir when she transferred to Hardy Junior High in 1966; school officials told her she was not allowed to join the singing group. Continued segregation in transportation of pupils was apparently the rule in most districts for the first few years of school desegregation. In Leake County in 1965, the twenty-six black students going to the white schools all rode the same beat-up bus, despite the fact that such an arrangement required the first black student on the route to be picked up at 5:40 in the morning so that the driver could complete his seventy-mile, one-way trip around the county, a circuitous journey on which he frequently crossed paths with buses transporting white students. Black students attending the previously all-white Fielding Wright Elementary School in Issaquena County in 1966 were also not integrated into the white bus routes. Many of the black children could have easily ridden on the buses that regularly passed their houses on the way to Fielding Wright. Instead, a separate bus first transported the black students to the all-black Issaquena Elementary School, where they waited until the white children arrived at Fielding Wright. Then, a second bus transported the black children to the desegregated school.[38]

The black students who survived the ordeal of the Grenada riots in September 1966 to desegregate that city's white schools faced the same types of problems that plagued freedom-of-choice desegregators statewide. White teachers ignored the black students in their classes; some teachers apparently even addressed their black students as "niggers." A number of the Grenada classrooms, technically desegregated, were, in fact, segregated by race, with a row of empty seats placed between black and white students in some classrooms. White teachers and administrators mandated that the two races use the restrooms at separate times and prohibited interracial seating in the cafeteria. On one occasion, a black boy eating lunch with a group of whites at Lizzie Horn Elementary was reportedly jerked out of his seat by the principal and sent to a table where a group of blacks were eating, with the admonition, "Nigger, you eat over there." A month of this discriminatory treatment led to a walkout by the black students on Friday, October 21, 1966. All of the black high schoolers and all but five of the black elementary students at the previously all-white schools left their classes. Many of the students, along with a contingent of black parents, returned to the white campus on Monday to protest the conditions for black children in the desegregated schools. Unlike the white mob that had surrounded the same school grounds a month earlier, the 250 black protesters were quickly arrested by local law enforcement. After filling the local jail and vacant cells in surrounding communities, sixty-nine of the prisoners (forty-three males and twenty-six females) were transported to Parchman Penitentiary, where they were processed into the general criminal population. In response, all but four hundred of the twenty-six hundred students in the city's all-black schools stayed home from school in a sympathy boycott, but the protest action in Grenada soon evaporated in the face of threats by federal district court judge Claude Clayton to force the black students to return to classes. Although blacks in Grenada did receive a hearing from Clayton about the unfair treatment of black students in the white schools, the burden remained squarely on the backs of black Grenadians to demonstrate what Judge Clayton quaintly called the "maladministration of the freedom-of-choice machinery."[39]

While whites relied on intimidation to keep down the numbers of black students desegregating their schools during the freedom-of-choice era, the slow pace of faculty desegregation could be attributed both to the difficult position black teachers had always faced in asserting their civil rights as employees of a Jim Crow operation and to the simple fact that school districts continued to resist this part of the school desegregation equation until literally forced to act. School districts felt little pressure to transfer black teachers to white schools if black teachers did not clamor for such transfers, and many of them remained reluctant to cross the color line. On the whole, the state's black teaching corps, through no fault of its own but due to the warped logic of Jim Crow, had less training than the state's white teachers. As a result, many black teachers had doubts about their "professional competence." Others worried about what kind of authority they could exercise over white children in a society only beginning the process of unlearning the long-taught and time-honored homilies of white supremacy and black deference. At the same time, white school officials expected their black teachers to be part of the bulwark against racial change, not trailblazers for school desegregation. As the superintendent of the Canton public schools told Governor Paul B. Johnson Jr. in the summer of 1964, "We have got to work through the negro principals and teachers to try to help us keep our schools segregated." This kind of attitude, common in some districts well into the late 1960s, continued to chill civil rights activism among black educators. As in earlier years, those black educators who did not distance themselves from civil rights activity put their jobs in jeopardy. For example, in late 1967 the Sovereignty Commission investigated Eddie Lucas, principal of a school in Shelby. Lucas had been active in voter registration drives and had served the previous summer as the campaign manager for Kermit Stanton, who was elected as the first black supervisor in Bolivar County. At the end of the school year, Lucas's contract was not renewed.[40]

While black teachers had good reasons not to press the issue of faculty desegregation, Mississippi school districts came up with any number of reasons of their own for why their supposedly unitary school systems still assigned teachers based solely on race. A good example is the Benton County school system. After three years of freedom-of-choice school desegregation for the district's three schools (two white, one black), the only faculty desegregation during the 1967–68 school year involved one of the white assistant principals going to the black school, Old Salem, to administer achievement tests. School officials claimed that no white teachers needed to be transferred or placed at Old Salem because no white child had ever chosen to go to that school. Using the same reasoning, school officials believed that since student desegregation had only occurred at the previously all-white Ashland Attendance Center, there was also no need for black teachers to join the faculty at the still all-white Hickory Flat Attendance Center. As for Ashland, where black students had been attending for three years, all the vacancies (at least six during the 1966–67 and 1967–68 school years) were filled with white teachers. School officials made no effort to recruit any new black teachers for these openings, even though Rust College, a traditional source of black teachers for the county, was right down the road. At the same time, school officials did not approach any of the Old Salem teachers about transferring to Ashland, although most of the Old Salem faculty, unlike in other districts, had indicated a willingness to move to the white schools. Oftentimes, to satisfy federal mandates for some start toward faculty desegregation, school districts would arrange programs that provided for the most minimal intermingling of the black and white faculties. For example, in the 1969–70 school year, four years into a freedom-of-choice arrangement, faculty desegregation in the Drew school district involved little more than a month-long teacher swap at the end of the school year. The white teachers went to the black schools for two weeks (one week of observation and one week of teaching), then the black teachers took the same tour of duty at the white schools, although classes actually ended before the black teachers got to take their turn teaching white students.[41]

Because freedom-of-choice school desegregation in Mississippi placed excessive burdens on black parents and children to dismantle a dual school system that whites seemingly had no real intention of relinquishing, by the late 1960s many black Mississippians despaired of efforts to integrate the schools. At the same time, Black Power advocates, increasingly influential, also questioned the value of racial integration. Instead, they stressed the need for black control over the resources and institutions that shaped the lives of black Americans and called for black pride in black achievement. The notion that all-black institutions were suitable, as long as they had appropriate resources, received renewed support from black Mississippians.[42]

As the state of Mississippi continued its school equalization program into the late 1960s, black citizens were of a divided mind on the continuation of the separate building project, much as they had been ever since the campaign first began in the late 1940s. On the one hand, blacks viewed the continuing effort to make improvements to the black schools as clear evidence of the basic insincerity of the claims by white school boards that they had dismantled their dual school systems. For instance, black plaintiffs in the Jackson school desegregation lawsuit attacked the state's largest school district for using equalization as a way to avoid additional school desegregation. In 1968, Jackson had about ten thousand black students and eleven thousand white students in its elementary schools; however, the district had twenty-six white elementary schools but only thirteen black elementary schools, a situation that meant serious overcrowding at the black schools but unused capacity at the white buildings. So while all-black Reynolds Elementary was crammed to capacity, nearby Poindexter Elementary, a desegregated but formerly all-white school, had thirteen classrooms but only nine teachers. In some cases, black elementary students were being bused past traditionally white schools in their immediate neighborhood to distant all-black schools simply because their parents had not requested a transfer to the white schools. When the Jackson school board proposed in 1968 to build twenty-two additional classrooms at four all-black elementary schools to relieve some of the overcrowding, the black plaintiffs protested that the move merely perpetuated school segregation. Indeed, they were correct. The Jackson school district favored freedom-of-choice desegregation, which led to about nine hundred black students (5 percent) in all grades attending the previously all-white schools in the 1968–69 school year. Had the district supported another type of school desegregation, such as a carefully designed geographic pairing plan (linking specific locales in the city to pairs of white and black schools), much of the overcrowding at the all-black schools would have been relieved. Such a procedure, however, would have led to more school desegregation, which is precisely why Jackson school leaders avoided the logistically simple adjustments of utilizing an alternative method of school desegregation in favor of trying to launch massive black school construction projects.[43]

Other black Mississippians, however, believed that the pressure to desegregate had already forced the state to upgrade black education and sought to focus future battles on continuing this effort to improve black schools. In 1967, the Mississippi Freedom Democratic Party concluded that "faced with the immediate needs of the Black community, we call for immediate and massive efforts to correct the inadequacies of black schools." Owen Brooks, director of the Delta Ministry, in 1968 urged "black people to improve the black schools in Miss. and not depend on the white racist schools to either integrate or educate black children." In the Mississippi Delta, where most schools would remain largely black simply because of the region's demographic profile, blacks in a number of communities initiated direct-action campaigns demanding improvements to black schools. Blacks in Leland launched a five-month boycott of their school, the Lincoln Attendance Center, from October 1968 to March 1969, to demand a host of changes, including a reduction of class sizes; improvements to the school's restrooms, lunchroom, and gymnasium; and the addition of a black history course and "curriculum materials that do not violate the integrity of Black people." A boycott of the two black schools in Indianola, Carver Elementary and Gentry High, was launched to pressure school officials to make similar upgrades. The high school cafeteria had desks instead of lunchroom tables, an indication of the overcrowded conditions at the school. Both schools were unaccredited; Gentry needed improvements to its business, language, and home economics departments before it had any chance of securing accreditation. Carver had no gym, and neither school had "adequate library facilities" or provided any medical attention for students.[44] These campaigns, while certainly understandable and justifiable given white resistance in the state to abolishing the dual school system, represented an endorsement of the state's continuing equalization program, a stratagem, if recent history was any guide, doomed to failure.

Freedom-of-choice school desegregation succeeded in confining the vast majority of Mississippi's black children in the underfunded, second-class black schools of the state for five years after the passage of the Civil Rights Act of 1964. Black parents who tried to exercise freedom of choice were intimidated; black students who crossed the educational color barrier were harassed and humiliated. Despite the valiant efforts of these school desegregation pioneers, the dual school system in Mississippi stood, slightly dented but undeniably entrenched. The real destruction of Mississippi's segregated school system did not begin until early 1970. Although within a year Mississippi had converted to a unitary school system, the goal long sought by some black Mississippians, the end to segregated and second-class education was not achieved without negative costs, many of which no one could have anticipated.

CHAPTER SEVEN

SCHOOL INTEGRATION

We Do Not Want Our Children Going to School with Yours

The integration of Tunica County's school system in 1970, which in the 1969–70 school year enrolled over three thousand black children but just over four hundred white children, did not end the tradition of separate schools that had long characterized education in this Delta district of northwest Mississippi. In the late 1960s, whites had accepted fewer than two hundred of the county's black children in their school through a freedom-of-choice program (there was only one white school in the district, Tunica School, which served grades one through twelve), and Tunica whites proved unwilling to go beyond this token desegregation. After the intelligence-testing procedure approved by Judge William Keady in the summer of 1969 substantially raised the numbers of blacks who would attend Tunica School—the "smart ones" only—school leaders asked the judge to postpone implementation of the strategy in favor of retaining a basic freedom-of-choice plan. The judge denied this motion, and the Tunica school board appealed, only to have the Fifth Circuit Court of Appeals order an even more thorough integration plan, one that required geographic zoning, which meant the complete integration of the Tunica County schools, since there was no ironclad residential separation of blacks and whites in the county. The school district had to implement the court's order by February 1970.[1]

Whites responded to the sudden collapse of segregated education in their district with fear and defiance. A white teacher in Tunica County described the scene there in the winter of 1969–70 as "total chaos," as scores of houses owned by whites went up for sale, while other white families declared that their children "were going to stay home and do without education." White seniors at Tunica School were summarily declared through with their studies, and they graduated in January 1970; the remainder of the white student body at Tunica School received instructions from school officials to take their textbooks home with them at Christmas break in order to use them at whatever private school they might attend the following semester. White teachers reassigned to the two previously all-black schools, Dundee and Rosa Fort, because of the integration order were allowed to resign yet were still paid by the county for the remainder of the school year. When the semester began in February 1970 with a unitary school system, all but a handful of Tunica whites abandoned the public schools for three church schools characterized by their organizer as essentially "baby-sitting" facilities. Some of the white teachers still receiving pay from the Tunica County schools served as teachers, including the superintendent's wife.[2]

Whites in Tunica County continued to hold out hope that freedom of choice could be restored in the area's public schools, for they could not envision, and would not allow, having their small enclave of white children attend school with an overwhelming black majority. Their black neighbors were considered so "inferior" that whites truly believed their children were better off in makeshift private schools or no school at all. When school officials met with black parents at a PTA meeting in January 1970, Tunica County superintendent George Petty bluntly explained to the black parents that he and other whites did not want their children going to school with black children. School board president Wesley Bailey added that black teachers were "not qualified to teach white children." In late January, white parents staged a vain protest against the court's school integration order, while the school board continued to seek a rehearing on the court's ruling. The board's argument hinged on the fact that whites in Tunica would not accept anything beyond the token desegregation of freedom of choice and that "the only way to recapture the white students is by permitting them to choose the school they will attend." The court answered that if "hostility to school desegregation" were used to determine the school board's obligations, then "white parents would become the ultimate arbiters of the Constitution."[3]

Whites in Tunica County and throughout Mississippi could not prevent the long-dreaded specter of school integration from becoming a reality.

After sixteen years of delays and token desegregation, a steady stream of legal action by black parents and federal intervention finally toppled the ninety-five-year-old system of segregated schools in Mississippi. By the end of 1970, the dual school system had been eliminated in all of the state's school districts. Even so, school integration for white Mississippians generally meant finding a way to satisfy the latest federal mandate while maintaining white supremacy in the operation of the state's educational system. Most whites in the state surrendered this dearly cherished part of their segregated world only under duress. They resisted the change in every way still possible and generally retained their belief in the notions of white supremacy that had built and nourished a segregated school system, one in which "racial integrity" had always stood as a synonym for educational quality. As a result, the possibility of creating a truly unitary and integrated school system in Mississippi was decisively diminished. Though forced in 1970 to end the system of dual education, white Mississippians continued to search for ways, whenever possible, to avoid having their children attend the same schools as black Mississippians.

The efforts of white Mississippians and the Nixon administration during the summer and fall of 1969 to delay once again the implementation of *Brown* came to a screeching halt in late October 1969, when the Supreme Court essentially said enough is enough. In a landmark decision in *Alexander v. Holmes*, the High Court said that " 'all deliberate speed' for desegregation is no longer permissible. . . . The obligation of every school district is to terminate dual school systems at once and to operate only unitary schools." In short, no more delays would be tolerated. Within weeks, in addition to the thirty-three *Alexander* districts, all in Mississippi, a number of other school districts in the state, including Tunica County, were ordered by the federal courts to begin complete integration of their school systems after the Christmas holidays. Every other school district in the state had to implement the *Alexander* decree by the fall of 1970.[4]

The official white response in Mississippi to the *Alexander* decision echoed the response to the original *Brown* decision: state leaders became dedicated converts to the approach previously scorned and recently outlawed. In other words, Mississippi officials proclaimed their desire to proceed with freedom-of-choice school desegregation. State officials argued that the federal courts had pushed Mississippi and other southern states far beyond any constitutional mandate. On the day of the *Alexander* decision, Mississippi representative Charles Griffin told the U.S. House of Representatives that "freedom of choice is the only way to save quality public education. Freedom of choice—what can be more American? Or more democratic?" In early January 1970, Governor John Bell Williams spoke to a statewide television audience and railed that "the children of Mississippi, white and black, have been denied the right to attend the school of their choice by an arbitrary edict of the United States Supreme Court." Calling the crisis "the most trying times that have faced us since Reconstruction," the governor also pledged that "our fight has been for freedom of choice, and that fight will continue on and on until we have gained an ultimate victory." Senator James Eastland chided his colleagues in the U.S. Senate that "these white parents and students in Mississippi and the other Southern States are being asked to endure conditions which more than 95 percent of all of the white parents and students in the United States of America will never voluntarily accept," that is, something more than token school desegregation.[5]

In a sense, Mississippi political leaders were right; the Supreme Court's latest decision had gone beyond both the *Brown* decision and the Civil Rights Act of 1964 by calling for a results-oriented remedy that required evidence of racially balanced schools to demonstrate the creation of unitary school systems. Also, since segregation in the North and the West had been deemed de facto rather than de jure, northern schools would seemingly escape the implications of this latest mandate. What the script of Williams and Eastland refused to acknowledge, however, was that the state's resistance to all attempts to end the dual school system—including the token desegregation of freedom-of-choice plans—had led the Supreme Court to impose a results-oriented test. Black Mississippians recognized the protestations of the state's white politicians as merely another attempt to delay the implementation of *Brown* and preserve the state's dual school system. A black woman from Chickasaw County noted simply that "they got all this screwed up here. They had sixteen years, now they say it is too quick and they have had sixteen years to had [*sic*] the thing fixed." Another black Mississippian, seventy-five years old in 1970, took an even longer historical view of the recent conversion of white Mississippi leaders to the inherent value of freedom-of-choice school desegregation: "Now you're asking for freedom of choice. You have had freedom of choice for a hundred years and did wrong with it." Even some white Mississippians recognized that it "rings terribly hollow when . . . so many white Mississippians . . . speak of 'a loss of freedom' in the recent court decisions, . . . when, in fact, the greater portion of the blame can be carried to our own door because we were so unenlightened to the human needs and basic rights of Negroes within our state."[6]

Most white Mississippians, however, remained reluctant in 1970, and for many years thereafter, to sever the deep-seated belief that one-race schools were the only way to maintain quality education for whites. Few agreed with the sentiments of Jere B. Nash Jr., a white man who served on the Greenville school board in the early 1970s, who thought strong public schools were essential to Mississippi's future and that integrated education would transform race relations in the state. Among other benefits, Nash believed that white children in the integrated public schools would be prepared "for the future in which they must deal with blacks in a much different manner than that in which you and I have dealt with them." Instead, most Mississippi whites continued to believe that freedom-of-choice school desegregation represented the outer limits of their ability to comply with *Brown* and that the kind of total integration now ordered by the federal courts would mean the end of "quality" education for their children. Given the state's success in delaying school integration for a decade and a half, many white Mississippians truly believed that once again a way could be found to avoid all but the most token forms of school desegregation. As Claude Ramsey, head of the state's American Federation of Labor and Congress of Industrial Organizations (AFL-CIO), noted in late 1969, "For over fifteen years now, the self-serving, demagogic politicians of Mississippi have misled many white citizens into believing that the Supreme Court's decision on the public school issue in 1954 could be circumvented and that a dual school system could be maintained. . . . The false hand of hope was continually held out and many people actually thought their public schools could be maintained on a segregated basis."[7]

The actions of state leaders to continue the sixteen-year-old crusade to circumvent the requirement to dismantle the state's dual school system, even in the wake of the *Alexander* decision, kept these white hopes alive. Governor Williams and Senator Stennis lent their support to an organization started in early 1970 by former Jackson mayor Allen Thompson: Freedom of Choice in the United States (FOCUS). At a rally of the group in February

1970 at the Jackson Coliseum attended by more than four thousand people, Williams told the crowd that "we have not surrendered and we will not surrender. We will fight to the last man. We have exhausted every remedy available to us thus far in the courts, but we are not giving up the fight." Gycelle Tynes, superintendent of the Clarksdale public schools, urged local white parents to keep their children in the public schools as the midyear transition began there in February 1970—despite the requirement for massive school integration—"while they tried to persuade the federal government to let the schools revert to their old system." Many whites believed that such a result might actually be achieved. [8]

In one of the most bizarre strategies to counteract the *Alexander* decision, state attorney general A. F. Summer, with the support of Governor Williams, sent twenty-eight hundred letters to Mississippi lawyers seeking to enlist them in an effort to go north and west and file school desegregation lawsuits to require those areas to follow the new Supreme Court guidelines. The goal was to prove the inappropriateness of the *Alexander* decision by "destroying"—to use Summer's term—school systems in other sections of the United States. Summer also asked every parent in the state to send in $5 to the state's coffers to help fund the legal campaign. Dr. Aaron Shirley, black physician and school integration advocate in Jackson, noted the irony in school officials bemoaning the destruction of Mississippi public schools by the recent court orders, while at the same time marshaling resources in an attempt to "destroy" school systems elsewhere in the United States. The state legislature, for its part, passed resolutions asking for a national constitutional convention to enshrine into federal doctrine the principle of free choice for schools and asking President Nixon to apply the nation's educational laws equally across the country. The legislature also considered a law that outlawed the assignment of school students to achieve racial balance, but the bill died in conference committee over concerns that the measure would primarily succeed in convicting local white school board members acting under federal court orders and HEW directives.[9]

Despite the desires of most white Mississippians and the maneuvers of state politicians, the *Alexander* decision was much less ambiguous than *Brown* on the timing of implementation, and Mississippi's dual school system came to an abrupt end in 1970. The details of how school districts accomplished the integration of dual schools into a unitary system varied across Mississippi depending on local demographics and local leadership, but some broad patterns can be discerned. In much of the Delta and a number of other black-majority or significant black-population school districts, in a scenario similar to the one that played out in Tunica County, whites simply could not imagine an integrated school system. Once school integration became a fait accompli, many whites in these areas opted to abandon the public schools in favor of often hastily organized, private segregated academies as the only way to preserve "quality" white education. Governor Williams blamed the federal courts for creating in Mississippi a new "dual system of education: one public; the other, private." Although the governor claimed the creation of private schools had nothing to do with school integration, he envisioned them as white schools, places where "the pupils will be given a quality education in circumstances conducive to learning." [10]

The notion that segregated private schools might be the best way to avoid the "scourge" of desegregated schools had, of course, circulated among white Mississippians since the days of the *Brown* decision, but the Supreme Court's 1969 mandate for totally integrated school systems throughout Mississippi reinvigorated the white private school movement. Between 1966 and 1970, the number of private schools in the state rose from 121 to 236, and the number of students attending these schools tripled. At least 61 of these new private schools were organized in the year following the *Alexander* decision. In many locales where whites represented a distinct minority of all school children, such as Tunica County, practically all white children departed the school system once school integration began. In Canton, for example, nearly every one of the district's twelve hundred white students left to go to the new Canton Academy in early 1970 rather than attend classes with the city's thirty-five hundred black children. In Indianola, in the Mississippi Delta, practically all of the nearly one thousand white students left the public schools when they were integrated in the winter of 1970. The students crowded into private Indianola Academy, in a building originally planned for three hundred. When schools reopened in September 1970, after a pro–public schools campaign by area white business leaders, over two hundred of the white students returned to the Indianola public schools.[11] Despite this reconsideration by a number of whites, the majority ultimately decided to flee the public schools permanently.

While not all whites in these areas supported the policy of abandoning the public schools, fear of social ostracism prevented most from bucking the solution advocated by the private schoolers. One Canton teacher who made the move to the new private academy recognized that "it would have been bad for my husband's business if I had refused." An Indianola man who declined to send his daughters to Indianola Academy was accosted downtown by a local lawyer who inquired why the man did not want "to get [his] girls an education." The lawyer called the parent a "nigger lover," and a fight almost erupted. In Wilkinson County, a black-majority county in the southwest corner of the state, Burnell Brown, a farmer and logger, initially kept his children in the public schools when most of his white neighbors fled, citing poverty as the reason for his decision. Though he confessed his opposition to school integration, he also emphasized that "the main thing I want them to do is get an education." National news media featured his story in reports about Mississippi's midyear integration as a kind of white hope in an otherwise bleak story concerning school integration in Mississippi's black belt. The glare of national publicity, however, proved too much, and within a week, the Brown children quietly joined other local white students at one of the church schools recently set up in the county. For the Browns and many other whites unable to afford private schools in the state's black-majority school districts, local churches and businesses stepped forward to provide financial assistance; other whites in these areas simply chose no school over an integrated school for their children. [12]

Significant white flight from the public schools also occurred in Mississippi's only major urban area. Although Jackson's public schools had a roughly equal enrollment of black and white students prior to court-mandated integration in the fall of 1970, ten thousand whites, or over 40 percent, left the Jackson public schools when school integration was implemented. Those whites who left the public schools had a number of options. Some moved to neighboring county districts, which had substantially whiter school populations than the capital city. Others chose from an array of private school options. Hard-core segregationists sent their children to one of the Citizens' Council schools in the area. The primary qualification of teachers at these schools was that they be willing to sign a contract that included a clause stating that "forced congregation of persons in social situations solely because they are of different races is a moral wrong, and . . . the proven educational results of such forced interracial congregation are disastrous for children of both the white and black races." While the Council schools maintained a strict color line, they were not known for their academic rigor. Even so, almost 60 percent of Jackson's private school students during the 1971–72 school year attended one of these schools. Other whites fleeing the Jackson public schools transferred their children to one of eight parochial schools in the city, which were generally desegregated but educated few blacks. Some of Jackson's wealthiest citizens established Jackson Preparatory School, which had ample resources and soon developed into a top-notch school, although it was only available to those who could afford the tuition. Those whites who stayed with the Jackson public schools in 1970 did so for a variety of reasons. Some were too poor to leave the city or pay for private school tuition. Others stayed because they believed integrated education could work, although as the district faced its share of troubles in the years following the transition to a unitary system, the number of whites in the Jackson public schools continued to dwindle almost every year. [13]

State officials tried to aid the growing private school movement in Mississippi by continuing their search for a way to create some kind of publicly funded system of private schools, a strategy that had been pursued by those in state government since 1954. Even before the *Alexander* decision, in the fall of 1969, Governor Williams had proposed a variety of measures, totaling $20 million, to aid private schools. One of the proposals the state legislature passed in September 1969 sought to revive the private school tuition-grant law—originally created in 1964 but declared invalid by the federal courts earlier in 1969—by renaming the funds given to parents to pay for private schools "loans" rather than "grants." Similar efforts resurfaced when the legislature reconvened in January 1970. Mississippi leaders perhaps saw nothing illogical about public support for private white education, since the state had actually long succeeded in publicly funding an educational system that had primarily benefitted only white students. As one Mississippi school official cogently noted in early 1970: "The private all-white school is nothing new in Mississippi. We've had a private school system all along, but the state supported it. Now we have to find private support for it." Some of the proposals by officials in the wake of the *Alexander* decision made no effort to conceal public efforts to support private white education. A Jackson city commissioner favored the adoption of a city tax to support local white private schools, but Mayor Russell Davis nixed the idea, labeling it an "exercise of futility" that would actually undermine the whole rationale for establishing private schools by causing "private schools to be made public." State senator Robert Crook of Ruleville even called for the formation "of a statewide system of private schools," complete with the creation of a new state agency "to establish the private schools." Other officials remained more willing at least to preserve the fiction that "private" meant something short of state-run schools. Governor Williams urged public school officials to work closely with those trying to establish private schools, for example, to make public facilities available to private schools "at times and hours when they are not required for public school purposes." [14]

At the same time, many state political and business leaders believed that private schools could only be a partial solution. Although Governor Williams ultimately opted in 1970 to send his own children to one of Jackson's Citizens' Council schools, he also recognized that a permanent, mass abandonment of the public schools would damage the state's continuing effort to attract industry to the state. He hoped the state might find a way to fund both public and private education, in other words, a new dual school system. Williams proposed to the legislature in early 1971 that in school districts with growing private school enrollment, and consequently less need for state funds, parents who put their children in private schools be granted "relief commensurate, as far as possible, to the reduced cost of public education in their districts." Business groups, such as the Mississippi Economic Council, also endorsed the state's public school system as "indispensable" to the state's economic health, especially after a major industrial plant (with a potential employment of two thousand workers) hesitated in 1970 to commit relocating to central Mississippi "because of management reservations over the unstable school situation." Like the governor, however, business leaders often saw the necessity of private schools. Jackson business leaders, for instance, both championed the integration of the city's public schools and offered financial support for the establishment of the Citizens' Council schools. Jackson banks reportedly loaned $600,000 to the Citizens' Council in 1970 for their private school projects. The heads of two of the banks were members of the biracial committee for the Jackson public schools and also members of President Nixon's twelve-member state advisory panel to the Cabinet Committee on Education, organized to smooth the transition to a unitary school system throughout the South.[15]

Aside from a few well-financed enterprises, the private schools that hastily developed around the state in 1970 ultimately depended on public resources to operate in the short run. As a result, as in Tunica County, public assets were pilfered or acquired at a discount. Jackson school officials allowed city school buses to be "repainted white and marked Council Schools." At one Jackson public school, the principal allowed representatives from the Citizens' Council schools to come in the summer of 1970 and collect excess supplies, from sports equipment to soap to pencils. To name but a few other examples, in Canton, the public schools sold the local academy desks for fifty cents each and three school buses for $500; in North Pike County, officials provided a gym used by the public schools to a private school for $500; and at previously all-white Indianola High, which became largely black after integration in February 1970, white students used the facility for classes at nights because of the overcrowding at Indianola Academy. The hasty formation of many private schools led to some odd instances of cooperation between the public schools and the private academies. The white Canton seniors who moved to Canton Academy for the second semester of the 1969–70 school year still received their diplomas from Canton High, primarily because Canton Academy did not receive accreditation until 1971. Much like Tunica County, in a number of other school districts where the transition to unitary schools occurred in midyear, such as Benton County, Greenwood, and West Point, white teachers refused to transfer to the black schools. Claiming that the teachers had binding contracts but could not be forced to transfer to a different school in midyear, public school officials in these districts continued to pay teachers from public funds, although a number of teachers took jobs in private segregated schools for the second semester of the 1969–70 school year.[16]

Private school advocates also hoped to preserve their federal tax-exempt status, which helped keep many of the fledgling institutions financially afloat. Although private schools had long received an automatic exemption from federal taxes because of their standing as nonprofit educational establishments, that policy came under increasing scrutiny after the passage of the Civil Rights Act of 1964. In January 1970, a group of black parents in

Holmes County forced a decision on the issue when they secured a temporary injunction against Treasury Secretary David Kennedy and Internal Revenue Service (IRS) commissioner Randy Thrower, barring them from granting tax-exempt status to Mississippi private schools without some statement of nondiscrimination from the schools. Essentially, the federal courts recognized the inconsistency in requiring school integration while at the same time granting financial favors to institutions created for the sole purpose of avoiding those rulings. Although the Nixon administration initially debated whether to challenge the ruling in the Holmes County case, *Green v. Kennedy and Thrower*, the administration ultimately decided to enforce the ruling, at least in Mississippi, and in July 1970 the IRS moved to revoke the tax-exempt status of the Mississippi private schools covered by the *Green* case. Thirty-eight all-white academies and one all-black private school were affected. Nine of the institutions (including the one all-black school) agreed to submit the mandatory nondiscrimination pledge; the other thirty schools unsuccessfully tried to appeal the ruling to the Supreme Court. Most of these schools steadfastly refused to submit any type of nondiscrimination statement and lost their tax-exempt status in March 1971. Even so, the Nixon administration, always mindful of the benefits of its southern strategy of tacking just to the left of the racial conservatism of George Wallace (the former Alabama governor whose American Independent Party had won five Deep South states in the presidential election of 1968, largely because of his hostility to the cause of black civil rights), moved much slower to extend this policy to the rest of the South. [17]

Despite the white abandonment of public schools in many of the state's black-majority districts, whites typically continued to control school systems that few of their children or those of their white neighbors attended. As a result, whites increasingly had little incentive to make the improvements to black education already long postponed. As Robert Clark, a former teacher in Holmes County, noted on the eve of the implementation of the total integration orders in Holmes County: "It's very likely we'll have an all-black system, and that will be bad as long as the whites control it. I expect they will try to make the system as rotten as they can."[18]

Holmes County at least had a mobilized black citizenry to fight against such injustice; in other locales where the civil rights movement had not sunk deep roots, white abandonment of the public schools often provided the unfettered license to dismantle the public schools. For example, in the east Mississippi county of Kemper, where schools became more than 90 percent black following the white flight of 1970, those who ran the public schools were among the leaders in building a private school system for whites. One lawyer served both the public and private schools. One public school board member sat on the finance committee of the new private academy, while the wife of another board member was a member of the academy's board of trustees. In addition, the children of all the public school board members attended the private school. Even the assistant superintendent of the public schools there noticed that "some of the school board members aren't interested in public education." This lack of interest translated into a dwindling tax base for the public schools. In 1967, when school integration seemed only a distant threat, the county board of supervisors had set the local millage for public schools at almost 15, but by 1971 the millage rate had been slashed to 9.5, below the minimum suggested by the state. In Wilkinson County, almost total white flight reduced school enrollment by one-fourth between 1969 and 1971, but officials there cut the local millage rate by one-half during the same period. Other school districts that lost most or all of their white students, such as Hollandale and Greenwood, also took swift action to reduce local school taxes.[19]

Many white Mississippians in the state's black-majority school districts, similar to the white parents in Tunica County, believed that the abandonment of public schools in heavily black areas might only be a temporary necessity. Much like the strategy to "destroy" public schools in the North by urging the application of the *Alexander* mandate to school districts with de facto segregation, Mississippi private school advocates believed that if enough whites left the public schools, making them all-black, the federal courts would be forced to reconsider their total integration orders. It is unlikely that the federal courts would have accepted the logic of such an argument, but in any event, the white flight from the public schools never reached the anticipated critical mass the private school supporters had projected. Statewide, only about 8 percent of the white students left the public schools for private education in 1970; by 1979, almost 91 percent of Mississippi children still attended public schools. The private school phenomenon remained confined to large parts of the Delta, where blacks outnumbered whites by significant majorities, and a few urban areas, such as Jackson. Public schools continued to flourish in much of the state after integration for a number of reasons. The state's poverty meant that many whites could not afford private schooling, and white majorities in many parts of the state meant that school integration involved little beyond the token desegregation of the 1960s.[20] Equally important, in those areas where blacks and whites did attend classes together in integrated schools, with whites firmly in control of the operation of the public schools for many years after 1970, they were able to pursue policies that preserved as much white supremacy in public education as possible.

If white abandonment of the public school system represented the most common response to the arrival of total school integration in black-majority districts, other strategies were also utilized in these areas. At least four school districts—Amite County, Carroll County, Coffeeville, and Senatobia—developed sex segregation plans. Such plans perhaps had some potential educational value, but they were devised primarily to allay white fears about interracial sexual contact in integrated schools with large numbers of blacks, not to promote any perceived benefits of same-sex education. Though federal judge William Keady originally approved such plans for Coffeeville, Senatobia, and Carroll County and later pronounced them as "ingenious," he ultimately overruled the stratagems when masses of black parents protested and when irrefutable evidence surfaced that the plans clearly were racially, not educationally, motivated. In Coffeeville, about 75 percent of black parents kept their children out of the public schools for three months in the fall of 1970 in protest of Keady's sex segregation order. School officials in Coffeeville acknowledged that they "do not feel this is the best plan as for [sic] as education is concerned but with the ratio of 2 Negroes to 1 white this appears to be the only workable plan that would achieve the racial balance so required." In Carroll County, during a rehearing on the district's integration plan, the superintendent testified in court that the sex segregation mechanism was primarily designed "to keep the black teenage boys away from the white girls." Only the Amite County sex segregation plan survived for any length of time; it was utilized until 1977, when a group of local blacks successfully challenged this method of school integration. Although the Amite County sex segregation plan, like those in other locales, had been designed to limit white flight, by 1977 the number of whites in the school system was only 20 percent, down from 36 percent in the last year before full integration.[21]

In the white-majority areas of Mississippi, whites also frequently opposed the court orders for complete school integration, but rather than run from the requirement for school integration, whites in some of these locales sometimes decided to try and fight back. In Jackson and Forrest County, white parents adopted the tactics of the civil rights movement, organizing protest marches, mass rallies, student boycotts, and sit-ins at white schools to protest the integration orders. At Lake Elementary in Jackson, for example, when school began in fall 1970 under an integration order that paired white and black elementary schools, white mothers first marched on city hall, then picketed the school and sat-in at the school's library, next tried to teach classes in an unused portable classroom until evicted, and finally held classes for several weeks in an old school bus parked across the street from the elementary campus. White parents and teachers launched similar, though less comprehensive, protests at three other previously white Jackson elementary schools; none of these protests stopped Jackson's school integration from proceeding as ordered by the federal courts, and the whites involved in the opposition either eventually joined the white exodus from the city's public schools or accepted the new reality of integrated education.[22]

In the south Mississippi county of Forrest, one of the *Alexander* counties, white parents also mobilized to oppose the required reorganization of the county's schools. After a number of white students in the community of Petal, in grades five, six, and seven, were ordered to attend classes at Earl Travillion, six miles away in the black Palmers' Crossing neighborhood, white parents formed Citizens for Local Control of Education (CLCE). The group held a rally in December 1969 attended by one thousand supporters. The day after the rally, four-fifths of the white students in the Forrest County schools stayed home in a one-day boycott. In early January, the CLCE sponsored a protest march in downtown Hattiesburg, a town with its own separate school district, one not required to begin complete school integration until the fall of 1970. Despite rainy weather, the march attracted a large crowd, complete with Confederate flags, a volunteer band, and plenty of banners and placards, with slogans such as "How Can Freedom of Choice Be Wrong in a Free Country," "Down with HEW, Support CLCE," and "Bury the HEW in Mississippi Mud." Although Earl Travillion would have had 270 white and 90 black students under the new school integration plan, a three-to-one white majority, all the white students stayed in Petal when classes began in early 1970, sitting-in at their old school. The tactic worked, for in the wake of the Petal protest, county school officials reworked their original school integration plan; the new plan allowed the Petal students to remain in the Petal school, and the community soon incorporated as a town and formed its own separate school district. The new plan, however, proposed to move white students in the fifth through eighth grades from two other white schools, Dixie and Central, to Earl Travillion. Not surprisingly, white parents in these areas, also affiliated with CLCE, tried the sit-in approach that had worked so well in Petal. For a couple of weeks, white students sat in at empty classrooms and school auditoriums at both Dixie and Central schools, without teachers or books and with white mothers serving as chaperones. When the Forrest County school officials ran out of maneuvering options, however, most of the white Dixie and Central students eventually moved to a new private school rather than accept the transfer to Earl Travillion.[23]

Although state officials praised the efforts of Forrest County's CLCE, similar protest efforts in other south Mississippi locales failed to garner widespread white support. As Petal whites boycotted their assignment to Earl Travillion, forty-eight state legislators sponsored a resolution praising the actions of the white parents of CLCE for their "personal courage" and "love of liberty and freedom." CLCE efforts to organize white protests in nearby counties, however, generally fizzled. Despite an effort to get one thousand mothers in neighboring Covington County to picket against the massive integration orders, only fifteen to twenty protestors showed up when the county opened its new unitary schools in early 1970. Likewise, when black and white students began attending school together in large numbers for the first time that January in Columbia (about thirty miles west of Hattiesburg), they only had to walk past fewer than ten protestors outside their schools.[24]

Covington County and Columbia, as well as a number of other white-majority county or small-town school districts, successfully integrated their schools in 1970 without massive white flight or white protest. For example, in Tupelo, located in northeast Mississippi, with a school population 75 percent white, school integration proceeded smoothly; few whites left the public schools, and within a few years the integrated schools of the town were actually a source of civic pride among whites. Other white-majority school districts, however, especially urban ones, devised school plans in 1970 that surrendered their long opposition to school integration but still maintained some semblance of segregation. One blueprint used in a number of school districts focused on preserving segregation in the elementary grades by appealing to the concept of neighborhood schools. President Nixon gave explicit support to these sentiments in his March 24, 1970, statement on the school integration issue. Although the president reiterated his support for ending "deliberate racial segregation of pupils by official action," Nixon also told the nation in this key speech just six weeks after many Mississippi school districts had converted to unitary schools at midyear that "the neighborhood school will be deemed the most appropriate base" for a system of integrated schools. Nixon also promised that busing "for the purpose of achieving racial balance will not be required." Perhaps most troubling for black Mississippians about the president's remarks was his suggestion that local school officials play the "key" role in "developing local plans." Such officials, of course, had managed for a decade and a half to disobey all edicts demanding the elimination of dual schools. State legislator Robert Clark expressed his displeasure with Nixon's suggestion that the school integration problem be worked out by local officials by noting that blacks would have to "beg" for what was right, as they had in previous years. Even though Nixon's March 24 statement was designed primarily to allay the fears of whites in northern cities that the federal government would not attack de facto segregated schools through the use of busing, the statement also provided words of seeming moderation on the school integration front for the white South.[25]

Many white Mississippians heard Nixon's statement and had their hopes renewed that integrated schools might be a temporary inconvenience and that segregated education might eventually be restored. After all, if President Nixon was urging limits on school desegregation policy, perhaps the federal courts would eventually back off from what many white Mississippians viewed as an ill-conceived attempt to change their racial attitudes. The chief justice of the Mississippi Supreme Court, Robert Gillespie, noted two years after forced integration that "people are going to associate with whom they want to and you can't force people against their will; it might work for awhile but you just can't do that." Dave Dunaway, white principal in the Greenville public schools, agreed that "you can't legislate the law of brotherhood. . . . I don't think you can gain anything by forcing that issue." Dunaway, like Senator John Stennis and numerous other white Mississippians, believed a respite from school integration might come once the court orders that had forced school integration on Mississippi and the rest of the South were applied to other parts of the country. Dunaway remembered that he and others hoped that "the political powers up there [the North], that they'd find some way to change it or not obey it [the federal court's school integration rulings]."[26] Such thinking echoed Attorney General Summer's effort in the days after the *Alexander* decision to undermine federal court orders on school integration by "forcing" them on an unwilling North.

These ideas were far from fanciful. Although the Supreme Court initially pressed for more action on completing school integration after 1970, as these new remedies for integrating schools, such as busing, were approved by the federal courts, whites outside the South did become increasingly disgruntled about judicial efforts to force school integration on any school district. By 1974, federal support for forcing compliance with school integration had significantly diminished. The Supreme Court's 1971 decision *Swann v. Charlotte-Mecklenberg County Board of Education*, which permitted busing to achieve school integration, crystallized opposition outside the South to further court-mandated action to create racially balanced schools. Even though the *Swann* decision implicitly applied only to the de jure segregation of the South, whites outside the South feared an extension of the case's holdings to the North and the West would undermine the residential segregation that supported the de facto school segregation of their metropolitan areas. President Nixon steadfastly opposed the *Swann* decision, and he also instructed HEW to abandon efforts to force compliance with school integration decrees through its fund cutoff powers granted in Title VI of the Civil Rights Act of 1964.[27]

At the same time, the House of Representatives, backed by the Nixon administration, passed a number of measures attacking the judicial enforcement of school integration and the busing that might be used to achieve such outcomes, including bills that would have eliminated gasoline supplies for school buses, allowed southern schools that recently integrated their schools to resegregate, and set limits on what the Supreme Court might decide in the area of school integration. The Senate turned all such stratagems away, but the Supreme Court, which had become increasingly conservative in membership during the Nixon years, took heed of the huge white backlash outside the South to forced school integration and in a series of decisions in 1973 and 1974 set limits on what school districts could do to achieve school integration, culminating in the 1974 decision *Milliken v. Bradley*, which disallowed an effort to achieve school integration by busing students between the mostly black schools of Detroit and the white suburbs that surrounded the city. Though fierce battles over school integration continued to erupt outside the South in the mid-1970s, *Milliken* essentially signaled that de facto school segregation in the North and West would be preserved.[28]

In Mississippi, whites also complained about the destruction of neighborhood schools through mechanisms such as busing, although the protests over busing in the state were disingenuous. Even before the *Swann* decision, whites in Mississippi objected to the "tyranny" of using busing to achieve school integration. A Taylorsville man told President Nixon in December 1969 that "I would not object to my child going to school if it was integrated by 'freedom of choice' but for him to be picked up and bussed across the county *I will not do*." A group of "concerned citizens" in Greenville asked the president in the fall of 1970 "to use your influence on the Supreme Court to prevent busing in our schools. Also, to keep neighborhood schools and quality education in the U.S.A." Whatever anxieties the remedy of busing might have aroused nationwide, it is clear that the fears of white Mississippi parents during the early 1970s really had little to do with transportation arrangements. As one black Mississippian noted, "As long as riding the school buses served to segregate in Mississippi, everything was OK, but just as soon as bus riding started for integration it was the wrong thing." Indeed, in a largely rural state, most districts had bused the vast majority of their students for years. Statewide, 58 percent of all Mississippi children rode a bus to get to their schools in 1967. Black students often endured the longest bus rides. For example, before integration, black children in the east Mississippi community of Sturgis rode about thirty miles each way to attend a black school in Maben. According to the State Department of Education's supervisor of pupil transportation, the typical district ended up transporting fewer students after integration.[29]

Busing was even proposed as a method to achieve "school integration" whenever the procedure actually helped preserve segregated education within unitary schools. The East Tallahatchie school district, for instance, satisfied the demand to end its dual system in 1970 by keeping both the black and white high schools and holding classes in some subjects in the previously all-white East Tallahatchie High and other courses in the previously all-black Allen Carver High. Buses transported students between the two campuses, and most students had to make at least one trip a day. Although the U.S. Justice Department approved the East Tallahatchie plan, a majority of blacks in the district boycotted the schools because of the strange busing requirement. The Mississippi House of Representatives also supported school busing in its 1970 legislative session, approving a measure to use public funds to aid private schools in transporting their students, many of whom had substantial bus rides once they left the public schools.[30] Outside of most of the state's urban areas, the creation of true neighborhood schools without regard to race would have resulted in largely integrated schools, which is one reason why most Mississippi school districts had long favored freedom of choice over geographic zoning desegregation plans. The real institution white parents and officials in Mississippi sought to preserve was the white neighborhood school. Ironically, in much of rural Mississippi, busing was often an effective mechanism for achieving this goal.

After the *Swann* decision, a busing controversy did erupt in the state's largest school district. Even though Jackson's schools were integrated in the fall of 1970, the shape of the city's school plan remained tied up in litigation during the 1970–71 school year. In the summer of 1971, the Fifth Circuit Court of Appeals finally decreed that because of the loss of so many white students (over 40 percent during the first year of school integration) and the resulting concentration of the city's black population in the central part of the city, intracity busing was needed to integrate Jackson's elementary schools successfully. The court's plan had the "active support of a large part of the community" in Jackson; what opposition existed actually came from the black community (two of the four black members of the biracial committee for the schools voted against implementing the Fifth Circuit's plan). After the appeals court announced its decision in the Jackson school case, Governor John Bell Williams issued an executive order cutting off $8 million of the school district's $20 million in state funds. Williams stated that he wanted to end all busing in the state "and return to the neighborhood school concept," and the governor based his fund cutoff on a 1953 law that prohibited cities from busing students, a measure seemingly superceded by the federal doctrine embodied in *Swann*.[31]

When schools officials sought an injunction to keep the governor from freezing the district's funds, federal district court judge Dan Russell granted their motion. Russell claimed that the governor's executive order was merely a ploy to "re-open the approved integration plan," which would only "delay the inevitable" and prolong a court case that had been in litigation since 1963. Governor Williams called Russell's decision an "unbridled" act designed to spend Mississippi's money "as the court sees fit without the people's consent." While Williams certainly wanted to make a point about federal-state relations, his portrayal of school busing as an inherent evil neither described the Jackson situation nor the transportation arrangements that prevailed around the state in the early 1970s or in Mississippi's past. School busing in Jackson only involved about one-fourth of the district's students in the 1971–72 school year, and school officials were using local, not state, funds to pay for the transportation. In the end, busing was a crucial factor in successfully ending Jackson's dual school system, though it also undoubtedly accounted for some of the white flight from the district.[32]

While Governor Williams's call for an end to all busing was both impracticable in a state as rural as Mississippi and not necessarily a strategy that would have achieved the governor's real goal of preserving segregated education throughout the state, his plea for the preservation of neighborhood schools did represent a possible way for whites in a number of towns and cities to preserve one-race schools within a unitary system. In some locales with segregated housing patterns, school officials constructed plans that focused on preserving neighborhood schools, often by keeping racial segregation in elementary schools. In some cases, these neighborhood school proposals were blocked by federal officials, though in several other cases such plans were allowed to go forward for a number of years. For instance, the Picayune school board initially adopted a plan in June 1970 that would have created one integrated high school and one integrated junior high but seven segregated elementary schools. After HEW rejected the plan and threatened the district with a lawsuit, school officials pondered their options, concluded that court-ordered plans led to "almost daily changing and unworkable" situations, and adopted a plan that incorporated "the basic requirements for approval" by HEW, one that integrated the town's schools at all levels, in part through the use of busing.[33]

On the other hand, HEW and the Justice Department allowed Hattiesburg to create a school integration plan in 1970 that maintained one-race elementary schools, a school integration proposal the school district claimed "follows the principles as outlined by President Nixon's statements on March 24, 1970." The different result in the two towns rested on two important factors. For one thing, the Hattiesburg plan that maintained racially identifiable neighborhood elementary schools initially had the backing of the school district's biracial committee, the local chapter of the NAACP, and many other local blacks. At the same time, the city of Hattiesburg had important political connections in Washington. Mayor Paul Grady, one of the few Republicans holding local office in the entire state of Mississippi, served as an intermediary between federal bureaucrats in Washington and Hattiesburg school officials to ensure that the school district received a favorable response to a school plan that preserved a large measure of school segregation. One black critic of the Hattiesburg plan claimed that its approval demonstrated that the Nixon administration was "using its Southern Strategy to show a Republican town they can get a better deal than a George Wallace one." But other communities, such as Laurel and Columbus, were also allowed to develop school integration plans in 1970 that preserved segregated elementary schools.[34]

While the partially segregated, unitary school systems created in Laurel, Columbus, and Hattiesburg in 1970 were allowed to stand for a number of years, all were eventually overturned. When the elementary schools in these cities were finally integrated, another round of white flight ensued. In Laurel, where the white and black population was neatly divided by the Southern Railway tracks, the preservation of seven one-race elementary schools in 1970 kept the majority of whites in the public schools, although a significant minority left the district that year as school integration arrived for the higher grades. Black plaintiffs brought the district back to court in the early 1970s, and in 1975 Judge Dan Russell told the Laurel district that the pairing of the city's elementary schools appeared "inevitable." In late 1977, the Fifth Circuit Court of Appeals confirmed Russell's hunch, and in the fall of 1978 the district was forced to open with integrated elementary schools. Whites in Laurel renewed their exodus from the city school district soon after Judge Russell's warning about the coming specter of elementary school pairing. Between 1976 and 1979, the Laurel schools lost over eight hundred students, mostly white children. By 1995, the city had almost the same black student population as it had in 1968, but white enrollment had declined by almost twenty-three hundred, transforming the district from one with a 53 percent white majority to a system with a 25 percent white minority.[35]

The Columbus school district followed a similar path. Although the system signed a school integration consent decree in 1970 that allowed the city's six elementary schools (three black, three white) to remain neighborhood schools, and thus segregated, within the first few years after the school integration order took effect the district lost over fifteen hundred of its more than nine thousand students. While the 1970 integration plan kept most whites in the Columbus public schools, this unitary arrangement was almost immediately challenged. The Columbus school district, however, fought a seven-year legal battle to preserve this valued aspect of the city's school plan. When the federal courts finally ordered pairing of the city's six elementary schools, beginning with the fall semester of 1977, a biracial coalition of black and white parents and teachers objected. Some suggested that parents just keep sending their children to their neighborhood schools in defiance of the federal orders. White school board members, however, urged parents to accept the federal decrees and remain with the public schools. One of the board members, John East, told black and white parents that although there would be much about the pairing of the city's elementary schools that "you're not going to like," he reminded parents that "my child is going to be in public schools. . . . My child is going to get a good education and yours is too." Such reassurances apparently worked with many parents, but after 1977 a significant number of whites began once again to drift away from the Columbus city schools. After the first two years of completely integrated schools, overall enrollment in the city had only declined by about five hundred students. Yet by 1995, the number of whites who had left the city's schools since 1970 totaled almost four thousand. Most undoubtedly moved to the neighboring county schools, which had a larger white student population.[36]

Hattiesburg managed to keep its elementary schools segregated until 1987, although black support for the integration plan diminished after the first year of school integration. The Hattiesburg integration scheme originally provided for two integrated high schools, one previously white and the other previously black; four integrated junior high schools; and eleven elementary schools, all but two of which remained almost totally white or black. After one year, the plan was adjusted primarily to transform the white high school into an eleventh and twelfth grade center and to use the previously black high school to educate all tenth graders. This change was necessitated primarily because practically none of the whites assigned to the black high school showed up when the school year began; in a number of cases, parents in the white high school zone took out "legal guardianship papers" for white students who lived in the black high school zone. One family reportedly claimed twelve children through such procedures. Because of the changes in the high schools, several black members of the school district's biracial committee asked that all racially identifiable schools be eliminated in the revised plan, but that proposal was rejected, and the elementary schools in the city remained largely untouched in the revised plan. As a result, most whites stayed with the city schools; the Hattiesburg schools had been about 55 percent white before 1970, and after the first year of integration, they still had a student population that was 45 percent white.[37]

In 1984, a group of black parents reopened the Hattiesburg school integration case, eventually securing a ruling from the Fifth Circuit Court of Appeals in 1987 that required pairing of schools to achieve a racial balance at all levels of the Hattiesburg public schools. At the time of the 1987 ruling, the ratio of black students to white students in the city's schools stood at 57 to 43 percent, but four of the city's elementary schools were more than 90 percent black (one had no white students and another had five), and three of the elementary schools had student populations greater than 70 percent white. One of the these, Thames, had an enrollment of 526 whites and 57 blacks and, according to one observer, was "for all practical purposes—a heavily white private school in a public system." Whites in Hattiesburg, who had basically remained in the public schools as long as the lower grades remained largely segregated, began forsaking the system in droves following the Fifth Circuit ruling. Within a year, white enrollment dropped from 43 percent to 28 percent, and by 1995 the number of whites in the system stood at 22 percent. Some moved to private schools. Others fled to adjacent Lamar County, which in 1995 had a school system that remained 90 percent white; indeed, the economic expansion of Lamar County just west of Interstate 59 that began around 1990 followed close on the heels of the delayed massive white flight west, away from the integrated Hattiesburg schools.[38]

Not every school district that negotiated a partially segregated unitary school plan in 1970 was forced at a later date to abandon such arrangements. Most notable in this category was the Delta town of Cleveland, which managed to parlay its segregated housing pattern (whites primarily to the west of Highway 61, blacks primarily to the east) into a stable, semisegregated education layout, with all-black elementary schools, a middle school, and a high school in east Cleveland and integrated schools, from elementary schools to high school, in the western part of the town. Although some blacks in the town complained that the schools east of Highway 61 were frequently shortchanged, no formal legal challenge to the Cleveland integration plan emerged, and the system continued to remain in place into the twenty-first century. In 2003, the city had two high schools, the all-black East Side and Cleveland High, which was 61 percent white; two middle schools, the all-black Eastwood and Margaret Green, which was 57 percent white; and five elementary schools, three that were all-black or that contained only a handful of white students, one that was 70 percent white, and one that was 39 percent white. Able to maintain a thoroughgoing system of segregated schools, Cleveland stood as an aberration in the Mississippi Delta. Unlike most of the other districts in the area, whites remained in the public schools of Cleveland; in 2003, they comprised 25 percent of the town's student population.[39]

During and after the conversion to a unitary school system in 1970, state and federal officials declared the process an unqualified success. Mississippi's state superintendent of education publicly crowed in the summer of 1970 that the state had the most desegregated schools in the nation. President Richard Nixon counted the desegregation of southern schools as the crowning achievement of his administration's civil rights record. If one looks only at the numbers, the extent of change in Mississippi, and across the South, was indeed striking. At the end of the 1966–67 school year, over a third of Mississippi's districts had achieved no school desegregation and less than 3 percent of the state's black children attended classes with whites; by the end of 1970 all of the state's public schools had been integrated. And this transformation was generally accomplished without the violence associated with the earlier desegregation and voting rights battles of the 1960s.[40]

School integration in Mississippi, however, was not as successful as some observers at the time suggested. In areas of the state with sizable black populations, public school integration had indeed occurred, but only because education still remained separate, as whites fled from the public schools and formed separate private educational institutions for their children to attend. In many other parts of Mississippi, whites either protested against the efforts to create unitary schools or strove to find ways to maintain as much segregated schooling as could be accommodated within the confines of federal demands, requirements most white Mississippians in any event hoped would soon be overruled. In addition, school integration always occurred on white terms, with the primary objective often being to keep white children, as much as possible, out of the same schools black children attended. For black Mississippians, school integration under such strictures represented something less than the total victory they had long believed would come with the abolition of Mississippi's dual school system.

CHAPTER EIGHT

SCHOOL INTEGRATION

A Pyrrhic Victory?

At the end of the 1971–72 school year, the second full year of school integration in Meridian, the local chapter of the NAACP registered complaints about a number of problems in the public schools. The group charged that black students were unfairly disciplined and subsequently suspended for lengthy terms. Black leaders in Meridian suggested that a biracial student and parent committee develop "uniform disciplinary rules" and that suspensions last no longer than three days for each infraction. Black citizens in Meridian also pointed out that many schools had no black administrators and that the number of white teachers had increased in the district even as the number of white students declined. Blacks demanded more black administrators and a "freeze" on hiring white teachers. In addition, blacks in Meridian perceived that their children were "being labeled 'retarded' and 'unteachable' by white administrators and forced out of regular classroom situations"; the parents called for an end to such practices. Other problems cited by the local NAACP chapter included a lack of black history offerings and the failure to develop biracial social activities "that will help the students of both races become better acquainted with the other."[1]

The ongoing battles between blacks and whites in the Meridian public schools after integration were stoked by the fact that whites continued to exercise total control over the schools and neglected to ask for or heed black input on how to operate an integrated school system. After the first year of school integration in Meridian, for example, the local chapter of the NAACP sent the Meridian school board, an all-white body, a list of problems that parents and students had pointed out concerning the integrated schools. The NAACP claimed that overall, "progress has been made, but existing problems tend to overshadow such progress." During the second year of school integration, these concerns merely continued to fester, since the school board failed to address any of the problems or even respond to the complaints. As the NAACP pointed out, blacks in the city had a "different view point of school matters" than the all-white school board; without any real communication between whites and blacks, school difficulties continued to plague the Meridian schools for many years after integration.[2]

The problems identified by the Meridian NAACP were not unique to that school district. Indeed, the Meridian catalog of complaints about the state of integrated education resonated with blacks in many of the state's school districts during the 1970s. Although the dual school system was eliminated in Meridian and throughout Mississippi in 1970, blacks across the state found that racial discrimination did not suddenly disappear merely because the state's separate but equal educational arrangements had been dismantled through forceful federal action. Eight years after the transformation to unitary schools, Aaron Henry delivered what by then was becoming a familiar message to NAACP members at their annual state meeting: segregation and discrimination in education were still problems in Mississippi. He specifically cited the "push out of Black students particularly Black males," the demotion or loss of black teachers and administrators, and "the many hostilities and discourtesies heaped upon Black children daily by school authorities."[3]

For black Mississippians, the achievement of school integration in 1970 represented a giant step forward in their century-long battle to secure the best-possible education for their children, but many soon recognized the often staggering price exacted for this triumph. School integration occurred largely on white terms, typically with a diminution of black control over education, a loss of black institutions nurtured during the years of enforced racial segregation, and a thinning of the ranks of black teachers and administrators. For many, the integration of the state's public schools represented a pyrrhic victory over Mississippi's dual school system.

White leaders had the power to shape school integration in ways that suited their concerns, primarily how to allay the fears of their white constituents, since they remained firmly in control of the state's public school system when the U.S. Supreme Court issued its *Alexander* decision in October 1969. Faced with a mandate to abolish the dual school system immediately, or at least by the fall of 1970, many school districts had to act quickly to come up with acceptable school integration plans. While some districts sought black input, in most areas, and certainly on a statewide level, white leaders made no effort, or only the most minimal one, to involve black citizens in formulating plans for the dismantling of dual school systems. Black Mississippians had long argued that any meaningful school integration would require a serious black-white dialogue in the state. Indeed, at the July 1954 meeting with Governor Hugh White, black leaders proposed a biracial committee as one of the centerpieces of their proposal to implement the *Brown* decision. White leaders, however, never seriously considered offering black Mississippians a voice in how to dismantle the dual school system, primarily because most whites never accepted the legitimacy of such a task and battled against all efforts to undermine segregated education. Even so, black leaders in 1970 still remained willing to negotiate with whites on how to create a unitary school system. As Robert Clark, a former teacher and the state's only black legislator, noted in early 1970, even if integration led to the closing of black schools and the loss of black educators, "if we can go into this thing shoulder to shoulder, we are willing to try to make a go of it." In other words, black Mississippians might have accepted their share of the dislocations if the inevitable losses associated with combining two school systems into one had been shared equally and agreed upon in real negotiations.[4]

Some districts did make an effort to incorporate black input into the construction of plans to move toward unitary school systems by creating biracial committees to advise school boards. Federal judges often counseled school districts to utilize such committees. When Judge Griffin Bell of the Fifth Circuit Court of Appeals met with a number of the defendant school boards in the days after the *Alexander* decision, he suggested that biracial committees would go a long way toward ensuring the crafting of viable school integration plans. In many communities, however, especially those where the civil rights movement had established a minimal presence, the admonitions to consult with blacks in developing school integration blueprints were

totally ignored. When Jefferson Davis County's all-white school board negotiated an acceptable school integration plan with the Department of Justice
in the summer of 1970, the board had no mechanism for black input. As a
result, the plan called for the closing of black schools in the district and
converted one black high school to an elementary school, even though, due
to the state's equalization campaign, the black high school was one of the
most modern schools in the county.[5]

In locales that did utilize biracial committees, the outcomes varied. In
Hattiesburg, the school district actually had a biracial committee with a
black majority. The committee endorsed a plan favored by most whites that
also had the backing of the local black community: one that preserved
neighborhood, one-race schools at the elementary level. In Jackson, the biracial committee represented a wide range of black opinion. One black member opposed crafting a plan that focused on maximizing racial balance,
fearing that it would merely lead to black teacher displacement. Another
black member proposed that all historically black schools be closed as part
of the city's integration plan, seeing such action as the key to ensuring equal
treatment of black and white students. Still other black members supported
the primary concern of the white members on the committee: keeping white
students (and ultimately, white tax dollars) in the public schools.[6]

In a number of places that utilized biracial committees, the panels
merely highlighted the divergent ideas of what a successful school integration strategy looked like. Greenville is a good example. A Delta town with a
reputation for moderation in race relations, Greenville nevertheless had
seen growing frustration by the black community over the inadequacies
of public education in the months prior to the *Alexander* decision. In
September 1969, a group of teachers in the black schools and local black community groups—dismayed by a long string of broken promises by school
officials—joined forces to create the Ad Hoc Committee for Quality Education to address "the subtleties of racial discrimination and the failure of
Greenville to provide quality public education for all its citizens." White
leaders were invited to attend the group's meetings, but they never showed
up. After the *Alexander* ruling, Willie Long, a biology teacher and chair of
the Ad Hoc Committee, asked school board president Hugh Alexander, a
local dentist, for black representation in any meetings held to draw up plans
for the transition to unitary schools. Alexander said "no," but within weeks,
HEW threatened to cut off the school district's funds, and the board agreed

to the creation of a biracial committee. The group consisted of eleven blacks (including Long) and eleven whites. The black teachers' organization and the local black PTA group selected the black members, while the separate white teachers' organization and white PTA chose the white members. The all-white school board instructed the biracial committee that the board's primary concern was keeping the white students in the schools, and at one of the first meetings of the committee, the board secured a pledge that neighborhood schools would be preserved at the elementary level where possible.[7]

The school board submitted two plans to the biracial committee, a sex segregation plan, quickly shot down by both black and white members of the committee, and a geographic zoning plan that would retain a number of both largely black and largely white elementary schools. Black members on the biracial committee disliked the segregation preserved in the board's plan, and the committee grew increasingly polarized, with most of the black members soon boycotting the committee's deliberations. Meanwhile, black parents affiliated with the Ad Hoc Committee tired of the seemingly one-sided negotiations and filed a lawsuit against the Greenville public schools. The plaintiffs suggested the use of a system of pairing black and white schools to eliminate the one-race schools that the board's geographic proposal preserved. After two months of meetings, the biracial committee voted on the board's plan, but only three black members remained involved. The committee endorsed the board's geographic zoning scheme by a ten-to-three vote. In a separate tally held later, all eleven black members of the biracial committee endorsed the plaintiffs' school integration plan.[8]

In the end, the Greenville biracial committee was mere window dressing, adopted by a school board under duress. The panel had little real chance to negotiate with an all-white school board unwilling to compromise on its ultimate objective of maintaining one-race schools for as many whites as possible, especially for the more affluent whites. After federal judge Orma Smith approved the board's plan, Willie Long noted that the final blueprint for school integration actually contained more segregation than the design originally submitted by the board to the biracial committee. After most of the black members had left the biracial committee, some white parents complained about the integration plan, and the committee made further changes in the geographic lines. As a result, most of the whites placed in the largely black elementary schools were poor, working-class whites who did not have the time to seek exceptions for their children or did not know they could. Even with all the efforts to create a school integration process acceptable to Greenville whites, approximately six hundred white students left the Greenville schools.[9]

Under pressure from federal officials, many communities maintained biracial committees well into the 1970s. The committees were supposedly impaneled to oversee the transition to unitary schools, but school leaders frequently completely ignored the groups when making decisions. In Clarksdale, for example, in the first two years after integration, the school district hired a new superintendent, shifted administrators around the various schools, and adjusted the busing plan, all without consulting the city's court-mandated biracial committee. One of the committee members, Bennie Gooden, claimed at the time that "it is obvious that school officials continue to ignore that a Bi-racial Committee exists. ... [T]o my knowledge, our committee has not even been advised and by no means consulted" about the changes in the operation of Clarksdale's new unitary schools. When the Clarksdale school board attorney, Semmes Luckett, sought to make some changes to the city's school integration plan in the summer of 1974, rather than present his proposal to the biracial committee, Luckett contacted a local black attorney, Charles Stringer—whom Luckett later described as "a good black"—as well as other blacks in town, seeking approval for his scheme. Luckett's handpicked group of black leaders, however, rebuffed his effort to tinker with the city's school integration setup. Luckett thought that "the blacks simply think that any white man is just trying to sell them a bill of goods." Stringer, however, objected to Luckett's approach primarily because Luckett did not make "use of [the] Bi-racial committee ordered by the courts to deal w/ such matters."[10]

Biracial committees, whether whites consulted them or not, had little real power. The real decision makers were school board members and school superintendents. In most Mississippi school districts, school boards remained all-white in 1970, the year when the plans for the new unitary schools were being crafted. Even in locales where the newly enfranchised black population had succeeded in electing a black school board member or two, whites sometimes still thwarted black input. When the Wilkinson County school board met to draw up an integration plan in the wake of the *Alexander* decision, the three white members met privately, failing to notify their two black colleagues of the gathering.[11] Almost completely shut out from a share of power over the public schools in 1970, black Mississippians only gradually secured positions that allowed them to make decisions and set policies concerning the public schools.

In 1970, many school board members, as well as school superintendents, were appointed by city or county officials, and the white politicians who primarily made these appointments during the 1970s and beyond were often reluctant to tap black leaders for school management positions. Although some school districts had appointed a black school board member before 1970, for the most part white officials viewed such appointments as problematic. When blacks in Jackson asked in early 1970 for the appointment of a black board member in a district with a school population almost evenly divided between whites and blacks, they were told that the white folks were going through enough at the time without having to deal with a black board member. When the city council appointed yet another white to fill a vacancy on the school board in February 1970, black Jacksonians complained. Mayor Russell Davis replied that although the council could not please everyone, it "has demonstrated that it does want to move in the direction of unity within the city." In fact, Mayor Davis had secured local business support for school integration a month earlier by privately pledging to avoid appointing a black board member "in the near future."[12]

In Hattiesburg, city leaders maintained an all-white school board until 1972, despite the pleas of blacks and even some whites. Black leaders had asked for the appointment of a black school board member every year since 1966. In 1969, fifty whites in the town even approached the city council (composed of the mayor and two city commissioners) about appointing a black school board member. Each time, the supplicants were promised such an appointment would be made at the next opportunity, pending the nomination of a suitable black man or woman. In 1967, the city council claimed that its appointments were always made without "respect to race, creed or color," but year after year the council appointed only white men, primarily from the Thames district, the most affluent white neighborhood in the city. In early 1970, after school board member Red Galey indicated he did not want to serve another term, the local NAACP branch submitted a list of names for possible appointment. City leaders only deemed one of the candidates suitable, but he refused to serve. So Galey was convinced to stay on

the board for another term. In early 1971, during the first year of total integration, two school board seats became vacant. Although Mayor Paul
Grady, the black community, and even much of the white community
believed at least one of the seats should go to a black citizen—in a supposedly integrated school district one-third black—the two city commissioners outvoted the mayor and appointed two white men to the board. One
Hattiesburg woman noted the absurdity of maintaining a lily white school
board: "What a fake our unitary school system is when no black person can
help determine school policies." One year later, city leaders did appoint
Jesse Parker to the board. A black World War II veteran who worked for ten
years as an educator in the state's public schools before becoming an executive with the Boy Scouts, Parker's appointment was made possible only
because one of the white board members, Ralph Milloy, resigned his term
early due to the widespread community sentiment that the city needed a
black board member. Despite their initial hesitations, whites in Hattiesburg,
a white-majority school district, had more sensitivity on the issue of sharing
power with blacks than many other school districts across the state.[13]

The failure to appoint black school board members or black superintendents in black-majority districts seemed an especially egregious attempt
by whites to limit black power. For example, an all-white school board continued to direct the Yazoo County schools in the late 1970s, even though the
board members, like many whites in the district, sent their own children to
private schools. In Drew, when the job of superintendent became vacant,
school officials in this overwhelmingly black district decided not to adver-
tise the position; instead, they privately appointed a new leader. Jimmy
Langdon, a black educator, filed a complaint with the Equal Employment
Opportunity Commission, and a federal judge eventually installed Langdon as Drew superintendent. The Drew school board, dominated by two
white members who served continuously from the 1960s through the 1990s,
responded by battling Langdon on every issue during his tenure. After he
served one term, the school board fired the unwanted black administrator.
In Jackson, which was transformed into a district with a black student majority immediately after the total integration of 1970, city leaders appointed one
black board member in the early 1970s but did not name a majority-black
school board until 1994. By that date, black students constituted 84 percent
of the student body.[14]

Almost two-thirds of Mississippi's school boards and about one-third of its superintendents were elected rather than appointed, but until the late 1970s the number of blacks elected to any political positions in the state remained small, despite the passage of the Voting Rights Act of 1965. State legislators continued their massive resistance of civil rights, throwing up roadblocks for more than a decade to limit the impact of the newly enfranchised black vote.[15] As a result, ten years after the Voting Rights Act, black candidates for school offices still faced stiff resistance from an entrenched white power structure. Reecy Dickson's experience is instructive. In 1975, Dickson decided to run for school superintendent in Noxubee County, a black-majority county in east-central Mississippi. Dickson was a music teacher in the county's schools, and after school integration—when all the white students left but none of the white administrators did—she "didn't like the way the kids were being educated because they [white school officials] didn't really care." She initially tried to qualify to run in the 1975 Democratic primary against the incumbent white Democratic superintendent, A. R. Koon. After being barred from the primary on a qualifying technicality, Dickson ran as an independent. Pregnant during the campaign, she canvassed the county, asking for support and bringing numerous black citizens who had never voted to the courthouse to register to vote. She remembered that many blacks in Noxubee County in 1975 "were afraid of the courthouse." Her opponent portrayed her as a crazy pregnant woman during the campaign; she received threatening phone calls, and her car was vandalized. Not all blacks supported her candidacy, as many educators backed the status quo of Superintendent Koon. Dickson did receive some support from local whites, who told her, "You're the best thing that ever happened to race relations. Don't give up. Don't let them do that to you." But she lost the election, in part because county officials and white leaders intimidated black voters. The county attorney went to the houses of blacks asking if Dickson had done "something illegal" to get their vote; whites at the polling places vocally abused black voters by telling them things such as, "You can't read."[16]

Reecy Dickson, however, persevered in her quest to right the wrongs she saw in the integrated schools of Noxubee County, despite ongoing opposition from white school leaders. After her defeat in 1975, the school system tried to fire her from her teaching job. Dickson managed to fight off this blatant attempt to intimidate her, and then she ran for superintendent again in 1979, this time defeating the incumbent, Koon, becoming the first black elected to countywide office in Noxubee County in the twentieth century and the first black woman to serve as a school superintendent in Mississippi's history. Getting elected, however, proved to be only part of the battle for Dickson. When she walked into the superintendent's office in 1980 after her election, all but one of the all-white staff walked out. The elected school board, composed of four whites and one black member, who according to Dickson, "was really just a token on the board," refused to approve any measure she proposed for most of the eight years she served as top school administrator. In fact, the school board would meet in the offices of the board attorney, without Dickson, before the scheduled public meetings of the school board. Dickson countered this effort by whites to maintain their control over the Noxubee County schools by working to change the racial composition of the school board. By the time she left office in 1984, four of the five board members were black.[17]

The fight by black Mississippians to secure a share of control over integrated schools was crucial to the construction of a unitary school system that would treat black students and black citizens fairly. As long as whites controlled the operation of the public schools, they frequently pursued an agenda that focused solely on making school integration palatable to whites by preserving as much of the legacy of segregation as possible within now "unitary" schools and by ensuring that schools remained as white as possible. State officials proved eager to help with these efforts. As the integration of many school districts began in February 1970, Governor John Bell Williams instructed the State Sovereignty Commission to keep close tabs on the proceedings. W. Webb Burke, Sovereignty Commission director, told his investigators to be on the lookout for such things as black instructors teaching black history and "reports pertaining to improper advances made by Negro males to the white girl students." Sovereignty Commission spies also continued to scrutinize any teachers suspected of supporting integrated schools, despite the fact that all schools in Mississippi had been legally ordered to integrate. In Coffeeville, school board president Chapel Sides asked a commission investigator for information on "how they could fire two Negro teachers" who had opposed the district's sex segregation plan. Blacks recognized that this approach to school integration represented something less than true integration. Pearl Garrett of Ripley indicated that she favored the changes 1970 brought "if they would integrate it full like it ought to be. But, you see, they hadn't integrated the schools[,] they just pretending to integrate." For her, full integration would have meant "for the black man to have jest [sic] as much say so and right as the white man got."[18]

The easiest way for whites to accede to the *Alexander* mandate in 1970 without relinquishing segregation, of course, was simply to segregate students by race within desegregated schools. In Yazoo City, heralded as a successful model of school integration by the national media in January 1970, most classrooms initially remained almost totally segregated. At least thirteen other school districts that adopted a unitary school plan in midyear 1970 also maintained segregated classrooms. Kemper County took the idea of segregation in a nominally desegregated school to perhaps its most ridiculous lengths. The superintendent of the county schools, E. G. Palmer, claimed, "We're fully integrated, that's for sure." Yet at the county's DeKalb High School, black and white students attended classes in separate wings of the same building; changed classes at different times to the sounds of a "black" bell and a "white" bell; ate lunch at different times; and even drank water from separate fountains. One school district claimed that its maintenance of segregated classrooms in a supposedly integrated school sprang from the fact that black and white students had used different editions of the same textbook before integration, so the students were at different levels of study for similar subjects. Unspoken was the fact that this practice of the "separate but equal" years, passing down the old editions of books to the black schools when the state bought new textbooks for the white schools, had persisted in the state for sixteen years after the *Brown* decision.[19]

Blacks quickly and successfully attacked such obvious evasions of the mandate for unitary schools, but more subtle attempts to continue forms of segregation within "integrated" schools proved more difficult to eradicate. As one black student noted in the fall of 1970, "I can truly tell you that the schools here are supposed to be black and white together, but the white people act as though it is all theirs. The white teachers only stand on one side of the classroom (the white side because that is the way they have it, the white on one side, the Negro on the other, or rather that it [sic] is the way we sit)." Reports circulated that year about a number of other troublesome practices, including continued segregation on school buses and the adoption of "departmentalization" of instruction in elementary schools, so a black teacher would not teach a white child all day long. A black observer of some of these problems associated with school integration in Greenwood despaired that the process ultimately "hurt us" and thought black students were "better off when they were in an all-black school."[20]

School integration plans in 1970 also often called for the closing of black schools or the alteration of their identity as black schools in order to allay white fears, such as that of a Hattiesburg woman who believed that her children's "lives will be jeopardized by going to a Negro community for their schooling." In West Point, school officials chose to have students attend classes on a split session rather than utilize two schools located in black neighborhoods, which remained closed until a federal court invalidated the city's plan. In 1970, 127 black schools were closed or lost their identity (primarily by changing their names) as black schools; only 57 white schools suffered this fate.[21]

While black Mississippians certainly shouldered more than their share of the necessary school closings required by the transition to unitary school systems, the closing of black schools in Mississippi actually happened less often than in some other southern states because Mississippi had invested so much in black school plants through its equalization campaign of the 1950s and 1960s. When Canton had to merge its two school systems in the winter of 1970, the school district closed the white high school rather than the all-black one, because the latter building was a more modern facility. Some districts that utilized often newer black schools to implement desegregation plans frequently organized campaigns to "clean up" or "improve" black schools in preparation for the arrival of white students. These efforts gave many black schools the complete upgrade they had long been denied, since in many cases the state's extensive building program had succeeded in building new black school buildings but had neglected to furnish them adequately. The upgrade to the previously all-black Carver School in the south Mississippi town of Picayune during the summer of 1970 began with a change of the school's name to South Side Elementary. In addition, school officials undertook a "full scale revamping of the . . . school grounds and renovation of the classrooms and general rehabilitation of the furniture,

fixtures and all equipment," improvements heralded as converting "the former Carver Elementary school into a unitary school"; they also decided to
build an eight-foot-high chain-link fence around the school grounds.[22]
Once the center of the local black community, the integrated South Side Elementary School would now essentially be sealed off from that community.

As in many other locales, the elimination of the dual school system in
Picayune meant removing only the black vestiges of the old order. While
any neighborhood, black or white, that lost a school because of school integration suffered, the dislocations such closures caused in black neighborhoods were perhaps greater because of the often exaggerated importance
blacks, by necessity, invested in their schools, many times the strongest
institution, along with local churches, in their communities. Lynda Davis of
Monroe County noted that because of school integration in 1970, "by taking the schools out of the community, it did something to the community.
Seems people here have just lost heart of, lost interest in the progress of the
community with the school [a]way."[23]

With whites setting the agenda for school integration, black students
became embroiled in a number of visible clashes with white teachers and
administrators during the first year of the transition to unitary schools in
Mississippi. Major protests, boycotts, or walkouts by black students erupted in
a number of locales, including Jackson, Hattiesburg, Clarksdale, Greenville,
Belzoni, Moss Point, Coffeeville, Kilmichael, Charleston, and Rankin County.
The substance of the disputes varied from town to town. In Clarksdale,
eighty black students staged a walkout at Clarksdale High School after the
school refused to allow a black history week, an event that had been a traditional highlight of the school year in the black schools. In Belzoni, hundreds
of black students boycotted Humphreys County High School to protest
a whole range of "discriminatory practices" by school officials, including
a white principal who yelled at the black students, the use of the words
"nigger" and "nigra" to refer to the black students, and the mass failure of
black students by white teachers. In Hattiesburg, three hundred black students staged a series of demonstrations to protest both the lack of black
representation on the school board and the failure to include black students
in extracurricular activities.[24]

In Hattiesburg, Belzoni, and most of the other places where black student protests occurred during the 1970–71 school year, the biggest issue of

contention was over disciplinary procedures in the integrated schools, an issue that continued to fester for much of the 1970s. Black students often believed that new rules were created just for them or that school regulations were not enforced the same for black and white students. Such inequities did occur. For instance, when a black girl at Greenville High School got into a fight in the lunchroom with two white girls in the fall of 1970, only the black girl was suspended. White administrators and teachers claimed that they had to discipline black students more often than white students because the white schools had always had higher and stricter standards of behavior, and blacks had to adjust to this more orderly environment. Dave Dunaway, principal at Greenville High School, believed that part of the mission of having unitary schools was "to upgrade the black pupil," including their deportment. Miriam Vance, a white teacher at Hattiesburg High School, thought that the black students who came to the school after integration "resented discipline and considered suspension for failure to honor 'white' rules of school too radical." These claims that black discipline had not existed at the previously all-black schools seem wildly at odds with the black oral tradition that black schools during the era of segregation maintained strict control of student behavior, often through the liberal use of corporal punishment. Perhaps the conflict between black youth and white educators more truly reflected white resentment at having to deal with students perceived as "inferior." Helen Nicholson, a black teacher at Hattiesburg High School, remembered a different source of conflict between black students and white teachers than the one suggested by her white counterparts. She thought that white teachers often taught just to the white students and ignored the black pupils. To get attention, black students sometimes engaged in disruptive behavior. These students would then be labeled discipline problems and possibly suspended.[25]

The conflicts between black students and white teachers and administrators in the 1970s were undoubtedly heightened by two other important factors. First, these early years of the transition to unitary schools took place at the height of the student movement, when all students, black and white, dressed and acted much differently than students of even a few years earlier. Part of the changing attitudes of students included a greater willingness to challenge all forms of authority, a disposition that surely puzzled and perhaps frightened the older generation of educators. Indeed, black students (and sometimes white students) were often suspended simply for failing to follow personal appearance codes established by the schools.[26] Second, the phenomenon of dealing with more rebellious students was certainly amplified in the setting of unitary school systems that had virtually eliminated all black authority figures.

The first year of school integration was perhaps the most traumatic one for black students. Some of the black children who became involved in the racial conflicts of 1970–71 never recovered. Donnell Monix of Clarksdale, for example, joined in the black student protests at Clarksdale during the first year of school integration. He was arrested and went to jail because of his activism. His mother remembered that her oldest son was traumatized by the experience. "After that year," she recalled, "he didn't go to school anymore." The other nine Monix children who followed Donnell found the experience of integrated schooling in Clarksdale to be much less racially charged; they "didn't have to go through all that stuff."[27]

While daily racial tensions eased somewhat as blacks and whites extended their interaction in the public schools on a regular basis, many integrated schools in Mississippi still experienced racial conflict between black and white students and between black students and white school officials for a number of years after 1970. In Clarksdale, as late as 1973 the local NAACP branch reported that it received "complaints of being treated unfairly" from black students "almost daily." Black students continued to believe that white teachers treated them differently than white students, and the circulation of documents asking white teachers to discriminate against black students and push them out of the public schools did little to allay such fears. In 1972, a document sent to white female teachers in Jackson offered $500 "to any White women responsible for the permanent elimination of Black males from our Public Schools." The suggested method for accomplishing this task was to "maneuver a black male into a compromising position" and then report the incident to school officials, whose names and phone numbers were included in the document. Aaron Henry got hold of a similar document circulating around the state in the years after the beginning of full-scale integration; that document suggested that while whites had lost the battle to preserve dual schools, white teachers could still help the cause by flunking out as many black students as possible. Blacks also believed that whites often displayed little interest in allowing black students to play an equal role in shaping the life of the integrated schools. Participation in extracurricular activities, for instance, continued to be a point of contention in many integrated school districts for years after 1970.[28]

Other controversies arose over what blacks perceived as white attempts to stamp out unwanted expressions of the "black way" of doing things or the black perspective. Clarksdale is a good example. In February 1973, three black male students were expelled by the Clarksdale school board after they pressed, yet again, for a black history observance. After Clarksdale High School authorities denied a request from the school's black students for the program, three boys organized the assembly without permission, a program 127 students at the school attended. The three were expelled for the remainder of the year; all were accomplished students, one with a college scholarship already in hand. The local NAACP took the matter to court, and a federal judge eventually reinstated the three boys and required the school to stage the black history event, but not before the three boys had missed over a month of school. In 1978, one of the black members of Clarksdale's biracial committee, busily involved in talks with whites about the contours of biracial education in the city, was shocked by how white school officials structured the annual commencement ceremony. In a graduating class that included ninety blacks and sixty whites, the ceremony involved no blacks in the program. White students directed the processional, gave the welcoming comments, and introduced the speaker; in addition, "Every single program personality was white."[29]

One of the most serious points of contention between blacks and whites in the aftermath of school integration was the grouping of students by abilities, or tracking. This practice was widely adopted throughout the South in conjunction with school integration; by the 1973–74 school year, two-thirds of Mississippi's school districts utilized ability grouping. The policy might have actually represented a real remedy for boosting lagging black educational performance caused by years of second-rate schools and instructional materials and poorly trained teachers, assuming that the notions of white supremacy that historically produced such unequal educational opportunities for whites and blacks no longer existed. In Mississippi, such attitudes clearly did not disappear just because the federal courts ordered unitary school systems. In fact, many whites at the time school integration began still believed intellectual ability was racially determined. One Avon woman lamented in 1970 that "quality education" was impossible in integrated schools when "the blacks are so dumb and so behind the teachers are having to go back and try to catch them up." Many Mississippi whites believed in the innate connection between race and intellectual ability expressed by a Jackson man in 1970: "Years of educational research has proved that there is a distinct gap in learning capacity between the races. A teaching program suited to one race is not suited to the other. . . . Education will still progress best where students are assigned according to their race, character, desire, and *ability*." Because of these beliefs that blacks were "inferior" intellectually, whites blamed the end of dual schools for declining educational standards in the public schools; this "fact" then provided a further rationale for whites to distance themselves from blacks in all matters involving learning. Thomas J. Tubb of West Point thought that with school integration, "Our school standards are gone. . . . I'm sure that's all over Mississippi where you have a heavy black population." Former governor John Bell Williams described school integration to an interviewer in 1974 as "a very, very bad and almost impossible situation." One of the by-products of this disaster, according to Williams, was that "the quality of instruction and learning in our public schools now has suffered a very visible decline, a deterioration."[30]

In reality, whites in integrated schools did come in contact with black students who had been subjected to a second-class education in the all-black schools of the dual education era. In addition to complaining about a problem they had largely created, however, white Mississippians mistakenly faulted school integration as *the* educational apocalypse. Most social science research in the three decades after school integration, however, did not back up the impressions of white Mississippians about the impact of school integration on educational achievement. Study after study concluded that the impact of school integration on black and white achievement was negligible, having only a limited positive effect on black students and almost no discernable consequence for the educational accomplishments of white students. At the same time, white Mississippians tended to ignore broader changes that affected public education during the years of transition to unitary schools. For instance, all levels of education throughout the United States seemingly experienced a "dumbing down" of educational standards during the 1970s and 1980s, and this transformation obviously had a number of political, social, and economic causes unrelated to school integration.[31]

As long as beliefs of innate black intellectual inferiority persisted among whites in Mississippi—and they still persist today, not only in Mississippi but throughout the United States—having whites in the state determine black "abilities" for the purpose of differential instruction and devising remedies for eliminating the disparities remained highly questionable. Mississippi state NAACP chairman Aaron Henry suggested in 1969 that he could level the playing field by designing an achievement test himself: "I'd talk about chitlins and two rooms and a path versus six rooms and a bath. I'd talk about black-eyed peas and collard greens and the whites wouldn't know nothing."[32]

Whatever educational possibilities ability grouping might have held in the abstract, in the aftermath of school integration in Mississippi, school districts that turned to tracking students frequently seemed more concerned about using the device to maintain racial segregation than with improving the performance of students with weaker skills. For example, in the Delta town of Drew, school officials located special education classes for "slower" students in a separate school building. These classes were largely filled with black children, assigned not on the basis of some form of testing but because of the way certain black children were dressed or after others had been disciplined for some violation of school rules. Like the Drew schools, other school districts sometimes created their "slow" classes simply based on teacher recommendations. Especially in the first several years after school integration, these appraisals often came from white teachers who at best had less interest in the black students than the white students and at worst considered all black children to have inferior brains compared to their white counterparts. Many school districts, however, did use achievement tests to develop their tracking hierarchies, and black students typically scored lower than white children. Convinced that such testing proved the innate intellectual disparities between blacks and whites, Mississippi school officials utilized ability grouping as a way to warehouse the weakest black students in dead-end remedial classes. Such a practice merely reinforced the white view of black intelligence in the students slotted for the "slow" class; these students were often stigmatized at an early age as mental failures. In a sense, the integrated schools of the 1970s, with their segregated tracking systems, simply wrote off a whole generation of slow black learners. Many of these students simply gave up. In the 1970s, Mississippi had a serious problem with students dropping out of school; nearly fifteen thousand a year left before graduation, almost 75 percent of whom were black children.[33]

Tracking of students, as practiced in Mississippi schools subsequent to integration, failed to consider that the disparity between black and white intellectual abilities was not the result of genetics but rather was caused by the centuries of oppression and discrimination blacks had endured during slavery and segregation. Such a realization would have required school districts to devote maximum effort and resources to diminishing the inequities. Perhaps the integrated schools should have adopted the model of the black segregated schools, which had been among the first promoters—though without the necessary resources—of the "no child left behind" idea. Instead, relatively half-hearted efforts characterized the remedial education that many blacks were now consigned to receive. At Greenville's high school in the early 1970s, for example, the largely white "smart" sections of English had a significantly lower student-teacher ratio than the overwhelmingly black "slow" sections, not exactly the best deployment of the instructional staff if the strategy was to help slow learners catch up with their smarter peers. Federal Title I programs provided additional funds for remedial classes, but school districts used little of their own resources to attract their best and brightest teachers to staff these classrooms.[34]

If school integration often worked to marginalize black students, the impact of the transition to unitary schools on black school employees was even more dramatic. Indeed, the loss of jobs or status by black teachers and administrators represented perhaps the most unmistakable evidence that the wholesale integration of schools occurred on white terms. C. J. Duckworth, executive secretary of the black MTA, reasoned in late 1969 that "if you need [black teachers] today with the dual system, you will need them tomorrow with a unified system." But such logic did not anticipate the white flight that accompanied the school integration of 1970. Declining public school enrollments meant that teaching staffs had to be reduced. In districts that became all-black, the number of black teachers actually increased, as white teachers voluntarily abandoned the system, but in many other locales, black teachers lost their jobs as school integration became a reality. While integration also displaced some white teachers, black educators ultimately became the primary victims of diminished enrollments caused by the white abandonment of the public schools. Overall, between 1970 and 1973, the number of white public school teachers in the state increased by almost 9 percent, while the number of black public school teachers fell by almost 12 percent.[35]

Some school officials used the opportunity of the conversion to a unitary school system to weed out black teachers perceived as poorly qualified; other white administrators sought to rid their districts of teachers who had supported the civil rights movement. Most white school leaders paid little attention to the qualifications of black teachers until school integration became an inescapable reality in late 1969. Assistant state superintendent W. S. Griffin admitted that the concern over the training of black teachers only drew notice once they started "teaching the white kids." This new interest in the abilities of black teachers was manifested in some newly integrated schools by not allowing them to teach certain subjects, especially English and math. Many other school districts, however, tried to scale back the number of black teachers by suddenly adopting more rigorous, "objective" forms of teacher evaluation. While the new plans often relied on supposedly impartial standardized tests, such as the NTE or Graduate Record Examination (GRE), the white-controlled school districts that adopted these instruments did not necessarily use these measures of teacher ability in a race-neutral way.[36]

A good example is what happened in the Starkville public schools. In March 1968, after HEW turned down the district's school desegregation plan, the school board adopted policy 13-69, requiring all teachers to make a certain NTE or GRE score, unless they held a master of arts degree. The school superintendent, B. Hall Buchanan, later admitted that the district, which had only sent a couple of black instructors to teach in the white schools prior to mandated integration, adopted policy 13-69 over concern about black teachers instructing white children and in the belief that blacks would generally score low on the standardized tests. Although policy 13-69 had been adopted in 1968, it was not actually implemented until the spring of 1970, after the *Alexander* mandate for integrated schools. Among the teachers who left the Starkville system at the end of the 1969–70 school year were nine white and sixteen black teachers, released because they did not meet the newly implemented requirements of 13-69. The district had to hire thirty-two new teachers for the 1970–71 school year, and all the instructors hired were white, even though at least six of the black applicants had the requisite test scores.[37] Despite Superintendent Buchanan's beliefs, standardized tests did not prove to be a panacea for ensuring the elimination of black teachers, at least not if fairly applied as an "objective" measure of teacher competency.

Black school teachers who supported the civil rights movement had long felt the wrath of white school officials, and the reduction in the teaching staff necessitated by the white flight of 1970 offered whites yet another opportunity to purge the schools of black teachers who favored changes in the racial status quo. Even after the *Alexander* decision, school superintendents still retained lists of local blacks who favored school integration, rosters to be consulted when hiring and firing black educators.[38] After *Alexander*, however, no superintendent could explicitly fail to rehire a teacher because of his or her support of school integration; rather, white educators seeking to rid their districts of perceived racial "troublemakers" simply labeled such teachers as ineffective, a hard accusation to disprove, as Don Jennings of Meridian discovered in 1970. Although L. O. Todd, superintendent of the Meridian schools, claimed that his district's failure to rehire science teacher Jennings after the first semester of school integration (spring term 1970) was solely "because of incompetence," much of the evidence suggests that Jennings's support for a student boycott at the newly integrated Northwest Junior High during April 1970 likely played a more prominent role in the school authorities' decision to dispense with his services. Jennings had taught in the Meridian schools for nine years, all at the black schools until the midyear reshuffling in January 1970, when he was transferred to Northwest Junior High, previously a predominantly white school. After two months at his new school, his new principal, George Cannon, told him that he would be rehired. That promise of support turned to a recommendation of nonrenewal following the walkout of twenty-four black students at Northwest a month later. Many of the students came from Jennings's first-period class, the time the walkout began, and Cannon accused Jennings "of having a direct hand in the boycotting and other demonstrations." Jennings denied any prior knowledge of the walkout, though he admitted that he sympathized with the students' grievances, which revolved around a variety of complaints about the treatment of black students at Northwest. When Cannon failed to recommend the renewal of Jennings's teaching contract in

May 1970, the principal cited as the reason that Jennings's teaching was "weak." Other evidence, however, suggested that Jennings was a valuable member of the Meridian teaching corps. He had won several teaching awards while at all-black Magnolia, and after his transfer to Northwest, he had been selected to attend a summer course at the University of Southern Mississippi to learn how to teach a new science class.[39]

While the loss of black teachers associated with the beginnings of school integration was quite significant, the wholesale dismissal of black administrators was even more stunning. Obviously, unitary school systems did not need two sets of administrators, but the solution devised in 1970 meant the almost complete elimination of black principals. In 1969–70, Mississippi had 168 black secondary school principals; that figure had declined to 19 by the 1970–71 school year. School districts generally demoted or reassigned black principals rather than fire them, many becoming assistant principals or classroom teachers or given impressive-sounding though essentially meaningless titles, such as director of buildings and grounds. Decisions about whether to employ a white or black principal in the new unitary schools did not always turn on the question of qualifications. In Rankin County, a white coach with no administrative experience replaced one black principal. At Okolona High School, a white counselor received the top job over a black principal with a master of arts degree and fifteen years administrative experience.[40] In addition to the loss of jobs caused by these displacements, both black and white students in integrated schools received the not-so-subtle message that only whites could be leaders.

The elimination of black teachers and administrators continued to be a problem throughout the 1970s. Although the number of Mississippi public school teachers increased over the course of the decade, the number of black teachers in the state's schools increased at a much smaller rate than the growth of the white teaching corps. In the 1967–68 school year, black teachers had comprised 42 percent of all educators in public schools; by 1978–79 that figure had dropped to 37 percent. When black teachers retired or moved, they were frequently replaced by whites. In Vicksburg, for example, a district that in 1976 had a black student enrollment of 72 percent, practically all of the new teachers hired between 1973 and 1976 were white; by the latter year, over half of the teachers were white. Much of the decline among black teachers in the state was related to the method of recruiting new teachers. In many locales, vacancies were rarely formally announced; new teachers typically found their jobs by "word of mouth referrals." Since most administrators were white, they often did not hear about the qualified black teachers looking for jobs. Blacks also remained shut out of much of not only school administration but also counseling and extracurricular leadership jobs such as coaching sports teams and directing bands, in other words, all positions of authority. By the end of the 1970s, in a state with a slight black-majority student population (54 percent), only one in five principals and assistant principals was black, only one in four guidance counselors was black, and only one in twelve coaches, band directors, and so forth was black. In Vicksburg during the 1976–77 school year, there were no black principals or assistant principals, although the district did have a black tennis coach and black band director. For many white parents who continued to send their children to integrated schools, student integration was only tolerable as long as whites continued to hold most positions of authority in the unitary schools and as long as most of their children continued to receive instruction and supervision from white educators.[41]

The end of school segregation did represent an achievement for black Mississippians. As Fred Banks, an NAACP attorney who litigated many school cases, explained, the school integration fight was "the major thrust in breaking the back of governmental apartheid" in Mississippi, an accomplishment that ultimately "affected other aspects of our society" and "had ramifications way beyond just education." Despite the necessity for dismantling segregated schools and the positive impact the change had on altering the racial foundations of Mississippi society, as the process of converting Mississippi's dual system of education to a unitary system unfolded in 1970 and the years that followed, many black Mississippians perceived that achieving their goal of ending school segregation was in many ways a pyrrhic victory. Whites generally offered black citizens little input on how the conversion should proceed, even in areas where only a few whites remained in the public schools. As a result, the transition to a unitary school system primarily revolved around ways either to continue to preserve some semblance of segregation in integrated schools or shield whites from the perceived negative impact of having to attend biracial schools. Many blacks ultimately despaired over the way school integration occurred, and some even called for a return to separate but this time truly equal education. For example, Doretta Boston of Buena Vista thought in 1970 that "since it is like it is, they don't want to be with us and we don't want to be with them, it ought to be a letter sent to Washington asking for our part. They build their schools and if we could get the money to build ours and get the things we need to go in them, it wouldn't be all this upsteam." Hezekiah Braddock of Tippah County in northeast Mississippi agreed that there "won't be a bit of harm" in separate but equal education, as long as "[i]t could be equally divided and equal opportunity to each school." On further reflection, however, Braddock concluded that such arrangements would not work for the same reasons they never had in the past: black schools would always be "deprived" of their fair share of educational resources.[42]

While the dual school system was eliminated in 1970, blacks for much of the 1970s faced what Rims Barber, who worked for the Delta Ministry, called "a new discriminatory system," one where whites exercised almost complete control over the unitary schools, eliminated black teachers and administrators, adopted draconian disciplinary policies for black children, and segregated black students through tracking procedures. Many black Mississippians came to realize, in the words of a veteran of school desegregation litigation in Mississippi, Derrick Bell, that segregation was merely a symptom of white racism, which could be "as viable and as pernicious a force for harming the hearts and minds of Black children in a racially balanced school as it ever was under . . . 'separate but equal.'" Ultimately, the problem in Mississippi in 1970, and in the years that followed, was that the state, under duress, created a unitary school system, but black and white education was not truly integrated. Looking back on the transition of 1970 from the vantage point of 1974, Harry Bowie, who had also worked with the Delta Ministry, summed up the problem: "We've massively integrated the school system in Mississippi. . . . We have not accomplished massive integration in the truest sense. We still have a great deal to do on that front."[43]

EPILOGUE

In December 1982, the Mississippi legislature, meeting in special session, passed the Education Reform Act of 1982. The legislation provided $106 million of new money—during a recession—for public kindergartens, a 10 percent pay raise for public school teachers, and the placement of reading aides in the public schools. The law also reinstated the compulsory education requirement abolished after the *Brown* decision, tightened teacher certification requirements, and reorganized the State Department of Education. New sales and income taxes financed the reforms. Governor William Winter was the driving force behind this sweeping education package. Winter had pressed for the changes after becoming governor in 1980, but an initial attempt to pass the reforms during the 1981 legislative session had gone down to defeat. The proposed kindergartens generated the most opposition. Both religious fundamentalists and some outspoken white supremacists resisted state sponsorship of early education, the former on the grounds that families should provide such instruction and the latter because they "didn't want preschool age white and black children mixed." Despite the early setback, Governor Winter persevered and took his cause to the people of Mississippi. He campaigned tirelessly across the state, holding community meetings and delivering scores of speeches. He found Mississippians "standing up for what is good for Mississippi in the Education bill," and a groundswell of popular support for the education act brought initially reluctant legislators back to Jackson in December 1982 for a special session to reconsider and ultimately pass the reform legislation.[1]

While education reform succeeded in large part because of the political skill and determination of Governor Winter and his staff, the measures never would have become law without biracial support for the reforms among Mississippi's citizens, most of whom continued to send their children to public schools. Despite the initial flight from the public schools in 1970, the number of white Mississippians who turned to private education to avoid school integration never exceeded 10 percent; in 1999, almost 91 percent of Mississippi school children still attended public schools.[2]

In fact, beyond the Delta and some of the state's largest urban areas, where the white exodus from public education was sometimes total, most whites had stayed with the public schools after 1970, even if they objected to the principle of school integration and how it had been forced on the state. As a result, in 1981 and 1982 many whites saw the battle over Governor Winter's education measures as a referendum on the preservation and improvement of their state's public school system in the postintegration era. Ted Alexander, the leader of the Mississippi Association of School Superintendents, believed the act demonstrated that "we've had racial disorder and disharmony, but we are willing to make this kind of investment for black children in Mississippi, for white children in Mississippi." A history teacher from Brookhaven noted that "Mississippi's public education is in a contest with private education and we've got to win. What the governor's program says is public education is going to survive and do well." Robert Fortenberry, superintendent of the Jackson city schools, called the legislation "a recommitment on the part of the public to public education." Much of the opposition to Governor Winter's attempt to improve public education came from private school supporters, who, according to one white observer, used arguments against the reforms that "had a racial overtone." Even the discussion over how to fund the education program in part revolved around what opponents of the improvements saw as a contest between public and private education for the hearts and minds of whites in the state. Governor Winter had originally proposed that an oil and gas severance tax pay for most of the program, but conservative legislators, such as Ellis Bodron of Vicksburg, had successfully argued for the use of the sales and income taxes. Bodron believed that since "[t]he primary beneficiaries [of the education legislation] will be people who cannot afford to put their children in private schools," they should pay for the improvements.[3]

White opponents of Governor Winter's education reform program such as Bodron saw the program as primarily designed to improve the public schools for whites who unfortunately had to send their children to such institutions. Interestingly, Bodron's calculations did not consider that black Mississippians might also derive some benefit from the reforms. Yet black Mississippians typically believed that the momentous legislation of 1982 represented a positive step forward for them. It promised to improve public education in the state, long a goal of the generations of black men and women who had agitated for better schooling for their children. Aaron Henry, long-time state leader of the NAACP and a member of the state legislature in 1982, claimed that "this legislation is color blind. It will have, I think, a tremendous impact upon the academic strength of the whole population."[4]

Did the passage of the Education Reform Act in 1982 signal that Mississippi, despite its long battle to preserve a dual education system for whites and blacks in the state, had successfully made the transition to a unitary school system? How one answers that question depends on the standard of comparison. The striking scope of change was, in many ways, undeniable. The convening of a special session in 1982 to appropriate public funds to improve a unitary public school system was certainly a far cry from the special sessions of the legislature Mississippi governors regularly assembled in the 1950s and 1960s to devise ways to preserve segregated education and waste the state's precious funds on the mirage of dual schooling. In the late 1990s and into the twenty-first century, the state legislature continued to support pro–public education legislation, passing another major reform, the Adequate Education Program, designed to equalize funding between the state's richest and poorest school districts and committing to a multiyear program to boost the salaries of teachers in the public schools. Also, by the 1980s, outside of the Mississippi Delta and a number of urban areas, blacks and whites in many small towns and rural districts attended school together in some of the nation's most integrated schools, a remarkable development in a state that had spent so many years and wasted so much money fighting to save segregated schooling.[5]

On the other hand, a perfectly integrated unitary education system had not been created in Mississippi by 1982. The long struggle between black and white Mississippians to define the nature of public education persisted. Indeed, throughout the next two decades, racial battles in the state's integrated schools continued to break out sporadically over a number of issues, everything from claims of racially motivated hiring of school personnel to accusations of racial discrimination directed at black students, from charges of whites illegally crossing school boundary lines to get into whiter schools to the clustering of white children within certain classrooms at black-majority schools.[6] In addition, as in much of the country, some school districts in Mississippi, which had integrated under federal pressure in 1970, had begun to resegregate by the 1990s. In recent years, several studies have noted the increasing resegregation of public schools throughout the United States. In large part, this trend developed because of evolving court decisions on what constituted successful school integration. By the early 1990s, a more conservative Supreme Court completed the retreat from the *Alexander* decision's requirement for racially balanced schools, ruling that racially identifiable schools were permissible if the racial characteristics of these schools were created solely because of seemingly nonracial factors, such as housing patterns.[7]

In Mississippi, such decisions had little effect in the most rural parts of the state, where segregated living arrangements generally did not exist, and in much of the Delta, where the relatively small white population of most communities meant there was little chance for the establishment of white-majority schools, whatever housing patterns might exist. As in many other parts of the South, the trend toward resegregation was most notable in urban areas. The arguments advanced in the immediate aftermath of forced school integration about the sanctity of neighborhood schools ultimately prevailed. In a number of Mississippi cities outside the state's black-majority areas, the neighborhood became increasingly black in the thirty years after the beginning of school integration, as whites fled to nearby county systems that had sizable white populations (see table 5). Although the 1982 Education Reform Act had sought to prevent this kind of resegregation, that effort failed. The legislation commissioned a study through the State Educational Finance Committee, which generated a school reorganization plan that proposed to combine Mississippi's 154 school districts into 91. While the plan would not have tried to combine a very large school district, like Jackson, with neighboring county systems, the proposal would have mandated the combination of separate school districts in small cities with neighboring county districts. For instance, under the committee's recommendations, Hattiesburg would have been merged with both the Petal and Forrest County school districts. The result would have undoubtedly been more integrated schools for the Hattiesburg area, which had an educational landscape that included a largely black Hattiesburg system and the largely white Petal and Forrest County systems.

Table 5. Comparison of White Public School Enrollment in Mississippi Cities, 1968–69 and 2001–2

School district	Percentage white enrollment, 1968–69	Percentage white enrollment, 2001–2
Biloxi	86	55
Brookhaven	58	39
Columbus	58	18
Hattiesburg	55	11
Jackson	54	4
Laurel	53	13
McComb	49	21
Starkville	54	32

Sources: MEA Statistics, 1968–69, RG 48, vol. 185, MDAH; 2001–2 Mississippi Report Card, available at http://www.mde.k12.ms.us/Account/RC2B/RC2b.htm (accessed on July 29, 2004).

The committee's recommendations, however, never received serious consideration by the legislature, perhaps precisely because they would have eliminated what had become one of the most effective ways that some communities could maintain some semblance of separate schools in the post–school integration era.[8]

By the 1990s, black Mississippians had conceded that some school districts in the state would never be racially integrated. Of course, the goal for blacks had never been the abstract principle of integrated schools; rather, unitary schools were seen as the only way to ensure that resources spent on education in Mississippi were equally distributed to benefit both black and white students. When school districts that were ordered to integrate began to resegregate because of the flight of white students, black leaders were often quick to approve less integration in favor of assurances that improvements to black education would continue. In Jackson, that compromise came just five years after school integration began. After most whites left the Jackson public schools in the early 1970s, black leaders proposed a revised settlement in 1975, one that permitted an end to the busing of white students to inner-city, black-majority schools in exchange for guarantees from the school board that additional funds would be spent to improve those black-majority schools and that changes would be made to "school district employment policies" that had diminished the number of black teachers and administrators in the district.

In 1983, after years of struggling first to eliminate dual schools and then to make integrated schooling work fairly, Aaron Henry and other black leaders in Clarksdale gave their blessing to a return to neighborhood elementary schools, a move that brought more whites back to the public schools but that ultimately created a resegregated school system. In exchange for agreeing to the new plan, the Clarksdale school district agreed to employ more black teachers, administrators, and coaches and renamed one of the junior highs after a prominent black educator.[9]

In Hattiesburg, although the school district had to abandon its neighborhood elementary school plan in 1987 because of a court challenge, the district was released from court oversight in the late 1990s and decided to reinstate the neighborhood elementary school arrangements in 1999. While almost all whites remaining in the district supported the plan, blacks in the town were divided on the change. Some believed that crosstown busing made little sense in a district that was largely black anyway. Others, however, worried that the schools that had the most white students, like Thames Elementary, would receive more resources than the schools with only black children. A biracial committee, with the black members appointed in part by the NAACP and the SCLC, was created to oversee the transition to neighborhood schools and ensure that it proceeded fairly.[10]

As in Hattiesburg, blacks elsewhere in the state remain divided on whether the resegregation of the public schools that has occurred since the 1970s is a good or bad development. Certainly, eliminating separate schools in Mississippi was an absolutely necessary objective, not only for ensuring improvements in black education but also for ending the wasteful duplication of educational services that Mississippi's limited resources could never afford and, in the process, improving public education for all Mississippians. While the transition from separate schooling to integrated education has not been a total failure, it has not been a total success either. The resesegregation of education in some communities of the state and the lingering battles over the persistence of racial discrimination in integrated schools at the beginning of the twenty-first century highlight the fact that not all white Mississippians have yet accommodated themselves to the idea that integrated schools can provide quality education, especially when white students are in the minority.

The shortcomings of the process of school integration have been felt most sharply by black Mississippians, so it is not surprising that many now remember the days of segregated schooling with a certain amount of nostalgia, as almost a golden age of black education.[11] Some scholars, such as Derrick Bell, a law professor who worked on school desegregation cases for black plaintiffs in the 1960s, have even suggested that blacks would have been better served had the U.S. Supreme Court in 1954 moved to enforce the separate but equal doctrine rather than require integrated education.[12] To be sure, separate black schools during the years of racial segregation did provide valuable education to black youth, despite the massive obstacles they faced. And there is no reason to doubt that, with adequate and equitable funding, black Mississippians could have received a top-quality education in one-race schools. However, the history of public education in Mississippi makes clear that the state would have resisted the demand to make separate education truly equal with as much vigor as it opposed the call for an end to segregated schools. In fact, even as Mississippi fought all efforts between 1954 and 1970 to end its system of dual schools, the state tried but failed to equalize white and black education, because of both a lack of resources and a lack of will.

Ideally, the project of public education in a state with Mississippi's demographic makeup would be a biracial concern. However, as long as significant numbers of Mississippi whites remain convinced that their children cannot be educated adequately in an environment populated by significant numbers of black students, that ideal will remain unrealized. After a century of struggle over integrated education, a deplorable system for educating Mississippi youth was destroyed, but the long-anticipated solution of school integration has proved, in many ways, equally unworkable. Ultimately, the state of Mississippi can only advance when all of its citizens receive an adequate education. How that will be achieved is almost as unclear as when the enterprise of public education was first conceived during Reconstruction.

NOTES

INTRODUCTION

1. Although most of the evidence suggests that about ten blacks were injured during the riot, some reports at the time suggested that the number of injured children was significantly higher, as many as forty. See, for example, "The South: Intruders in the Dust," *Time*, September 23, 1966, 26.

2. Gale Wilborn, September 21, 1966; unidentified black child involved in the September 12 march to the white schools, September 21, 1966; unidentified black parent involved in the September 12 march to the white schools, September 21, 1966; and A. Rosen to Mr. Deloach, September 13, 1966, all in FBI-GRN; "Trials: 'I Never Hit Nobody,'" *Time*, June 16, 1967, 48; Rosie Washington, interview by Worth Long, April 2, 2000, Civil Rights Documentation Project: The Grenada Movement, TCA. The beating of the black workers and the delivery of metal pipes to the mob were witnessed by an unidentified white man. See the statement of this individual to the FBI, September 21, 1966, FBI-GRN.

3. James Bonney, "School Mix Brings Grenada Violence," *Jackson (Miss.) Clarion-Ledger*, September 13, 1966; "Trials"; injury report furnished by Battle Rankin, n.d.; Richard Sigh, September 21, 1966; and two unidentified FBI agents, both dated September 21, 1996, all in FBI-GRN.

4. Robert Gordon, September 21, 1966; Jack Cantrell and Jim Reid, September 15, 1966; unidentified white man, September 21, 1966; and unidentified Grenada County policeman, September 19, 1966, all in FBI-GRN.

5. Unidentified white man, September 21, 1966; unidentified FBI agent, September 21, 1996; Sheriff Suggs Ingram, September 27, 1966; unidentified Grenada city policeman, September 23, 1966; unidentified Grenada County policeman, September 19, 1966; Robert Gordon, September 21, 1966; three unidentified white women, all dated September 21, 1966; unidentified white woman, September 19, 1966, all in FBI-GRN; Homer Bigart, "Grenada Official Gets Jail Term," *New York Times*, September 17, 1966.

6. Charles E. Sondgrass, "Grenada Detail," [September 1966], Box 148, PBJ; report of A. D. Morgan, September 16, 1966; and FBI report, September 30, 1966, both in FBI-GRN; Charles Edmundson, "Hasty Desegregation, Pressure of Marches Struck Violent Spark, Says Ex-City Manager," *Memphis Commercial Appeal*, September 14, 1966; "Grenada Whites Condemn Recent Racial Violence," *Jackson (Miss.) Daily News*, September 21, 1966; "Petition Hits Mix Violence in Grenada," *Jackson (Miss.) Clarion Ledger*, September 21, 1966.

7. "Petition Hits Mix Violence in Grenada"; John Bell Williams to Mrs. Walter L. McMullen, September 19, 1966, RG 59, vol. 204, MDAH; David J. Garrow, *Bearing the Cross: Martin Luther King Jr., and the Southern Christian Leadership Conference* (New York: William Morrow, 1986), 530–31; Andrew Jaffe, "Grenada, Mississippi: Perspective on the Backlash," *New South* 21 (Fall 1966): 15–27.

8. James Bonney, "Negro, White Crowds Dispersed at Grenada," *Jackson (Miss.) Clarion-Ledger*, July 11, 1966; Bill Crider, "City Officials Refuse Grenada CR Demands," *Jackson (Miss.) Clarion Ledger*, July 12, 1966; Informative Note, July 15, 1966; and Memo to the FBI Director, August 11, 1966, both in FBI-GRN; Highway Patrol Reports, September 2, 1966, Box 148, PBJ; Henry Peacock III, interview by Worth Long, April 2, 2000, transcript, Civil Rights Documentation Project: The Grenada Movement. Sovereignty Commission investigators were surprised to find that local black educators had played a leadership role in the development of the Grenada movement. See Roger Baker, "Memo on Grenada," September 30, 1966; and Sovereignty Commission Report, October 31, 1966, both in LF.

9. Report to the Director, September 13, 1966; and Report of Elizabeth Payton, September 21, 1966, both in FBI-GRN; telegram from Elmer Lower (ABC News president) to Governor Paul B. Johnson, September 13, 1966, Box 148, PBJ; "Sunday Was Peaceful in Race-Tense Area," *Jackson (Miss.) Clarion-Ledger*, September 19, 1966; "Trials."

10. Buck Wells, interview by Lawrence Kight, May 6, 1997, transcript, vol. 694, MOHP.

11. For an account of these discussions, see Peter Schrag, "The Near-Myth of Our Failing Schools," *Atlantic Monthly*, October 1997, 72–80.

CHAPTER 1

1. William W. Winter, interview by Orley B. Caudill, August 9, 1978, transcript, vol. 417, MOHP.

2. Annie Stewart, interview by Worth Long, March 22, 2000, transcript, Civil Rights Documentation Project: The Grenada Movement.

3. Edward Mayes, *History of Education in Mississippi* (Washington, D.C.: Government Printing Office, 1899), 278–82.

4. Report of T. Sargent Free to Col. Samuel Thomas, August 31, 1865; and State Superintendent's Annual School Report, August 4, 1867, both in MS-FB, reel 37; Joseph Warren to Lt. Stuart Eldridge, November 15, 1865, Letters Sent by Mississippi Superintendent

of Education, vol. 49, RG 105, NA; Monthly Reports of Subcommissioners, October 1865, MS-FB, Box 32; William C. Harris, *Presidential Reconstruction in Mississippi* (Baton Rouge: Louisiana State University Press, 1967), 84–86.

5. W. F. Smith, ed., "The Yankees in New Albany: Letter of Elizabeth Jane Beach, July 29, 1864," *Journal of Mississippi History* 2 (January 1940): 46; William C. Harris, "A Reconsideration of the Mississippi Scalawag," *Journal of Mississippi History* 32 (Spring 1970): 12–13; Robert W. Flournoy, *Testimony Taken by the Joint Select Committee to Inquire into the Condition of Affairs in the Late Insurrectionary States, Mississippi, 1871,* June 28, 1871, 42nd Congress, 2nd. Sess., U.S. Senate Reports.

6. Edward Fontaine to Maj. Gen. L. J. Wood, October 8, 1866; E. Kibbe to W. K. Douglas, October 28, 1866; and J. F. H. Claiborne to Maj. Preston, September 10, 1866, all in MS-FB, reels 13 and 14; William Preston Vaughn, *Schools For All: The Blacks and Public Education in the South, 1865–1877* (Lexington: University Press of Kentucky, 1974), 42.

7. Vaughn, 43; Joseph Warren to Lt. Stuart Eldridge, November 15, 1865; and Joseph Warren to Carl Schurz, November 28, 1865, both in Letters Sent by the Mississippi Superintendent of Education, vol. 49, RG 105, NA; R. F. Campbell to Col. Thomas, April 5, 1866; and Affidavit of John Field, September 4, 1866, both in MS-FB, reel 13; M. E. Gill to Rev. Edward P. Smith, June 17, 1869, Box 92, American Missionary Association Archives, ARC; Rev. J. P. Bardwell, "Mississippi," *American Missionary* 10 (October 1866): 219.

8. Henry Allen Bullock, *A History of Negro Education in the South* (New York: Praeger, 1967), 43; Margaret Hughes Fitzgerald, "Negro Education in Mississippi during Reconstruction" (master's thesis, Mississippi College, 1972), 25–28.

9. Fitzgerald, 41; "A Synopsis of Chapter 1, General Laws of Mississippi, 1870 which is the Reconstruction Act setting up the Public School System of the State," Box 2, J. M. Tubb Papers, MDAH; *Senate Journal*, 1870, 436–40.

10. William C. Harris, *Day of the Carpetbagger: Republican Reconstruction in Mississippi* (Baton Rouge: Louisiana State University Press, 1979), 311–52; S. H. Champney to Rev. Cravath, November 20, 1873, Box 92, American Missionary Association Archives; 1872 Reports from County Superintendents of Education, in *Senate Journal*, 1873, 806–916; Fitzgerald, 65–71.

11. Allen W. Trelease, *White Terror: The Ku Klux Klan Conspiracy and Southern Reconstruction* (Baton Rouge: Louisiana State University Press, 1971), 294–96; *Testimony Taken by the Joint Select Committee to Inquire into the Condition of Affairs in the Late Insurrectionary States, Mississippi, 1871,* 42nd Congress, 2nd. Sess., U.S. Senate Reports.

12. WPA History, Tunica County (microfilm).

13. Quoted in Johnny L. Harris, "A Historical Analysis of Educational, Economic, and Political Change in Fayette, Mississippi, from 1954 to 1971" (Ed.D. diss., Florida State University, 1972), 39.

14. Thomas W. Cardoza Collection, ARC; "Testimony of C. E. Bent," January 26, 1876, RG 47, vol. 53, MDAH; T. S. Wood to M. E. Strieby, January 17, 1876, Box 92, American Missionary Association Archives; Eric Foner, *Reconstruction,*

1863–1877: America's Unfinished Revolution, 1863–1877 (New York: Harper and Row, 1988), 588–89; C. Vann Woodward, *Origins of the New South, 1877–1913* (Baton Rouge: Louisiana State University Press, 1951), 61–63.

15. *Laws of the State of Mississippi, 1878* (Jackson, Miss.: Power and Barksdale, 1878), 103; Stuart Grayson Noble, *Forty Years of the Public Schools of Mississippi, with a Special Reference to the Education of the Negro* (New York: Teachers College, Columbia University, 1918), 53–54.

16. "Mississippi Teachers Association," Subject File, MDAH; *Proceedings of the State Teachers' Association of Mississippi at Its Annual Meeting, 1887* (Jackson, Miss.: The Association, 1888); *Proceedings of the State Teachers' Association of Mississippi at Its Annual Meeting, 1889* (Jackson, Miss.: The Association, 1890); Lewis William Godlove, "History of the MEA" (Ed.D. diss., University of Mississippi, 1961), 52–62; Cleopatra D. Thompson, *The History of the Mississippi Teachers Association* (Jackson: Mississippi Teachers Association, 1973).

17. *Senate Journal, 1873*, 848–49; Jackson School System, Board of Trustees Minutes, December 1, 2, 1882, reel 1, MDAH; 1880 Manuscript Census for Hinds County, Mississippi. The 1869 law is quoted in Carroll Brinson, *Jackson/A Special Kind of Place* (Jackson, Miss.: City of Jackson, 1977), 128.

18. Jackson School System, Board of Trustees Minutes, September 3, 1887, July 5, 1888, reel 1, MDAH.

19. *School Law of Mississippi, 1892* (n.p.); correspondence and newspaper clippings, July 1892; and minutes of September 22, 1892, meeting, both in Jackson School System, Board of Trustees Minutes, reel 1, MDAH.

20. *Charles C. Chrisman, et al. v. Mayor and Board of Aldermen of Brookhaven, et al.* (1893), complaint, RG 32, case file #7284, MDAH; *C. C. Chrisman, et al. v. City of Brookhaven*, 70 Mississippi 477 (1893). The lead plaintiff in this case, Charles C. Chrisman, was actually a white man who sued the city over the bond issue on different grounds, claiming that some of the bonds had been sold to a city alderman and some to a school trustee.

21. Richard Kluger, *Simple Justice: The History of Brown v. Board of Education and Black America's Struggle for Equality* (New York: Knopf, 1976), 83.

22. Report by S. D. Redmond (Chairman, Steering Committee for Improved Higher Education for Negroes in Mississippi) to Governor Thomas L. Bailey et al., [1940s], Box 2, Kenneth Toler Papers, MSU; "Education in Mississippi," 1904, Box 4, Southern Education Board Records, SHC.

23. E. A. Rowan, *The Proposition to Amend Section 206 of the Constitution of Mississippi: Shall Mississippi Continue to Educate the Negroes at the Expense of the White Taxpayers* (Wesson, Miss.: Wesson Enterprise Print, 1903); BIENNIAL (1906); BIENNIAL (1911); George A. Sewall and Margaret L. Dwight, eds., *Mississippi Black History Makers*, rev. ed. (Jackson: University Press of Mississippi, 1984), 164; "Governor Vardaman's Stirring Appeal to Mississippi: Long Message Read to Both Houses at Jackson," *Memphis Commercial Appeal*, January 2, 1906.

24. Albert D. Kirwan, *Revolt of the Rednecks: Mississippi Politics, 1876–1925* (New York: Harper and Row, 1951), 144–47.

25. Spencer J. Maxcy, "Progressivism and Rural Education in the Deep South, 1900–1950," in *Education and the Rise of the New South*, ed. Ronald K. Goodenow and Arthur O. White, 52–53 (Boston: G. K. Hall, 1981); Summary of Reports of Mr. J. T. Calhoun, State Agent for Rural Schools in Mississippi, July 1, 1915–January 1, 1916, GEBR-MS, reel 77; Corey T. Lesseig, *Automobility: Social Changes in the American South, 1909–1939* (New York: Routledge, 2001), 76–77. Examples of white Mississippians objecting to school consolidation during this period can be found throughout the Department of Education records (RG 50) at MDAH and in W. F. Bond, *I Had a Friend: An Autobiography by Willard F. Bond* (Kansas City: E. L. Mendenhall, 1958).

26. *Twenty Years' Progress (1910–1930) and a Biennial Survey of Public Education in Mississippi (1929–1930 and 1930–1931)* (Jackson, Miss.: n.p., 1931), 13–15, 20; G. J. Cain, "Financing the Public Schools of Mississippi," August 1946, Box 48, J. M. Tubb Papers; 1944 pamphlet by Mississippi Board of Development, "Education, 1901–1949," Subject File, MDAH.

27. *Twenty Years' Progress (1910–1930)*, 14–15, 20; Cain.

28. Simeon Lafayette Stringer, "A Survey of Two Types of School Systems for Negro Education, a Semi-Consolidated School System without Transportation in Coahoma County, Mississippi, and a Consolidated School System with Transportation in Forrest County, Mississippi" (master's thesis, University of Mississippi, 1929); *Twenty Years' Progress (1910–1930)*, 51–53; Joseph W. Addison, "The Adaptability of the Forrest County Mississippi Program of Negro Education to Certain Selected Counties of the State" (master's thesis, Xavier University, 1942).

29. Addison, ch. 1.

30. The difference between black and white teacher salaries can be gleaned from "Salaries Paid to Teachers in Certain Mississippi Counties in 1889–90 and in 1936–37," GEBR-MS, reel 78. Redmond's comments on the effects of consolidation can be found in Report by S. D. Redmond.

31. Report by S. D. Redmond; Joe C. Brown to Walter White, November 29, 1937, I-C-201, NAACP Papers, LC. A mill is one-tenth of a cent, so a one-mill tax would be $1 for every $1,000 of property.

32. "Status of Negro Schools in Mississippi, 1939," in "Afro-American Education (to 1953)," Subject File, MDAH; Bullock, 172.

33. "Public School Enrollment and Expenditures in Six Southern States," 1944, GEBR-MS, reel 78; "Report by J. A. Travis, Assistant to Mr. Easom," *Mississippi Educational Journal* 15 (January 1939): 70–71; Field Report, November 1917, GEBR-MS, reel 78.

34. W. F. Bond to Dr. Abraham Flexner, February 17, 1917, GEBR-MS, reel 77.

35. R. B. Fulton, "Educational Progress in Mississippi," in *Proceedings of the Conference for Education in the South, the Sixth Session* (New York: Committee on Publication, 1903), 109.

36. BIENNIAL (1941), 16.

37. James D. Anderson, *The Education of Blacks in the South, 1860–1935* (Chapel Hill: University of North Carolina Press, 1988), offers the best description of the development of black education in the South during the early twentieth century; for Mississippi, see Neil R. McMillen, *Dark Journey: Black Mississippians in the Age of Jim Crow* (Urbana: University of Illinois Press, 1989), ch. 3.

38. Anderson, chs. 2–5; William A. Link, *A Hard Country and a Lonely Place: Schooling, Society and Reform in Rural Virginia, 1870–1920* (Chapel Hill: University of North Carolina Press, 1986), ch. 8.

39. Anderson; *Twenty Years' Progress*, 45–46; "County Training Schools," Extract from Report of Director, April 28, 1915; and "Some Results of the Work of the State Agent in Mississippi," January 1938, both in GEBR-MS, reel 77; NASC Interim Writing Committee, *The Jeanes Story: A Chapter in the History of American Education, 1908–1968* (Atlanta: Southern Education Foundation, 1979); Sadye Wier, interview by Kitty Galbraith, November 12, 1980, Robert and Sadye Wier Papers, Box 4, Mitchell Memorial Library, MSU; Annie Kelly Montgomery, interview by Clarence M. Simmons, July 24, 1970, vol. 9, MHC.

40. Anderson, ch. 5.

41. S. L. Smith to Mr. Harrell, September 9, 1929; "Bura Hilbun Faces Charges of Diverting Funds," undated article from unidentified newspaper; S. L. Smith to Edwin Embree, December 10, 1929; S. L. Smith to Mr. Stern, December 3, 1930; and S. L. Smith to Edwin Embree, January 2, 1931, all in Julius Rosenwald Fund Records, reel 60.

42. Bura Hilbun, "Report of Educational Activities in Negro Schools of Mississippi, 1923," RG 50, vol. 136, MDAH; Stringer, esp. chs. 3–6; S. L. Smith, *Builders of Goodwill: The Story of the State Agents of Negro Education in the South, 1910 to 1950* (Nashville: Tennessee Book, 1950), 126–29.

43. Francis W. Shepardson to S. L. Smith, March 17, 1922; and P. H. Easom to W. F. Credle, June 27, 1930, both in Julius Rosenwald Fund Records, reel 60; WPA History, Tunica County (microfilm); Edwin R. Embree and Julia Waxman, *Investment in People: The Story of the Julius Rosenwald Fund* (New York: Harper, 1949); Anderson, ch. 5.

44. *Mississippi Educational Journal* 16 (February 1940): 102; C. J. Duckworth, interview by Michael Garvey, December 12, 1975, transcript, vol. 352, MOHP; Lynda J. Davis, interview by Milan Green, July 23, 1971, transcript, vol. 5, MHC.

45. Ed and Edna Scott, interview by Chez Prince and Constance Curry, September 9, 2000, videotape, MCLA; Walter Reaves, interview by Aviva Futorian and Gloria Clark, December 12, 1995, transcript, North Mississippi Oral History Program Collection, MCLA; Rev. S. D. Washington, "The Department of Parent-Teacher Associations," *Mississippi Educational Journal* 2 (March 1926): 135. Information on fund-raising and celebratory events at black schools around Mississippi can be found scattered throughout the issues of the *Mississippi Educational Journal*. For examples, see "Mound Bayou Mississippi," *Mississippi Educational Journal* 3 (January 1927): 53; "The P.T.A.," *Mississippi Educational Journal* 18 (May 1942): 153;

and "Parent-Day Program a Success at Eureka, Hattiesburg, Miss.," *Mississippi Educational Journal* 22 (May 1946): 152.

46. Vanessa Siddle Walker, in *Their Highest Potential: An African American School Community in the Segregated South* (Chapel Hill: University of North Carolina Press, 1996), demonstrates that segregated black schools provided positive educational benefits for black children, despite the prevailing inequities.

47. Joe C. Brown to Walter White, November 29, 1937, I-C-201, NAACP Papers, LC; H. M. Ivy, interview by Orley Caudill, November 21, 1973, transcript, vol. 279; Charles Johnson, interview by Michael Garvey, August 26, 1975, transcript, vol. 344; and Dave Dunaway, interview by R. Wayne Pyle, March 24, 1981, transcript, vol. 411, all in MOHP; A. E. Coleman to J. H. Powers, November 18, 1908, RG 50, vol. 1, MDAH.

48. P. H. Easom to Joe May, March 12, 1938, GEBR-MS, reel 77; "State Normal Schools for Negroes in the Southern States—Report of the General Agent to the Special Committee," 1911, Box 7, Southern Education Board Records, SHC; Emily Mary Carouthers, interview by Alvin Thomas, August 27, 1971, vol. 3, MHC; Youth of the Rural Organizing and Cultural Center, *Minds Stayed on Freedom: The Civil Rights Struggle in the Rural South, an Oral History* (Boulder, Colo.: Westview Press, 1991), 47–48; *Mississippi Educational Journal* 21 (November 1944): 29–30; "Meridian Summer School," *Mississippi Educational Journal* 13 (November 1936): 35; P. H. Easom, "Some Results of the Work of the State Agent in Mississippi," January 1938, GEBR-MS, reel 77; Mississippi Department of Education, *Report of the Committee of Investigation of the Teacher Training Facilities for Negroes in Mississippi* (Jackson, Miss.: State Superintendent of Education, 1930), 35, 52.

49. Michael Fultz, "African American Teachers in the South 1890–1940: Powerlessness and the Ironies of Expectations and Protest," *History of Education Quarterly* 35 (Winter 1996): 416–21; Annie Blanchard, interview by Alvin Thomas, June 2, 1971, transcript, vol. 2, MHC; "The P.T.A. (Jones Chapel Public School Community)," *Mississippi Educational Journal* 18 (May 1942): 153; Douglas Conner, interview by Neil McMillen, December 2, 1993, transcript (copy in author's possession); and H. M. Ivy, unpublished autobiography, 65, vol. 279, MOHP.

50. Bernice White, interview by Kim Lacy Rogers, August 21, 1995, transcript, Delta Oral History Project, TCA; Adam Fairclough, *Teaching Equality: Black Schools in the Age of Jim Crow* (Athens: University of Georgia Press, 2001), ch. 1; Henrietta Shivery to W. E. B. DuBois, February 11, 1935, W. E. B. DuBois Papers, reel 44; Aaron Henry, unpublished autobiography, 61–66, 74–75, Aaron Henry Papers, Box 1, TCA.

CHAPTER 2

1. James T. Patterson, *Grand Expectations: The United States, 1945–1974* (New York: Oxford University Press, 1996), ch. 13.

2. W. W. Whitaker to J. M. Tubb, May 12, 1950, RG 50, vol. 234, MDAH.

3. Bond, 108–11; *W. J. McFarland et al. v. Robert Goins*, case file, RG 32, case #13990, MDAH.

4. *Survey of the Schools of Hinds County, Mississippi* (Jackson: Hederman Bros., 1917); Jackson Public School Board Minutes, January 18, 1902, June 25, 1906, February 6, 1907, January 5, October 4, 1909, October 17, 1910, May 8, 1911, April 18, 1922, reel 2, MDAH. The Hinds County survey makes no mention of any black school in the county.

5. *Mississippi Educational Journal* 18 (October 1941): 2–3; A. L. Johnson to NAACP, November 6, 1941; and A. L. Johnson to NAACP, March 24, 1943, both in III-B, NAACP Papers, reel 9; A. L. Johnson to A. J. Noel, April 6, 1950, Gladys Noel Bates Papers, TCA. Neil R. McMillen, in *Dark Journey*, 169, notes that in 1935, the five black lawyers in the state were generally powerless to handle matters involving "white interests."

6. T. R. M. Howard, "The Mississippi Negro in Our Changing World," January 4, 1945, Box 3, Walter Sillers Papers, DSU; "Negro Teachers Threaten Equal-Pay Suit as Solons Ready to Convene Tuesday," *Jackson (Miss.) Daily News*, January 7, 1946; Kenneth Toler, "Mississippi Negroes Ask School Equality," *Memphis Commercial Appeal*, February 18, 1946; L. O. Todd to Walter Sillers, February 21, 1946, Box 111, Walter Sillers Papers.

7. "A Timely Warning," *Jackson (Miss.) Daily News*, November 14, 1938.

8. Report of the Committee on Improvement of Negro Education, Mississippi Education Association, March 28, 1940, Julius Rosenwald Fund Records, reel 146; Andrew Anthony Workman, "The Rejection of Accommodation by Mississippi's Black Public Elite, 1946–1954" (master's thesis, University of North Carolina at Chapel Hill, 1988), 28; Mildred S. Topp to J. S. Vandiver, May 2, 1940, GERB-MS, reel 77; Flyer, [Fall 1948?], Southern Regional Council Papers, reel 22, University of North Carolina Libraries, Chapel Hill.

9. P. H. Easom to Judge Joe May, March 12, 1938, GERB-MS, reel 77; "Easom Addresses Indianola Rotary," *Jackson (Miss.) Daily News*, July 25, 1946, in "Percy H. Easom," Subject File, MDAH.

10. H. M. Ivy to J. M. Tubb, January 4, 1949, RG 50, vol. 230, MDAH; Robert M. Mayo to John Bell Williams, January 18, 1949, RG 59, vol. 279, MDAH.

11. Rena L. Vassar, ed., *Social History of American Education, Volume II: 1860 to the Present* (Chicago: Rand McNally, 1965), 5–7; Daniel W. Crofts, "The Black Response to the Blair Education Bill," *Journal of Southern History* 37 (February 1971): 41–65; Diane Ravitch, *The Troubled Crusade: American Education, 1945–1980* (New York: Basic Books, 1983), ch. 1; Ward M. McAfee, *Religion, Race, and Reconstruction: The Public School in the Politics of the 1870s* (Albany: State University of New York Press, 1998).

12. Aubrey Williams to W. F. Bond, March 3, 1934, Box 153, FERA Central Files, State Series, RG 69, NA; "Hinds County Passing Through an Era of Good Felling [*sic*]" *Mississippi Educational Journal* 10 (January 1934): 86; P. H. Easom, "Mississippi's Negro Schools," Delta and Pine Land Company Records, File IX—History of Education of Blacks, MSU; Hattiesburg School Board Minutes, July 5, 1932, February 7, November 27, 1933, February 5, March 12, 1934, March 15, 1935, Hattiesburg Schools Administrative Offices, Hattiesburg, Miss.

13. The details of the politics surrounding this issue are ably covered in Gilbert E. Smith, *The Limits of Reform: Politics and Federal Aid to Education, 1937–1950* (New York: Garland, 1982). As Smith notes, religious concerns were perhaps as important as racial ones in stalling efforts to provide federal aid to education.

14. "School Needs in War Areas in Mississippi," [1945?], RG 50, vol. 214, pt. 2, MDAH; Erick LeRoy Lindman, *The Federal Government and Public Schools* (Washington, D.C.: American Association of School Administrators, 1965), 50–53; U.S. Department of HEW, *Administration of Public Laws 81-874 and 81-815: Eleventh Annual Report of the Commission of Education, June 30, 1961* (Washington, D.C.: Government Printing Office, 1961); Harry S. Truman, Memorandum of Disapproval, November 2, 1951, RG 12, NA. The description of federal aid to education as a Trojan horse can be found in "Federal Aid to Education Checkup May Save a Life," *Charleston (S.C.) News and Courier*, April 3, 1949.

15. Numan V. Bartley, *The New South, 1945–1980* (Baton Rouge: Louisiana State University Press, 1995), esp. chs. 1–3 and 5; Davison M. Douglas, *Reading, Writing and Race: The Desegregation of the Charlotte Schools* (Chapel Hill: University of North Carolina Press, 1995), ch. 1.

16. Southern Regional Council, *Wanted: An Educated South* (Atlanta: Southern Regional Council, 1947), 20.

17. John Ray Skates Jr., "World War II and Its Effects 1940–1948," in *A History of Mississippi*, ed. Richard Aubrey McLemore, 2:131–33 (Hattiesburg: University and College Press of Mississippi, 1973); "Thomas Lowry Bailey Biographical Sketches," Subject File, MDAH; *Report of the Joint Legislative Education Committee on the Public School System of the State* (n.p., 1946); P. H. Easom and E. P. Littlejohn, "A Summary of the Main Legislative Enactments Pertaining to Negro Education in Mississippi, Passed by the 1946 Session of the Legislature," Southern Regional Council Papers, reel 22; *Mississippi Educational Journal* 17 (December 1940): 50.

18. "Our Disgraceful Negro Schools," *Jackson (Miss.) Daily News*, February 5, 1949; E. S. Bishop, "President's Annual Message to the Fortieth Annual Session of the Mississippi Association of Teachers in Colored Schools, March 28–29, 1946," *Mississippi Educational Journal* 22 (April 1946): 124.

19. J. M. Tubb to W. R. Nettles, October 24, 1946, RG 50, vol. 217, MDAH; Schools Applying for State Aid on Building Projects, October 27, 1947, Box 41; and A. H. Ramsey to Walter Sillers, February 10, 1951, Box 1, both in Walter Sillers Papers.

20. "Address by Governor Fielding L. Wright, Annual Meeting of Teachers in Negro Schools," *Mississippi Educational Journal* 25 (April 1949): 127; "Fair Deal for Negro Schools," *Jackson (Miss.) Daily News*, January 25, 1950; Tunica County Board of Education Minutes, September 9, 1946, September 10, 1947, reel 1, MDAH; John Martin to J. M. Tubb, September 10, 1947, RG 50, vol. 221, MDAH.

21. Tunica County Board of Education Minutes, August 3, 1955, July 3, 1957, reels 1 and 2, MDAH; Hattiesburg School Board Minutes, March 11, 1947, May 4, 1950. The 40 percent figure is listed in "Local Teacher's Action May Hasten Passage of

Salary Equalization Bill Now Before State Legislature," *Jackson (Miss.) Advocate*, March 13, 1948.

22. Easom and Littlejohn; BIENNIAL (1950), 11; "Number and Average Salaries of Classroom Teachers," [1960s?], RG 47, vol. 378, MDAH.

23. "State-Wide Mass Meeting Get No Answer on Request For Bi-Racial COMMISION [*sic*]," *Jackson (Miss.) Advocate*, March 27, 1948; Mrs. Gordon Patton and thirty-six others to Members of the State Building Commission, [March 1947?], Minutes of the Board of Trustees of the Jackson Public Schools, reel 4, MDAH; "Our Disgraceful Negro Schools."

24. Gladys Noel Bates, interview by Catherine Jannik, December 23, 1996, transcript, vol. 689, MOHP; "Statement by Mrs. Bates," May 16, 1992, Gladys Noel Bates Papers; Jess Wright, "Up and Down Farish Street," *Jackson (Miss.) Advocate*, June 4–10, 1981.

25. Bates, interview; Brief for Appellants, U.S. Fifth Circuit, *Gladys Noel Bates and Richard Jess Brown v. Board of Trustees of Jackson Separate School District and K. P. Walker, Superintendent of Jackson Schools*, [1950?], Gladys Noel Bates Papers; Catherine M. Jannik, "Gladys Noel Bates: Educator and Activist" (master's thesis, University of Southern Mississippi, 1999), ch. 3; Vicki Crawford, "Race, Class, Gender, and Culture: Black Women's Activism in the Mississippi Civil Rights Movement," *Journal of Mississippi History* 63 (Spring 1996): 8; Minutes of the Board of Trustees of the Jackson Public Schools, February 13, March 12, 1948, reel 5, MDAH; John C. Batte to Gladys N. Bates, February 11, 1948, Gladys Noel Bates Papers. The Fifth Circuit Court of Appeals upheld the district court ruling the following year. See *Bates et al. v. Batte et al.*, 187 F.2d 142 (1951), at 142.

26. "Statement by Mrs. Bates"; "Suits for Equal Pay for Negro and White Teachers to Be Filed on Every County in Mississippi," *Clarksdale (Miss.) Daily Press*, May 12, 1949.

27. G. N. Bates to L. F. Palmer, [Summer 1948?]; "Statement by Mrs. Bates"; and James A. Burns to Robert J. Carter, March 24, 1949, all in Gladys Noel Bates Papers; "Mrs. Gladys Noel Bates and Husband Denied Further Teacher Jobs in City School System," *Jackson (Miss.) Advocate*, June 15, 1948; "Suits for Equal Pay for Negro and White Teachers."

28. James A. Burns to A. J. Noel, December 22, 1948, Gladys Noel Bates Papers; BIENNIAL (1956), 64–66; BIENNIAL (1954), 14. Swango, quoted in Charles P. Smith, "Governor Fielding L. Wright's Legislative Program: 1946–1952" (master's thesis, University of Southern Mississippi, 1976), 60.

29. BIENNIAL (1956), 64–66; BIENNIAL (1954), 14; Lynda J. Davis, interview by Milan Green, July 23, 1971, transcript, vol. 5, MHC.

30. In the 1948–49 school year, the average salary for white teachers was $1,731.05 but only $659.49 for black teachers. See Number and Average Salaries of Classroom Teachers. Walker quoted in Linuel Duane Jayroe, "Kirby Pipken Walker, Superintendent, Jackson Municipal School District, 1937–1969" (Ed.D. diss., University of Mississippi, 1983), 106. "White and Negro Teachers Vote Down Proposed Plan to Equalize Salaries; Special Session Out," October 7, 1949, unidentified newspaper article in Box 91, J. M. Tubb Papers.

31. C. Smith, 50–52; Scott Baker, "Testing Equality: The National Teacher Examination and the NAACP's Legal Campaign to Equalize Teachers' Salaries in the South, 1936–63," *History of Education Quarterly* 35 (Spring 1995): 49–64.

32. Anyone familiar with standardized testing would have recognized that while the meager funds spent on black education certainly doomed blacks to perform worse on the whole on any test, some whites would inevitably score in the low percentiles and some blacks would make high scores, despite the legacy of inequalities. An example of this pattern can be seen in a test administered by the Benton County schools to its teachers throughout 1929. Twenty-seven whites took the test, and four of them failed it (14.8 percent), while twenty blacks took the test, and ten of them did not pass (50 percent). While six white teachers achieved scores in the highest percentile (22.2 percent), three of the black test takers achieved the same distinction (15 percent), and one of these three actually made the highest score of all those who took the test. See Benton County School Board Minutes, entries for April and September 1929, reel 2, MDAH.

33. Florence O. Alexander, "The Education of Negroes in Mississippi," *Journal of Negro Education* 16 (Summer 1947): 377; Hattiesburg School Board Minutes, November 6, 1951; "White and Negro Teachers Vote Down Proposed Plan"; Frances Baker, "Education Group Vote to Base Equal Pay on U.S. Teacher Exams," *Jackson (Miss.) Daily News*, August 25, 1949; "Better Negro Schools Are Now Imperative," *Jackson (Miss.) Daily News*, April 19, 1949; George Harmon, "Thigpen Predicts All Teacher Salary Bills Are Doomed," *Jackson (Miss.) Daily News*, January 25, 1950; C. Smith, 55–58.

34. BIENNIAL (1954), 163, lists the amount of the special appropriation for black teachers for 1952–53 as $2,241,938.80. Between the 1952–53 and 1953–54 school years, black teachers received raises averaging just over $90. With approximately sixty-five hundred black teachers in the state at the time, funds spent on increasing black salaries would have been about $585,000 if all teachers had received the average raise. See Number and Average Salaries of Classroom Teachers. While this calculation probably underestimates the amount of state funds actually spent on increasing black teachers' salaries during the period, my estimate that less than half of the funds appropriated were spent in the way they were intended seems a conservative one.

35. Address by Kenneth Toler, June 9, 1954, Box 1, Mississippi Education Collection, UM; A. H. Ramsey to Walter Sillers, March 25, 1953, Box 137, Walter Sillers Papers; Number and Average Salaries of Classroom Teachers.

36. BIENNIAL (1956), 64.

37. Applications Filed with the State Building Commission to March 24, 1947, Box 3, Walter Sillers Papers.

38. J. M. Tubb to George W. Stricklin, January 24, 1953, RG 50, vol. 246, MDAH; Mississippi Citizens Council on Education, "A Report on the Organizational Meeting Held in Jackson October 9, 1950," Box 3; Questionnaire Results, 1951, Box 1; and Total Number Completed Questionnaires by County, Box 3, all in Association of Citizens Councils of Mississippi Papers, MDAH; Committee Report, Recess

Education Study Committee, March 1953, 4, Box 7, George Washington Owens Papers, MDAH; BIENNIAL (1956), 18. The results of the 1951 questionnaire were not broken down by the race of the respondent, but a large number of the respondents were apparently white, since the only major black group involved in the MCCE was the MATCS. The small sampling of completed surveys in Box 2 of the Association of Citizens Councils of Mississippi Papers offers evidence that whites surveyed favored educational equalization between the races. For example, 57 of the 355 completed survey forms from Forrest County are included in these records, all from whites. To the question "Should equal services and facilities be provided" to black and white children, forty-two answered "yes," four said "no," and eleven did not respond to this question. For the 1948–50 Mississippi budget figures, see *General Fund Budget Discussion for the Fiscal Biennium 1950–52 for the State of Mississippi* (Jackson: State Budget Commission, 1949), 57, 59.

39. "Governor Says Tax Plans For School Support May Be Given at Special Session," *Jackson (Miss.) Daily News*, March 22, 1952; John E. Phay, "Report to the Recess Education Committee," [1953], Box 1, Mississippi Education Collection; "Number of People, by Counties, Listed by the U.S. Census of 1950 (Age 5–19 Inclusive)" and "Mississippi School Census of 1951; and Pecentages [*sic*] of Difference Between the Two Censuses," [1952?], both in RG 27, vol. 962, MDAH; Committee Report, Recess Education Study Committee, March 1953, 4.

40. Committee Report, Recess Education Study Committee, March 1953, 4; BIENNIAL (1956), 15–17; John Phay, "Estimate of Cost to Bring All Schools in County or Separate School Districts to Highest Level Now in Such District," December 7, 1953, Box 1, Mississippi Education Collection; Senate Bill No. 1204, Extraordinary Session 1953, Box 137, Walter Sillers Papers.

41. Committee Report, Recess Education Study Committee, March 1953, 57; Joe Wroten, interview by Yasuhiro Katagiri, November 4, 1993, transcript, vol. 476, MOHP.

42. Committee Report, Recess Education Study Committee, March 1953, 51; George W. Owens, interview by Chester Morgan, August 2, 1973, transcript, vol. 332, MOHP; *Journal of the House of the State of Mississippi, 1954, Including Extraordinary Session of 1953* (Jackson: Mississippi House of Representatives, 1954), 1269–72.

43. "Address by Governor Fielding L. Wright," 127; "2 Extra Sessions of Solons Possible," *Jackson (Miss.) Clarion-Ledger*, July 12, 1949; "Special Session on Teachers Set," *Jackson (Miss.) Clarion-Ledger*, August 17, 1949.

44. Kluger, esp. pt. 1; Mark V. Tushnet, *The NAACP's Legal Strategy against Segregated Education* (Chapel Hill: University of North Carolina Press, 1987).

45. John W. Cell, *The Highest Stage of White Supremacy: The Origins of Segregation in South Africa and the American South* (Cambridge: Cambridge University Press, 1982), ch. 7, suggests that once white supremacy had been well established and passed through its most violent stage (in Mississippi, the early decades of the twentieth century), moderate white segregationists (i.e., not radical, violent fanatics) and blacks generally collaborated in perpetuating a kinder, gentler form of white

supremacy. Humes's claim is in "What the Negroes Are Thinking," reprint of an editorial from the *Greenville (Miss.) Delta Leader*, May 11, 1949, RG 59, vol. 279, MDAH.

46. "Negro Teacher President Calls Segregation Closed Issue, Asks Improvements," *Jackson (Miss.) Daily News*, March 26, 1949.

47. "'Uncle Toms' Scored in Mississippi School Fight," Press Release, November 12, 1953, III-C, NAACP Papers, reel 1. The report of "no teachers" at the NAACP meeting is contained in a letter from H. H. Humes to P. H. Easom, November 13, 1953, in "Percy H. Easom," Subject File, MDAH.

48. C. R. Darden to Gloster B. Current, November 11, 1953, II-C-97, NAACP Papers, LC.

49. "State NAACP Conference Gets Rebuff," *Jackson (Miss.) Advocate*, April 4, 1953; J. D. Boyd and the Mississippi Teachers Association to the Governor and the Legislature of Mississippi, [1953?], RG 50, vol. 245, MDAH; "White Says Negroes Back Dual System," *Jackson (Miss.) Clarion-Ledger*, November 6, 1953; "Negro Leaders Conference Back [*sic*] Efforts to Raise and Equalize Education While Keeping Eye on Outcome of Segregation Cases," *Jackson (Miss.) Advocate*, November 7, 1953; "See Race Relations Set Back from Widely Published False Report on Negro Meeting Held Here Last Week," *Jackson (Miss.) Advocate*, November 14, 1953; "President of State Negro Teachers Ass'n. in Personal Visit Presents Letter to Governor and Members of the State Legislature," *Jackson (Miss.) Advocate*, November 28, 1953; Workman, 70–74.

50. Department of Educational Administration, Mississippi Southern College, *School Survey: Covington County, Mississippi* (Hattiesburg, Miss.: Department of Educational Administration, 1956).

51. University of Mississippi, Bureau of Educational Research, *The Report of a Survey of the Public Schools of Benton County* (University, Miss.: Bureau of Educational Research, 1956); University of Mississippi, Bureau of Educational Research, *The Report of a Survey of the Public Schools of Tallahatchie County* (University, Miss.: Bureau of Educational Research, 1955).

52. Press Release, [June 30, 1954?], III-C, NAACP Papers, reel 1.

CHAPTER 3

1. Various accounts of this meeting can be found in John Dittmer, *Local People: The Struggle for Civil Rights in Mississippi* (Urbana: University of Illinois Press, 1994), 38–40; Workman, 76–80; Numan V. Bartley, *The Rise of Massive Resistance: Race and Politics in the South during the 1950s* (Baton Rouge: Louisiana State University Press, 1969), 76; Bartley, *The New South*, 168–69; and James W. Silver, *Mississippi: The Closed Society* (New York: Harcourt, Brace, and World, 1964), 88.

The number of blacks who attended this meeting is not entirely clear. According to an invitation list in the Walter Sillers Papers, ninety-four black leaders were invited, but other accounts suggest that as few as eighty-five or as many as one hundred blacks met with the governor and his committee. See List of Those to Whom

Invitations Were Sent to Attend Meeting with Legal Advisory Committee on Friday, July 30, 1954, Box 112, Walter Sillers Papers.

2. "Construction of Equal Schools May Be Answer," *Jackson (Miss.) Daily News*, July 1, 1954; "Widespread Comment on Meeting with Governor," *Jackson (Miss.) Advocate*, July 10, 1954; Mrs. M. E. Tilly, "Report of Trip to Mississippi, November 14–20, 1954," Southern Regional Council Papers, reel 29; "Former President States Negro Teacher's Association Sees More Schools Now Paramount Need of State," *Jackson (Miss.) Advocate*, July 24, 1954. Tilly talked with Dr. Jacob Reddix about the June meeting with Governor White. The other white officials at this meeting were Superintendent of Education J. M. Tubb, Attorney General J. P. Coleman, and Speaker of the House Walter Sillers.

3. E. J. Stringer, interview by author, November 11, 1992, transcript, vol. 480, MOHP; List of Those to Whom Invitations Were Sent. Of those on the invitation list, 50 lived in the Delta. The occupational breakdown of the 76 of the 94 whose profession could be identified is as follows: educators, 25; businesspeople, 14 (including 6 funeral home operators); doctors/dentists, 11; ministers, 10; leaders of fraternal/civic organizations, 8; lawyers, 3; newspaper editors, 2; elected officials, 1 (mayor of Mound Bayou); railroad porter, 1; and farmer, 1 (some of the educators probably also worked part-time as farm workers, but only one individual was identified primarily as a farmer). Four of the 94 invitees were women. Governor White's recognition that Drs. Howard and Stringer would not go along with a voluntary segregation plan are revealed in Hugh White to Walter Sillers, July 19, 1954, Box 112, Walter Sillers Papers.

4. Stringer, interview; "Statement Issued by the NAACP Representatives from Every Area of the State of Mississippi," May 30, 1954, II-A-226, NAACP Papers, LC; note by A. Maurice Mackel attached to "The Jackson Declaration," III-C, NAACP Papers, reel 1; A. Maurice Mackel to Walter White, August 11, 1954, II-A-227, NAACP Papers, LC; Tilly. Mackel, a dentist from Natchez and an NAACP supporter, was apparently not invited to the meeting with the governor, but he did attend the meeting held the previous night, as did other black leaders not selected to attend the audience with the governor and the LEAC. At their next annual meeting, in March 1955, the MTA endorsed the *Brown* decision. See N. R. Burger, "The President's Corner," *Mississippi Educational Journal* 33 (February 1956): 97.

Numerous accounts of the July 30 meeting have suggested that it signaled the emergence of a more aggressive black leadership in the state, one unwilling to accommodate to the confines of a Jim Crow society. Indeed, when Mississippi blacks at the meeting announced their support for the *Brown* decision, white Mississippians expressed shock that the day of black accommodation to segregation had passed. The *Jackson (Miss.) Clarion-Ledger* blared the next day that "Negroes Insist Upon Integration." See "Negroes Insist Upon Integration: Speak Their Mind to Advisory Group," *Jackson (Miss.) Clarion-Ledger*, July 31, 1954. But black unity evident at the meeting barely concealed the tensions that continued to exist between accommodationists and those ready to fight to topple Jim Crow, and the declaration of black sentiment emanating from the meeting expressed a short-lived compromise between these two factions of the state's black leadership. White reaction in the state to the meeting—and subsequent historical accounts—generally failed to discern the ambiguities of the black response to the *Brown* decision embodied in the black leaders' meeting with Governor White.

5. At the meeting the previous night, Percy Greene had argued that the group should neither endorse nor renounce the *Brown* decision; for Greene, securing voting rights had long been more important than destroying segregation. See Henry, unpublished autobiography, 159.

6. Transcript of Meeting of Legal Educational Advisory Committee and Negro Leaders, July 30, 1954, 1–2, Box 7, George Washington Owens Papers.

7. Transcript of Meeting of Legal Educational Advisory Committee and Negro Leaders; J. H. White to E. J. Stringer, August 25, 1954, II-A-226, NAACP Papers, LC; Aaron Henry, interview by Neil McMillen, May 1, 1972, transcript, vol. 33, MOHP.

8. Aaron Henry, in his unpublished autobiography, 154, notes that many whites in Clarksdale immediately after the *Brown* decision believed the mandate would have to be obeyed. Whatever sentiment along these lines that did exist in Mississippi apparently evaporated quickly.

9. "Legislature Called on Schools Sept. 7," *Jackson (Miss.) Clarion-Ledger*, July 31, 1954; Transcript of Meeting of Legal Educational Advisory Committee and Negro Leaders; "Mississippi Moves to Close Schools," *New York Times*, September 8, 1954.

10. E. J. Stringer to Thurgood Marshall, October 7, 1954; and Ruby Hurley to Thurgood Marshall, September 21, 1954, both in II-A-226, NAACP Papers, LC; affidavit of E. W. Steptoe, 1964, in *Mississippi Black Paper: Fifty-Seven Negro and White Citizens' Testimony of Police Brutality, the Breakdown of Law and Order and the Corruption of Justice in Mississippi* (New York: Random House, 1965), 3; Neil R. McMillen, *The Citizens' Council: Organized Resistance to the Second Reconstruction, 1954–64* (Urbana: University of Illinois Press, 1971), esp. ch. 2; Charles Ray Fulton, "Racial Integration in the Public School System in Kemper County, Mississippi, 1954–1974" (Ph.D. diss., University of Mississippi, 1978), 93–95.

11. J. H. White to E. J. Stringer, August 25, 1954; and E. J. Stringer to Thurgood Marshall, October 7, 1954, both in II-A-226, NAACP Papers, LC; A. Maurice Mackel to Roy Wilkins, September 27, 1954, II-A-227, NAACP Papers, LC; "Dr. Stringer Quits Post in Council Negro Leadership," *Jackson (Miss.) Advocate*, October 2, 1954; Charles M. Payne, *I've Got the Light of Freedom: The Organizing Tradition and the Mississippi Freedom Struggle* (Berkeley: University of California Press, 1995), 36–43.

12. Bartley, *The Rise of Massive Resistance*, 77–78; "Committee Asks Lawmakers to Abolish Public Schools as Segregation Safeguard," *Jackson (Miss.) Daily News*, July 13, 1954; "Mississippi's School Problem," Report of LEAC Subcommittee on Planning, October 12, 1954, Box 7, George Washington Owens Papers; "Proposed Amendments to Constitution of State of Mississippi," [1954], Box 25, Walter Sillers Papers; *Southern School News*, January 6, 1955.

13. Maurice H. Black, interview by author, July 25, 1991, transcript, vol. 379, MOHP; "Mississippi's School Problem"; J. M. Ewing to Fellow Teacher, October 28, 1954, Box 3, George Washington Owens Papers. Walter Sillers's conception of how a publicly funded "private" school system would work can be found in Walter Sillers to J. O. Emmerich, November 9, 1954, Box 2, Walter Sillers Papers.

14. Statement by J. D. Boyd, [1954?], Box 2, Kenneth Toler Papers.

15. Transcript of Meeting of Mississippi Educational Advisory Committee and School Officials, August 12, 1954, Box 7, George Washington Owens Papers; George Evans, "Why I Am Against the Proposed Amendment," November 3, 1954, Box 2, Race Relations Collection, UM; "Teachers Approve School Abolishment," *Jackson (Miss.) Clarion-Ledger*, August 13, 1954; Walter Sillers to Hugh L. White, August 13, 1954, Box 3, Walter Sillers Papers.

16. Transcript of Meeting of Mississippi Educational Advisory Committee and School Officials; Walter Sillers to Hugh White, August 15, 1954, Box 3, Walter Sillers Papers; "Teachers Approve School Abolishment."

17. "Foes of Amendment Hold Meeting at Hattiesburg," *Jackson (Miss.) Clarion-Ledger*, October 29, 1954; Friends of Segregated Public Schools, "The Motives Behind the Proposed Amendment," [1954?], Box 2, Race Relations Collection; William Joel Blass, interview by Orley Caudill, March 26, 1977, transcript, vol. 639, MOHP; *Southern School News*, January 6, 1955.

18. The assessment of Walter Sillers was made by W. S. Griffen, interview by Thomas Healy, July 19, 1978, transcript, vol. 414, MOHP. Walter Sillers to J. J. Breland, May 26, 1954, Box 117; and Pat H. Eager Jr. to Walter Sillers, June 10, 1954, Box 112, both in Walter Sillers Papers. In 1957, Sillers urged Governor Coleman to have the Sovereignty Commission focus its resistance to school mixing toward "looking eventually to the resort to private schools." See Walter Sillers to J. P. Coleman, June 19, 1957, Box 1, Walter Sillers Papers.

19. *Southern School News*, January 1955; "School Amendment 'Pros' Ask Air Support by White," *Jackson (Miss.) Clarion-Ledger*, October 29, 1954.

20. *Southern School News*, June 1955; McMillen, *The Citizens' Council*, 28; Kenneth Toler, "Miss. Anti-Integration Group Is Vested With 'Court Powers,'" *Atlanta Journal*, January 30, 1955; John Herbers, "Legal Advisory Committee Says 'No Compromise' On Segregation," *Greenville (Miss.) Delta Democrat-Times*, June 8, 1955.

21. *Southern School News*, August 1955; "Vicksburg School Board Says Negroes' Petition Not Legal," *Jackson (Miss.) Clarion-Ledger*, July 20, 1955; "Those Who Signed," *Vicksburg (Miss.) Evening Post*, July 19, 1955; "Further Action in Local Segregation Case Threatened," *Vicksburg (Miss.) Evening Post*, July 20, 1955. Coleman apparently continued to believe the 1955 petitions were legally invalid. On NBC's *Meet the Press* in 1957, then-governor Coleman stated that "technically speaking, we have not yet defied the Supreme Court decision because we have not had a single petition to enter the white schools." Quoted in *Southern School News*, July 1957.

22. Minutes of the Board of Trustees of the Jackson Public Schools, August 16, 1955 (microfilm), MDAH; "NAACP Petition and Its Signatures," *Natchez Democrat*,

August 10, 1955; W. C. Shoemaker, "Integration Petition Is Received by Officials Here as Move Spreads South," *Jackson (Miss.) Daily News*, July 27, 1955; Henry, unpublished autobiography, 164–65; "Here Is an Authentic List of the Purported Signers to a NAACP Communication to Our School Board," *Yazoo City (Miss.) Herald*, August 25, 1955, in III-C, NAACP Papers, reel 1; "342 Names on NAACP Petition," *Clarksdale (Miss.) Press Register*, August 2, 1955; R. S. Lyells to Fred Routh, Monthly Report, August 1955, Southern Regional Council Papers, reel 145; A. M. Mackel to Roy Wilkins, July 18, 1955, II-A-226, NAACP Papers, LC; Jack E. Davis, *Race against Time: Culture and Separation in Natchez Since 1930* (Baton Rouge: Louisiana State University Press, 2001), 158–60; *Southern School News*, September 1955. The retraction letters of the Natchez petitioners can be found in Document 2-63-1-12, Sovereignty Commission Files, MDAH.

23. McMillen, *The Citizens' Council*, 28–31, 211; Jack Davis, "Deep South Reencountered: The Cultural Bases of Race Relations in Natchez, Mississippi, since 1930" (Ph.D. diss., Brandeis University, 1993), 251–53; unsigned to NAACP, [1955?]; and James Wright to NAACP, November 8, 1955, both in II-A-227, NAACP Papers, LC; David Halberstam, "A County Divided against Itself," *Reporter* 13 (December 15, 1955): 31–32; Report of A. L. Hopkins, December 18, 1964, Box 136, PBJ.

24. Keith Fuller, "Solons Set Up 'State Sovereignty' Group," *Greenville (Miss.) Delta Democrat-Times*, March 22, 1955; Kenneth Toler, "Miss. Sovereignty Commission Backs Up Interposition Stand," *Atlanta Journal*, March 25, 1955; Mrs. W. M. (Aubin) Newman to Judge J. Skelly Wright, February 16, 1956, Papers of J. Skelly Wright, LC.

25. "Mississippi Winds Up Legislative Session," *Memphis Commercial Appeal*, April 2, 1955; "Special Session Winds Up Work," *Jackson (Miss.) Clarion-Ledger*, April 2, 1955; *Southern School News*, March 1955; Ney M. Gore Jr. to Hugh White, October 12, 1954, Box 3, Walter Sillers Papers. Between 1956 and 1965, Mississippi did spend over $115 million of state funds, as well as an additional $243 million of local and federal monies, on school construction. See State Educational Finance Committee, *Mississippi's 300 Million Dollar School Construction Program* (Jackson: n.p., 1965).

26. *Report of the State Educational Finance Commission, July 1, 1955–June 30, 1957* (Jackson: State Educational Finance Commission, 1957); State Educational Finance Commission, "School Building Projects and Contracts Completed and in Process, December 31, 1959," Box 127, PBJ; Kenneth Toler, "Miss. Schools Near 'Equality'; Integration Could Ruin Setup," *Atlanta Journal*, July 29, 1956.

27. W. M. Drake (Jefferson County Citizens' Council), "The Public Schools of Mississippi," 1957, "Education, 1950–1956," Subject File, MDAH; Hugh White to Walter Sillers, October 14, 1959; and Walter Sillers to Hugh White, October 15, 1959, both in Box 3, Walter Sillers Papers; Erle Johnston, "The Practical Way to Maintain a Separate School System in Mississippi," 1962, Box 58, PBJ.

28. *Southern School News*, December 1955; Report to the Mississippi State Legislature on Activities of the State Sovereignty Commission, December 3, 1959, LF; Joe Patterson, February 5, 1959, RG 59, vol. 147, MDAH; Kenneth Toler, "Millions Spent to Bring

Negro Schools Up to Date," *Memphis Commercial Appeal*, September 11, 1960. Mississippi's official line on the success of the state's equalization program can be found in a 1964 pamphlet entitled "Mississippi Is Educating . . . without Integrating," a document prepared by the Mississippi State Sovereignty Commission but issued by the State Department of Education. See Sovereignty Commission Files, 99-133-0-1-1-1-1, MDAH.

29. Press Release, November 6, 1958, II-A-287, NAACP Papers, LC; Mississippi State Conference of Branches, "News and Views," March 25, 1959, III-C-75, NAACP Papers, LC; J. W. Grantham, "From Our President," *Mississippi Educational Journal* 33 (October 1956): 16; "Tells Negro Teachers Beware 'Uncle Toms,'" *Jackson (Miss.) State Times*, March 21, 1957; Zack J. Van Landingham, Sovereignty Commission File Memo 1–23, July 24, 1959, LF.

30. Confidential Report to Honorable J. P. Coleman from William Listen, State Sovereignty Commission investigator, [August 1956?], Box 21, J. P. Coleman Papers, MDAH; B. F. Smith to Ney Gore, February 27, 1956; and Zack J. Van Landingham to State Sovereignty Commission Director, April 30, 1959, both in LF; Report of L. C. Hicks, November 6, 1957, Sovereignty Commission Files, 3-2-04-1-1-1, MDAH.

The Sovereignty Commission also investigated several cases of potential school desegregation that would have occurred because mixed-race children, who were considered black under the logic of Jim Crow, whatever their actual physical appearance, tried to enroll in white schools. For examples, see the case of Roberta Vega, detailed in Report of Virgil Downing, September 29, 1961, LF, and the account of Louvenia Knight's children, recounted in Victoria E. Bynum, " 'White Negroes' in Segregated Mississippi: Miscegenation, Racial Identity, and the Law," *Journal of Southern History* 64 (May 1998): 274–76.

31. Report of Percy Greene through Hall DeCell, August 1958, Sovereignty Commission Files, 1-4-0-1-1-1-1, MDAH; C. R. Darden, interview by FBI, May 8, 1958, document in FOIPA No. 434554, in author's possession; Gloster Current to Roy Wilkins, May 15, 1959, II-A-287, NAACP Papers, LC; *Southern School News*, June 1959; "NAACP Head Out on Bond in Fracas," *Jackson (Miss.) Daily News*, May 15, 1959.

32. "Evers Hits 'Quisling' Leaders," *Jackson (Miss.) State Times*, June 1, 1959; John C. Melchor to T. R. M. Howard, Box 3, Race Relations Collection.

33. *Southern School News*, September 1956; Hattiesburg School Board Minutes, June 10, 1955.

34. "Let's Face the Facts," *Natchez (Miss.) Weekly Reporter*, September 15, 1955, in Natchez Public School Records 1950s, Historic Natchez Foundation, Natchez, Miss; "What Negroes REALLY Want—Jackson Colored Schools Chief Says They Want to 'Feel Good' in Public as White People Do," *Jackson (Miss.) Clarion-Ledger*, March 25, 1956.

35. Hattiesburg School Board Minutes, March 11, December 16, 1947, November 21, 1949, and March 6, 1956; "Scott County Board Plans New School to Serve Negroes," *School Board News and Cues* 2 (September–October 1958): 68.

36. An example of one of these Sovereignty Commission dispatches is the report of Tom Scarbrough on Benton County for September [1960, located in LF.

37. Advertisement and "Rogers School Dedication Gains Good Publicity," both in *Madison County (Miss.) Herald*, October 30, 1958.

38. Alexander's charge is detailed in Henry Kirksey, interview by Orley B. Caudill, January 27, 1977, transcript, vol. 613, MOHP. Constance Curry, *Silver Rights* (New York: Harcourt Brace, 1995), 33, recounts a similar operation working in Sunflower County during the days of segregated education.

39. N. R. Burger, "The President's Corner," *Mississippi Educational Journal* 33 (February 1956): 97; *Southern School News*, March 1956; Mississippi Council on Human Relations, Monthly Reports, August 1955 and April 1956, Southern Regional Council Papers, reel 145; N. R. Burger, interview by R. Wayne Pyle, May 11, 1982, transcript, vol. 356, MOHP; Josephine Bell, interview by Amy McPhail, October 22, 1996, transcript, vol. 675, MOHP.

40. For examples of Sovereignty Commission investigations of black teachers, see Reports of Tom Scarbrough, September 2, October 21, 1960; and March 27, 1961, all in LF. Needham Jones's Sovereignty Commission interview is recounted in Zack J. Van Landingham to State Sovereignty Commission Director, August 11, 1959, Box 21, J. P. Coleman Papers.

41. B. L. Bell's relationship with the Sovereignty Commission can be gleaned from the following documents: B. L. Bell to Governor J. P. Coleman, November 13, 1958; Zack J. Van Landingham to Governor J. P. Coleman, January 12, 1959; Zack J. Van Landingham to State Sovereignty Commission Director, January 26, June 30, October 22, 1959, all in LF. In a 1996 interview, Bell's son, B. L. Bell Jr., believed his father served as a Sovereignty Commission informer because "he was vehemently against" school desegregation since he did not think black teachers and students were "qualified enough" to attend the same schools as whites. See B. L. Bell Jr., interview by Kim Lacy Rogers and Owen Brooks, March 4, 1996, Delta Oral History Project.

42. Zack J. Van Landingham, Sovereignty Commission File Memo 9-9, January 26, 1960, LF; Aaron Henry to Gloster Current, November 25, 1961, III-A-231, NAACP Papers, LC; Kirksey, interview; unsigned report of March 4, 1964, LF.

43. Robert G. Clark, interview by Betsy Nash, February 18, 1991, John Stennis Oral History Collection, MSU. For Ernestine Talbert's story, see Ernestine Talbert, interview by author, October 1, 1997, transcript, vol. 702, MOHP; "Justice Asks Negro Teacher Who Tried to Vote Be Rehired," *Greenville (Miss.) Delta Democrat-Times*, June 17, 1962; and "Judge Cox to Hear Negro Teacher Suit," *McComb (Miss.) Enterprise-Journal*, June 18, 1962, both in Facts on Film, July 1961–June 1962, reel 5.

44. Publication of Coahoma County Branch of NAACP, [1962?], III-C-73, NAACP Papers, LC; *New Orleans Times-Picayune* 1963 article citing information from an unpublished report by the Mississippi State Department of Education, AFSC.

45. Aaron Henry to Boss Man, June 17, 1962, III-C-73, NAACP Papers, LC; *New Orleans Times-Picayune* 1963 article; Christopher Hexter, "What Is a Ruleville Education,"

[1964?], Christopher Hexter Papers, SHSW; Dr. W. B. Thompson, interview by Michael Garvey, October 7, 1976, vol. 270, MOHP. In 1962, only 5 of the state's 642 white schools failed to achieve approval by the state board of accreditation.

46. H. M. Ivy to W. M. Colmer, July 23, 1955, Box 363, William M. Colmer Papers, MCLA; University of Mississippi, Bureau of Educational Research, *The Report of a Survey of the Public Schools of Benton County* (University, Miss.: Bureau of Educational Research, 1956); Notes, Benton County, NAACPLDF, SCRLP, reel 136; Benton County School Board Minutes, June 30, 1964 (microfilm); Report of Tom Scarbrough, September 13, 1960, LF.

47. H. M. Ivy to W. M. Colmer, July 23, 1955, Box 363, William M. Colmer Papers; Tunica County Board of Education Minutes, January 14, August 1, 1958; October 2, 1963 (microfilm); *New Orleans Times-Picayune* 1963 article.

48. Mississippi State Department of Education, *Statistical Data, 1957–58* (n.p., [1958?]), 21; petition from Jefferson Davis County Parents to Jefferson County School Board, [late 1950s?]; and petition from Lauderdale County parents to Governor Coleman and the Lauderdale County School Board, [late 1950s?], both in Box 13, J. P. Coleman Papers.

49. Valerie Grim, "The Establishment and Implementation of Education in the Brooks Farm Community, 1920–1957," *Oral History Review* 23 (Summer 1996): 16–17; James Jones Jr., interview by M. G. Trend, April 13, 1982, transcript, MC-CPL; Emma Cooper, interview by Milan Green, August 1, 1971, transcript, vol. 4, MHC; Friendship PTA (Hoy, Miss.) to Mr. Tubb, August 30, 1957, RG 50, vol. 261, MDAH.

50. "Administration Highlights . . . Mississippi," August 6, 1964, Box 565, Office Files of Fred Panzer, LBJ; Statement, 1958, Box 8, George Washington Owens Papers.

51. U.S. Department of HEW, *Administration of Public Laws 81-874* and *81-815: Eleventh Annual Report*; U.S. Department of HEW, *Administration of Public Laws 81-874* and *81-815: Thirteenth Annual Report of the Commissioner of Education* (Washington, D.C.: Government Printing Office, 1963).

52. "NAACP Challenges HEW's Hands-Off Policy on School Desegregation," Press Release, March 6, 1958; and "NAACP Scores Failure to Insure Negroes Equal Benefits from School Aid," May 26, 1961, both in III-A-117, NAACP Papers, LC; Reed Sarratt, *The Ordeal of Desegregation: The First Decade* (New York: Harper and Row, 1966), 63–71; Abraham Ribicoff, March 30, 1962, Box 2, RG 12, NA.

53. Sarratt, 65; Jean Fairfax to Garnet Guild and Barbara Moffett (Mississippi Series No. 1), April 15, 1964, AFSC; Brief Summary of the Meeting with Local School Superintendents in the Southern States Held in Memphis, Tennessee, December 8 and 9, 1962, Box 2, RG 12, NA; "Biloxi's Officials Surprised," *Biloxi (Miss.) Daily Herald*, January 19, 1963; U.S. Commission on Civil Rights, *Public Education: 1964 Staff Report* (Washington, D.C.: Government Printing Office, 1964), 134–35.

54. "School-Military Crisis Is Moving Closer in Miss.," *Baton Rouge State Times*, August 28, 1963, in Facts on Film, July 1963–June 1964, reel 11; Lewis H. Walker to All Military Personnel, August 23, 1963, Series 4, Box 19, JCS; "School For Air Base Pupils Closed by Mississippi City," *Memphis Commercial Appeal*, August 23, 1963; "Air Base

Pupils Lack School Setup," *Memphis Commercial Appeal*, August 24, 1963; "Columbus Nearing School Agreement," *Jackson (Miss.) Daily News*, September 10, 1963; John R. Henry to Senator John C. Stennis, September 21, 1963, Series 4, Box 30, JCS.

55. "Report on 1960 Education Programs from State Organizations to Mississippi Coordinating Committee on Education," January 11, 1960, Box 51, J. M. Tubb Papers; "Aid to Education Hit By Miss. Farm Group," *Mississippi Free Press,* December 15, 1962; "75 Children in Biloxi Ask Desegregation," *Mississippi Free Press*, March 30, 1963.

56. Jim B. Collier to Albert Jones, February 26, 1962, LF; E. K. Windham to Walter Sillers, March 29, 1960, Box 40, Walter Sillers Papers; "MEC's School Stand Is Rare," *Jackson (Miss.) Daily News*, April 21, 1963; Sarratt, 296; C. E. Schmidt to Joe T. Patterson, February 7, 1963; C. E. Schmidt to Joe T. Patterson, March 14, 1963; and Joe T. Patterson to C. E. Schmidt, March 19, 1963, all in Box 17536, RG 48, MDAH.

CHAPTER 4

1. Telephone conversation between Lyndon Johnson and Robert F. Kennedy, July 10, 1964, 10:35 A.M., Citation # 4198; and telephone conversation between Lyndon Johnson and Nicholas Katzenbach, August 31, 1964, 2:35 P.M., Citation # 5288, both in Recordings of Telephone Conversations, White House Series, Recordings and Transcripts of Conversations and Meetings, LBJ; U.S. Commission on Civil Rights, 137–39; John Herbers, "Grade Schools in Mississippi Are Integrated," *New York Times*, September 1, 1964; "Rural School in Mississippi Enrolls One Negro Girl under Heavy Guard," *New York Times*, September 2, 1964; A. L. Hopkins, "Investigation of the enrollment of a Negro first grade student in the Carthage attendance center of Leake County a former all white school," September 8, 1964, Box 1, PBJ; Jean Fairfax to Barbara W. Moffett (Mississippi Report No. 7), October 2, 1964, AFSC.

2. Dittmer, ch. 11; Robert J. Norrell, *Reaping the Whirlwind: The Civil Rights Movement in Tuskegee* (New York: Knopf, 1985), chs. 9–10; Frank T. Read and Lucy S. McGough, *Let Them Be Judged: The Judicial Integration of the Deep South* (Metuchen, N.J.: Scarecrow Press, 1978), 611; Gilbert R. Mason with James Patterson Smith, *Beaches, Blood, and Ballots: A Black Doctor's Civil Rights Struggle* (Jackson: University Press of Mississippi, 2000), 157.

3. Dittmer, 86–87; Gilbert R. Mason Sr., interviews by James "Pat" Smith, sixteen interviews between March 12 and July 30, 1998, transcript, MOHP; Mason with Smith.

4. Jean Fairfax to Garnet Guild and Barbara Moffett (Mississippi Series No. 1), April 15, 1964, AFSC; Russell Quave, interview by R. Wayne Pyle, March 18, 1980, transcript, MOHP.

5. Fairfax to Guild and Moffett, April 15, 1964; Mason, interviews.

6. Mason, interviews; Mason with Smith, esp. ch. 8. Payne, in *I've Got the Light of Freedom*, ch. 7, suggests that many Mississippi civil rights activists came from "movement families."

7. Mason, interviews; Derrick A. Bell Jr. to Barbara Morris, May 21, 1963, III-D, NAACP Papers, reel 5. The Biloxi parents had asked for legal help from the NAACP as early as 1960 without success. See Medgar W. Evers to Robert L. Carter, October 11, 1960; and Robert L. Carter to Medgar W. Evers, October 25, 1960, both in III-D, NAACP Papers, reel 5.

8. Winson Hudson and Constance Curry, *Mississippi Harmony: Memoirs of a Freedom Fighter* (New York: Palgrave Macmillan, 2002), ch. 3; Dittmer, 256–57.

9. Hudson and Curry, ch. 3; Winson Hudson, interview by Thomas Dent, August 1, 1979, audiotape, Mississippi Oral History Project, ARC.

10. Complaint, March 1963; memo from Derrick A. Bell Jr. to Robert R. Ming, April 29, 1963; and letter from William R. Ming Jr. to Jack Greenberg, April 22, 1963, all in *Dian Hudson v. Leake County School Board*, NAACPLDF Litigation Files, SCRLR, reel 148; Hudson and Curry, ch. 3; "Leake Negro Educator Asks Name Removal from Petition," *Jackson (Miss.) Daily News*, April 5, 1962; "Leake County Parents File Desegregation Suit," *Mississippi Free Press*, March 16, 1963.

11. Dittmer, 87–89; Orbra Porter and J. B. Harrington, interview by author, December 17, 2001, transcript, MOHP; petition of black parents to Jackson Board of Trustees, August 15, 1962, case file, *Singleton v. Jackson Municipal School District*, U.S. District Court, Jackson.

12. Jeanne Marie Middleton, "The History of *Singleton v. Jackson Municipal Separate School District*: Southern School Desegregation from the Perspective of the Black Community" (Ed.D. diss., Harvard University, 1978), 65–69; Medgar W. Evers to Robert L. Carter, December 14, 1962, III-D, NAACP Papers, reel 5; "Courts to Be Asked to Open P.S. Here," *Mississippi Free Press*, March 2, 1963; *Fifteen-Year Report of the Superintendent of Schools, Jackson Municipal School District: July 1, 1950 through June 30, 1965* (Jackson, Miss.: n.p., 1965), 54–55; Jackson School Board Minutes, July 21, 1959, (microfilm), MDAH.

13. Mason with Smith, 153–54; Sarratt, 110; Louie Burton Barnes III, "The Embattled Judges: Cox, Mize, and Cameron, 1960–1965" (master's thesis, Mississippi State University, 1974), ch. 3.

14. Defendant's answer, March 31, 1964, *Dian Hudson v. Leake County School Board*; Judge Mize's decision, 5–11, July 1964, RG 50, vol. 285, MDAH; Jean Fairfax to Barbara W. Moffett and Garnet Guild, May 27, 1964, AFSC. Gooden's successor as Jackson's supervisor of black schools, Amos Wright, refused to testify for the defense. See Jean Fairfax to Barbara W. Moffett and Garnet Guild (Mississippi Report no. 7), October 2, 1964, AFSC.

15. Barnes, ch. 3; W. C. Shoemaker, "Mixing Ordered in Schools Here," *Jackson (Miss.) Daily News*, July 8, 1964; brochure of National Putnam Letters Committee, "The Evers Opinion," August 4, 1967, Facts on Film, July 1967–June 1968, reel 17; Read and McGough, 416–18, 472, 492–96; Fairfax to Moffett and Guild, October 2, 1964.

16. Aaron Henry with Constance Curry, *Aaron Henry: The Fire Ever Burning* (Jackson: University Press of Mississippi, 2000); "NAACP in Clarksdale, Miss., Seeks School

Desegregation," Press Release, September 20, 1963, III-D, NAACP Papers, reel 5; Jean Fairfax to Barbara Moffett and Garnet Guild, June 3, 1964, AFSC; U.S. Commission on Civil Rights, 133–39.

17. Nicholas Lemann, *The Promised Land: The Great Black Migration and How It Changed America* (New York: Alfred A. Knopf, 1991), 321–22; *Henry v. Clarksdale Municipal Separate School District* 409 F.2d 682 (1969) at 686–88; "Judge Clayton Orders Clarksdale to Integrate 1st Grade in 2 Weeks," *Tupelo (Miss.) Daily Journal*, August 20, 1964; Fairfax to Moffett and Guild, October 2, 1964, AFSC; Aaron Henry to Peter Labassi, September 25, 1967, IV-C-17, NAACP Papers, LC.

18. See school map that accompanies "Schools: Jackson, Mississippi, 1963," no author or publication information, "Jackson–Schools," Subject File, MCLA.

19. William Peart, "Conflict on Tuition Grants Unresolved," *Jackson (Miss.) Daily News*, June 30, 1964; U.S. Commission on Civil Rights, 136; Joe T. Patterson to John L. Barrett, November 9, 1964, RG 48, Box 17536, MDAH.

20. Selby Williams to Governor Paul B. Johnson, June 22, 1964, Box 119; Cleveland man (signature illegible) to Gov. Johnson, July 11, 1964, Box 116; Mavis Ervin Hollingsworth to Honorable Paul B. Johnson, July 8, 1964, Box 116, all in PBJ.

21. H. E. Pass to Governor Paul B. Johnson, June 6, 1964; Mrs. Bobby Perry to Gov. Johnson, June 23, 1964; T. Phillips Heard to Gov. Johnson, June 25, 1964; James Willie Carpenter to Gov. Johnson, June 23, 1964; Jerry Breazeale to Gov. Johnson, [June 1964]; Henry Edwards to Gov. Johnson, June 27, 1964; and L. C. Roebuck to Gov. Johnson, June 1964, all in Box 119, PBJ.

22. *William H. Green v. Kennedy*, Lawyers Constitutional Defense Committee, SCRLR, reel 26; Press Release, Jackson Citizens Council, August 11, 1964, Bill Minor Papers, MSU; "School Board Urged to Stand Firm," *EPIC* (April 1964), Facts on Film, July 1963–June 1964, reel 16; file memo from Erle Johnston Jr., November 17, 1964, Box 136, PBJ; School Committee, Jackson Citizens' Council, "Why Should I Join the Council School Corporation," [1964], Segregation-Integration Miscellaneous Collection, MSU. The federal government eventually filed suit in 1966 to have the tuition plan outlawed. See James MacNees, "Mississippi Tuition Plan Provokes U.S.," *Baltimore Sun*, March 15, 1966.

23. Speech by J. Oliver Emmerich to Mississippi Economic Council, April 5, 1965, in Facts on Film, July 1964–June 1965, reel 18; Curtis R. Walters, "A Parents Plea," [1966], Segregation-Integration Miscellaneous Collection.

24. *State-Wide Education Study: Phase I, State of Mississippi* (Chicago: Booz-Allen and Hamilton, 1966); "Remembering Jefferson Davis Academy, 1965–1987," in Lauderdale County Department of Archives and History, Meridian, Miss.

25. Motion for Supplemental Relief, September 1965, *Alexander v. Holmes County*, NAACPLDF Litigation Files, SCRLR, reel 133; "Durant Mayor Feels School Stand Responsible in Fire," *Jackson (Miss.) Daily News*, September 16, 1965; "Continued Investigation of the Racial Situation in the Holmes County Mississippi State Park, the town of Durant and Holmes County, as a whole," September 22, 1965, Sovereignty Commission Files, 2-54-2-24-1-1-1, MDAH.

26. Defendant's Answer to Plaintiffs-Intervenor's Interrogatories to State Educational Finance Committee, May 4, 1966; and Answer of Defendant-Intervenors to Complaint of Plaintiffs, May 16, 1966, both in *Coffey v. State Educational Finance Committee*, NAACPLDF Litigation Files, SCRLR, reel 140; "State of the Southern States," *New South* 22 (Spring 1967): 99; W. F. Minor, "Tuition Grants Not Used on Wide Basis in State," *New Orleans Times-Picayune*, February 26, 1967.

27. *Madison County (Miss.) Citizen*, March 9, 1964, Box 142; Students of Rogers High to Dean Allen, [March 1964], Box 135; and Erle Johnston Jr. to Governor Johnson, March 9, 1964, Box 135, all in PBJ; Oscar Chase to Matteo Suarez, [1964], Congress of Racial Equality, Madison County, Mississippi, Records, reel 4.

28. Mary Aickin Rothschild, "The Volunteers and the Freedom Schools: Education for Social Change in Mississippi," in *The Social History of American Education*, ed. B. Edward McClellan and William J. Reese, 352–55 (Urbana: University of Illinois Press, 1988); Staughton Lynd, "Mississippi Freedom Schools: Retrospect and Prospect," Appendix A, SNCC Papers, 1959–72, reel 38; Clayborne Carson, *In Struggle: SNCC and the Black Awakening of the 1960s* (Cambridge, Mass.: Harvard University Press, 1981), 119–21; Liz Fusco, "Freedom Schools in Mississippi, 1964," [1965?], James Mays Papers, SHSW; Payne; Sandra Adickes, "The Legacy of the Mississippi Freedom Schools," *Radical Teacher*, n.d., in Glenda Funchess Civil Rights Collection, MCLA; Glenda Funchess, interview by author, July 17, 1998, transcript; Glenda F. Funchess, "Freedom Summer," n.d., Glenda Funchess Civil Rights Collection, MCLA.

29. WATS [Wide-Area Telecommunication Service] Reports, August 3, 1964 (Shaw); August 4, 1964 (Shaw), both in FIS, reel 1.

30. WATS Reports, September 1, 1964 (Shaw and Marks); September 4, 1964 (Meridian); September 5, 1964 (Canton); September 9, 1964 (Marks); September 10, 1964 (Jackson); September 15, 1964 (Meridian); and October 1, 1964 (Shaw), all in FIS, reel 1; file memo from Erle Johnston, September 8, 1964; and report of A. L. Hopkins, September 8, 1964, both in Box 136, PBJ; Michael Churchill to R. Hunter Morey, September 4, 1964, *Barnhardt v. Meridian*, NAACPLDF Litigation Files, SCRLR, reel 136; petition to Roy E. Cox and Madison County School Board, September 1964, Congress of Racial Equality, Madison County, Mississippi, Records, reel 4.

31. WATS Reports, September 5, 1964 (Greenwood); September 9, 1964 (Summit and Moss Point); and September 24, 1964 (McComb), all in FIS, reel 1.

32. Jean Fairfax to Jacques Wilmore, October 16, 1963, AFSC.

33. Fairfax to Moffett and Guild, October 2, 1964; flyer from Jackson ministers, [August 1964], SNCC Papers, 1959–72, reel 68; Jean Fairfax to Dovie Hudson, August 5, 1964, *Dian Hudson v. Leake County*, NAACPLDF Litigation Files, SCRLR, reel 148; Mason with Smith, 155.

34. Glenda Elizabeth Gilmore, *Gender and Jim Crow: Women and the Politics of White Supremacy in North Carolina, 1896–1920* (Chapel Hill: University of North Carolina Press, 1996); Jacqueline Dowd Hall, *Revolt against Chivalry: Jessie Daniel Ames and the Women's Campaign Against Lynching* (Chapel Hill: University of North Carolina Press, 1979).

35. Marcia Kunstel, "Breaking the Conspiracy of Silence," *Southern Exposure* 7 (Summer 1979): 77–83; "History of Mississippians for Public Education," [July 1967?], Southern Regional Council Papers, reel 34; Pat Watters, "A Door Opens in Mississippi," *Progressive*, December 1964, 29–31; Winifred Green, interview by author, November 12, 1997, transcript, vol. 704, MOHP; American Friends Service Committee, "Community Relations Program in Mississippi, 1964–65," November 1964, AFSC.

36. Kunstel, 77–83; Watters, 29–31; Green, interview.

37. "A Delta Discussion—Issue III of a Series," [1964?], Box 3, Race Relations Collection. A number of letters to Governor Johnson from women associated with the MPE voicing opposition to the governor's tuition-grant plan can be found in Box 116, PBJ.

38. Public Notice about Jackson Municipal Separate School District Desegregation Plan, August 9, 1964, RG 50, vol. 285, MDAH.

CHAPTER 5

1. Presidential Message on Civil Rights and Job Opportunities to the Congress of the United States, June 19, 1963, Box 474, Office Files of Fred Panzer, LBJ; Lino A. Graglia, *Disaster by Decree: The Supreme Court Decisions on Race and the Schools* (Ithaca, N.Y.: Cornell University Press, 1976), 46–47; W. C. Shoemaker, "Segregation 'Out Window': Cox," *Jackson (Miss.) Daily News*, August 28, 1965; Frederick M. Wirt, *Politics of Southern Equality: Law and Social Change in a Mississippi County* (Chicago: Aldine, 1970), ch. 9.

2. "The South Far Behind in Education," *New York Times*, December 12, 1965; Department of Health, Education, and Welfare, "The First Work of These Times . . . : A Description and Analysis of the Elementary and Secondary Education Act of 1965," April 1965, Box 1, Office Files of Bill Moyers, LBJ; BIENNIAL (1969), 66–73.

3. Board of Directors, Ripley Junior Chamber of Commerce to South Tippah School Board, February 11, 1965, Box 110, PBJ. For evidence of similar sentiments, see Charles S. Whittington to Honorable Paul Johnson, January 13, 1965; and V. O. Campbell Sr. to Heber Ladner, January 12, 1965, both in Box 2, J. M. Tubb Papers.

4. Mrs. Loomis C. Giles to Governor Paul B. Johnson and Mr. J. M. Tubb, January 20, 1965; and Mrs. J. B. Dakin to J. M. Tubb, January 6, 1965, both in Box 2, J. M. Tubb Papers. Additional letters urging the state to refuse federal funds if the acceptance of such monies would lead to further school desegregation can be found in Boxes 1 and 2 of the J. M. Tubb Papers; and RG 50, vol. 288, MDAH.

5. Allan Wolk, *The Presidency and Black Civil Rights. Eisenhower to Nixon* (Rutherford, N.J.: Fairleigh Dickinson University Press, 1971), ch. 4; "Instructions to School Districts Regarding Compliance with Title VI of the Civil Rights Act of 1964: Nondiscrimination in Federally Assisted Programs," [December 1964], Box 111, PBJ; Special Committee of Mississippi Association of School Administrators to Francis Keppel, April 6, 1965, Series 29, Box 5, JCS; Henry Wilson to Larry O'Brien,

March 16, 1965, Box 7, Office Files of Henry Wilson, LBJ; Douglas Cater to the
President, April 23, 1965, Box 13, Office Files of S. Douglas Cater, LBJ; memo on call
from John R. Henry, July 30, 1965, Series 29, Box 8, JCS; "U.S. Demands Full
Integration by '67," *Jackson (Miss.) Daily News*, April 30, 1965; David Seeley, interview by Joshua Zatman, July 25, 1968, transcript, LBJ.

6. Gary Orfield, *The Reconstruction of Southern Education: The Schools and the 1964
Civil Rights Act* (New York: Wiley-Interscience, 1969), chs. 2–3, 6; "Status of School
Districts Either Failing to File Desegregation Plans or Having Serious Compliance
Problems Likely to Lead to Cut-Off of Funds," September 13, 1965, Box 53, Office
Files of S. Douglas Cater; Marion S. Barry and Betty Garman, "SNCC: A Special
Report of Southern School Desegregation," [1965?], Records of CORE, 4th District
of Mississippi, reel 4.

7. F. Peter Libassi to Douglas Cater, January 20, 1966, Box 2, Office Files of Lee C. White,
LBJ; "Amite Calls School Levy Referendum for July 17," *Jackson (Miss.) Daily News*,
July 12, 1965; "Amite Voters Pass School Tax Levy," *Jackson (Miss.) Daily News*, July 19,
1965. The twelve Mississippi districts that had federal funds cut off in the fall of 1965
(there were fifty-one nationwide) were Amite County, Copiah County, Covington
County, Greenwood, Grenada, Humphreys County, Leflore County, Noxubee
County, Sunflower County, Warren County, Wilkinson County, and Natchez.

8. Nina Dinkins, interview by M. G. Trend, April 29, 1982, transcript, MC-CPL; John C.
Stennis to President Johnson, November 3, 1965, Box 52; and Douglas Cater to President Johnson, September 13, 1965, Box 14, both in Office Files of S. Douglas Cater.

9. Seeley, interview; John W. Gardner to Members of Congress and Governors, April
9, 1966, Box 53, Office Files of S. Douglas Cater; Press Release, U.S. Department of
Health, Education, and Welfare, March 7, 1966, Box 8, MCHR; Gene Roberts,
"South Intensifies Resistance to U.S. Guidelines for School Integration," *New York
Times*, May 23, 1966.

10. Douglas Cater to President Johnson, February 19, 1966, Box 14, Office Files of
S. Douglas Cater; "Patterson Attacks Federal Guidelines," *Jackson (Miss.) Daily
News*, April 18, 1966; "State of the Southern States: Mississippi" *New South* 21
(Summer 1966): 97, in Facts on Film, July 1966–June 1967, reel 16; Eighteen south-
ern U.S. Senators to President Johnson, May 2, 1966, Box 53, Office Files of S.
Douglas Cater; Committee of Mississippi Educators to Harold Howe II, March 24,
1966, NAACPLDF General Office Files, SCRLR, reel 161.

11. Seeley, interview; Henry Aronson to Jean Fairfax, [March 1966?]; and Aaron Henry
to John Gardner, April 4, 1966, both in NAACPLDF General Office Files, SCRLR,
reel 161; Lyndon B. Johnson to Senators, May 16, 1966, Box 22, Office Files of Harry
McPherson, LBJ; Gary Orfield, *Must We Bus?: Segregated Schools and National
Policy* (Washington, D.C.: Brookings Institution, 1978), 239.

12. Douglas Cater to President Johnson, May 19, 1966, Box 14; Douglas Cater to President
Johnson, August 4, 1966, Box 15; F. Peter Libassi to Douglas Cater, Joseph Califano,
and John Doar, November 18, 1966, Box 53, all in Office Files of S. Douglas Cater.

13. Libassi to Cater, Califano, and Doar, November 18, 1966; F. Peter Libassi to Douglas Cater, November 30, 1966, Box 53; and F. Peter Libassi to Joseph Califano, Douglas Cater, and Nicholas Katzenbach, September 2, 1966, Box 52, both in Office Files of S. Douglas Cater. The fifteen Mississippi school districts where HEW enforcement proceedings were initiated in the fall of 1966 were Choctaw County, Coffeeville, Forrest County, Lincoln County, Montgomery County, Nettleton Line Consolidated, Oakland Consolidated, Pascagoula, Picayune, Pontotoc County, Poplarville, Rankin County, Richton, Simpson County, and Smith County.

14. This story can be followed in Wolk, ch. 4; and Gary Orfield, "Congress, the President, and Anti-Busing Legislation, 1966–1974," in *The Struggle for Equal Education*, vol. 7, pt. 1 of *Race Law and American History 1700–1990: The African American Experience*, ed. Paul Finkleman, 11 vols. (New York: Garland, 1992), 481–539.

15. Douglas Cater to the President, May 19, 1966, Box 14, Office Files of S. Douglas Cater.

16. A number of scholars have criticized the federal courts for their judicial activism in forcing the abandonment of freedom of choice and requiring the achievement of racial balance as proof that dual school systems had been eliminated. See, for example, Raymond Wolters, *The Burden of Brown: Thirty Years of School Desegregation* (Knoxville: University of Tennessee Press, 1984); and Stephen C. Halpern, *On the Limits of the Law: The Ironic Legacy of Title VI of the 1964 Civil Rights Act* (Baltimore: Johns Hopkins University Press, 1995). Given the white southern establishment's refusal to comply in any meaningful way with either *Brown* or the Civil Rights Act of 1964, the federal judiciary's actions seem reasonable and understandable.

17. Burk, 117–19; "Guidelines on Trial," *American Education* 3 (March 1967): 18–20; Patterson, *Grand Expectations*, 730.

18. Burke Marshall, interview by T. H. Baker, October 28, 1968, transcript, LBJ.

19. Burk, 133; Horace Barker, *The Federal Retreat in School Desegregation* (Atlanta: Southern Regional Council, 1969), 19–20.

20. U.S. Civil Rights Commission, "Federal Enforcement of School Desegregation," September 11, 1969, in Lawyers Constitutional Defense Committee, General Office Files, SCRLR, reel 93; Erle Johnston Jr. file memo, June 21, 1968, LF; William C. Keady, *All Rise: Memoirs of a Mississippi Federal Judge* (Boston: Recollections Bound, 1988), 114; *Anthony v. Marshall County Board of Education* 409 F.2d 1287 (1969).

21. *United States v. Hinds County School Board* 417 F.2d 852 (1969); Notes, [1968?], Box 6, Rims Barber Papers, TCA; Phil Hearn, "Expert Testifies Negro Less Able in Abstract," *Jackson (Miss.) Clarion-Ledger*, October 9, 1968; Phil Hearn, "Psychology Prof Testifies Negro Achievement Lower," *Jackson (Miss.) Clarion-Ledger*, October 11, 1968; "Educator Says School System Could Be Ruined," *Jackson (Miss.) Clarion-Ledger*, December 3, 1968. The twenty-five school districts were Amite County, Canton, Columbia, Covington County, Forrest County, Franklin County, Hinds County, Holmes County, Kemper County, Lauderdale County, Lawrence County, Leake County, Lincoln County, Madison County, Marion County, Meridian, Natchez-Adams County, Neshoba County, North Pike, Noxubee County, Philadelphia, Sharkey-Issaquena, Anguilla Line, South Pike, and Wilkinson County.

22. Betty Showell, "The Courts, the Legislature, the Presidency, and School Desegregation Policy," in *School Desegregation: Shadow and Substance*, ed. Florence Hamlish Levinsohn and Benjamin Drake Wright, 101–3 (Chicago: University of Chicago Press, 1979); John Morton Blum, *Years of Discord: American Politics and Society, 1961–1974* (New York: W. W. Norton, 1991), 332–35; Mel Leventhal, Conference on Public Education, April 26, 1969, Box 8, MCHR.

23. Gycelle Tynes to William Colmer, May 2, 1969, Box 194, William M. Colmer Papers (2nd accession); William B. Alexander to G. V. Montgomery, April 30, 1969, RG 50, vol. 175, MDAH.

24. Memo from Clarke Reed to Harry S. Dent, May 20, 1969; and memo from Harry S. Dent to the Attorney General, May 23, 1969, both in Box 1, Presidential Materials Review Board—Review on Contested Documents, Harry S. Dent, Nixon Project, NA; John Stennis to Richard Nixon, August 11, 1969, Box 34, WHSF-SMOF: Ehrlichman.

25. Stennis to Nixon, August 11, 1969.

26. A number of historians have recognized that on the issue of school desegregation, Nixon's policies were often contradictory and ambiguous. See, for example, Lawrence J. McAndrews, "The Politics of Principle: Richard Nixon and School Desegregation," *Journal of Negro History* 83 (Summer 1998): 187–200; and Hugh Davis Graham, *The Civil Rights Era: Origins and Development of National Policy, 1960–1972* (New York: Oxford University Press, 1990).

27. McAndrews, 189; Harry S. Dent, Memorandum for the President, June 26, 1969, Box 13, WHCF, Subject Files—Human Rights, Nixon Project; "President Vows to Enforce Edict on Desegregation," *New York Times*, October 31, 1969; Harry Dent to President Nixon, April 9, 1969, Box 30, WHSF-SMOF: Ehrlichman.

28. "Eastland Says GOP Lied on Mix Plans," *Jackson (Miss.) Clarion Ledger*, July 11, 1969; MEA Statistics, 1968–69, RG 48, vol. 185, MDAH; Charles R. Jacobs to President Nixon, August 17, 1969, Box 15, WHCF, Subject Files—Human Rights, Nixon Project.

29. Gary Orfield, "The Court, the Schools, and the Southern Strategy," *Saturday Review*, December 20, 1969, 62; Aaron Henry to Roy Wilkins, November 29, 1969, IV-C-17, NAACP Papers, LC; "Area Pupils Take Tests," *Clarksdale (Miss.) Press Register*, September 29, 1969; testimony of George Pettey, Hearing on Plan before Judge Keady, September 2, 1969, *United States of America and Driver v. Tunica County School District*, case file, FDCOX; Tunica County Board of Education Minutes, September 30, 1969 (microfilm). The other school districts where intelligence-testing plans were adopted in 1969 were Bolivar County, Sunflower County, Marshall County, and Holly Springs.

30. Mrs. R. R. Vance to John Stennis, August 18, 1969; Rudolph Harris and Mrs. Rudolph Harris to Senator Stennis, August 9, 1969; and Mrs. Lavon Wade to Senator Stennis, July 23, 1969, all in Series 53, Box 2, JCS. This box contains hundreds of similar letters.

31. Stennis to Nixon, August 11, 1969; Jack Rosenthal, "Stennis Linked to Desegregation Delay," *New York Times*, September 19, 1969; "Stennis Asks Uniform Integration Enforcement," *Jackson (Miss.) Clarion Ledger*, August 12, 1969.

32. Barker, 30–32; "School Mix Delay Welcomed at Top," *Jackson (Miss.) Daily News*, August 29, 1969; "Where Jim Crow Is Alive and Well," *Time*, September 19, 1969, 21. The case name had to be changed because the federal government switched sides in the litigation.

33. Leventhal, Conference on Public Education, April 26, 1969; *Franklin v. Quitman County Board of Education* 288 F. Supp. 509 (1968).

34. Ernest L. Brown to Dugas Shands, September 19, 1966, RG 48, Box 17486, MDAH.

35. Obie Clark, interview by author, September 30, 1997, transcript, vol. 699, MOHP.

36. Speech by J. M. Tubb to Jackson Civitan Club, September 21, 1967, Box 2169, Mississippi AFL-CIO Records, Southern Labor Archives, Georgia State University, Atlanta; Armand Derfner to Jerry J. Berman, December 4, 1969, Lawyers Constitutional Defense Committee, Papers from Mississippi, Alabama, and Louisiana for the 1960s, SCRLR, reel 79.

37. Neil Maxwell, "Integration Irony," *Wall Street Journal*, December 12, 1969; Derfner to Berman, December 4, 1969; General Young to John Gardner, August 30, 1967, IV-C-18, NAACP Papers, LC; Title I review by OEO of Mississippi school districts, July and August 1969, in Lawyers Constitutional Defense Committee, General Office Files, SCRLR, reel 95; testimony before the Senate Education Committee by Jake Ayers Sr. and Rims Barber, June 20, 1969, Box 5, Delta Ministry Papers, MSU. Of course, some districts refused to apply for the Title I funds to avoid federal oversight of their operations.

38. Report of Rims Barber on Yazoo County, Mississippi; and Complaint of Mrs. Emanuel Crystal, both in Title I review by OEO of Mississippi school districts, July and August 1969, in Lawyers Constitutional Defense Committee, General Office Files, SCRLR, reel 95; Complaint, *Taylor v. Coahoma County*, February 21, 1969, Lawyers Constitutional Defense Committee, Papers from Mississippi, Alabama, and Louisiana for the 1960s, SCRLR, reel 68.

39. Armand Derfner to Rev. Rims Barber, September 9, 1969, Lawyers Constitutional Defense Committee, General Office Files, SCRLR, reel 95.

40. Ibid.

41. Read and McGough, 612–14; "Negroes in Desegregated Schools in Mississippi, Autumn, 1966," Box 10, Delta Ministry Papers; MEA Statistics, 1968–69.

CHAPTER 6

1. Porter and Harrington, interview.

2. Ibid.

3. Ibid.

4. Isiah Thigpen, "Why People Are Not Sending Their Children to White School," [1966?], *Barnhardt v. Meridian*, NAACPLDF Litigation Files; Rims Barber, interview by author, August 21, 1997, transcript, vol. 690, MOHP; Green, interview.

5. WATS Reports, February 19, 1965 (Indianola); February 24, 1964 (Valley View and Moss Point); and March 10, 1965 (Benton County), all in FIS, reel 1; Report by Clay County MFDP, August 16, 1965, Box 7, MFDP Papers, King Library and Archives, Atlanta; "The Illegal School System of Liberty, Mississippi," list of demands from black students, [1965], Box 142, PBJ; Fusco; "No Freedom in School," February 18, 1965, Congress of Racial Equality, 4th District of Mississippi Records, reel 4.

6. Martin Nicolaus to Jim, February 16, 1965, Martin and Victoria Nicolaus Papers, SHSW; "No Freedom in School"; Cleopatra D. Thompson, *The History of the Mississippi Teachers Association* (Jackson, Miss.: Mississippi Teachers Association, 1973), 130; Affidavit of Harriet Diggs, May 6, 1965, case file, *Jeremiah Blackwell Jr. et al. v. The Issaquena Board of Education et al.*, U.S. District Court, Jackson, Miss.

7. Sovereignty Commission report on Issaquena-Sharkey Counties, March 11, 1965, LF; "School De-Segregation in Issaquena and Sharkey," [1965?], SNCC Papers, 1959–72, reel 58; Unita Blackwell, interview by Mike Garvey, May 12, 1977, transcript, vol. 334, MOHP.

8. Benton County School Board Minutes, June 7, 1965 (microfilm); "Physical Description of School Properties," *Baird v. Benton County*, NAACPLDF Litigation Files, SCRLR, reel 135; G. N. Reaves, interview by Aviva Futorian, December 11, 1995, transcript, North Mississippi Oral History Program Collection.

9. Aviva Futorian, "The Benton County Movement," 1999, in author's possession; Benton County School Board Minutes, January 4, March 8, 1965 (microfilm); G. N. Reaves, interview; Walter Reaves, interview by Aviva Futorian and Gloria Clark, December 12, 1995, transcript, North Mississippi Oral History Program Collection; *Benton County Freedom Train*, February 7, 1965, in Sovereignty Commission Files, 2-23-0-28-2-1-1, MDAH; *Benton County Freedom Train*, February 14, March 14, 1965, both in Box 142, PBJ; "The gang to fellow members of the great society," March 15, 1965; and "Let's Keep Our Children Out of School," March 1965, both in Aviva Futorian Papers, SHSW.

10. Futorian; Report of the Benton County Citizens Club, April 1965, Aviva Futorian Papers.

11. *Benton County Freedom Train*, February 14, 1965, Box 142, PBJ; Benton County School Board Minutes, March 3, May 3, 1965, (microfilm); Futorian; petition to the School Board for the Benton County Public Schools, 1965, *Baird v. Benton County*, NAACPLDF Litigation Files.

12. Interviews with a number of Mississippi blacks in 1968 revealed that the vast majority cared little about "complete desegregation" but wanted "equal facilities and educational opportunities regardless of the desegregation policy." See Mark Lowry II, "Schools in Transition," *Annals of the Association of American Geographers* 63 (June 1973): 173.

13. "Hearings Before the U.S. Commission on Civil Rights," vol. 1, Voting, Hearings Held in Jackson, Mississippi, February 16–20, 1965, Box 2166, Mississippi AFL-CIO Records, Southern Labor Archives; Mary Blackmon, interview by M. G. Trend,

March 16, 1982, transcript, MC-CPL; Loyal Thompson and Thelma Thompson, interview by Aviva Futorian, December 13, 1995, North Mississippi Oral History Program Collection; Lou Emma Shipp, "School Desegregation," September 1965, Congress of Racial Equality, 4th District of Mississippi Records, reel 4.

14. Kenneth L. Dean, "An Evaluation of School Desegregation in Mississippi," [1966?] NAACPLDF General Office Files, SCRLR, reel 161; Minutes of the Mississippi State Advisory Committee to the U.S. Commission on Civil Rights, January 11, 1966, Box 83, Claire Collins Harvey Papers, ARC; Mary Hightower, interview by Tom Dent, August 20, 1978, audiotape, Mississippi Oral History Project.

15. Harriet to Monica, Mike, Jesse, and Margie, May 20, 1966, Box 8, Mississippi Freedom Democratic Party Papers; form letter from Aaron Henry et al., April 4, 1966, Box 23, Delta Ministry Papers, King Library and Archives; untitled document, [1964], about the AFSC and NAACPLDF Leadership Training Institute on School Desegregation held on October 10, 1964, at Farish Street Baptist Church in Jackson, AFSC; memo from AFSC and NAACPLDF to John W. Gardner, November 15, 1965, Box 23, Office Files of S. Douglas Cater.

16. Fairfax to Moffett and Guild, October 2, 1964; Mason with Smith, 57.

17. Derrick A. Bell Jr., September 1, 1964, Facts on Film, July 1964–June 1965, reel 18; Affidavit of Derrick A. Bell Jr., [September 1964], *Dian Hudson v. Leake County School Board*, NAACPLDF Litigation Files, SCRLR, reel 148; "Mississippi Father Keeps Promise and Gets Fired," Press Release, September 4, 1964, III-A-231, NAACP Papers, LC.

18. "Mississippi Father Keeps Promise"; "How Debra Lewis Desegregated a School," *Southern Courier*, February 11–12, 1967, 4–5, AFSC; Affidavit of Minnie Lewis, March 1965, *Dian Hudson v. Leake County School Board*, NAACPLDF Litigation Files, SCRLR, reel 148.

19. Porter and Harrington, interview.

20. Ruby Nell Stancill, interview by Chea Prince and Constance Curry, July 7, 2000, videotape, MOHP; Amos J. Barron to William Colmer, May 22, 1965, Box 70, William M. Colmer Papers, 2nd accession; Mrs. J. B. Davenport Jr. to Governor Paul B. Johnson, September 1, 1966, Box 61, PBJ. David Higgs, a white teenager in Simpson County during the 1960s, also recalled that his parents believed black parents were paid to send their children to the white schools during the freedom-of-choice years. David W. Higgs, conversation with author, September 22, 1998.

21. Rev. A. H. Lambright to Dr. A. D. Beittel, June 14, 1965, AFSC; James H. McPhail, ed., *A History of Desegregation Developments in Certain Mississippi School Districts* (Hattiesburg: University of Southern Mississippi, 1971), 25, 78–80.

22. Dean. The evidence of white efforts to deny black choice in the matter of schools during these years through intimidation and chicanery is voluminous. For scores of examples of white intimidation and subversion of black "free choice," see the documents concerning school desegregation scattered throughout the 170 rolls of microfilm that make up the SCRLR.

23. Tommie Lee Williams Sr., interview by Don Williams, August 20, 1999, transcript, Civil Rights Documentation Project: The Vicksburg Movement, TCA; Barry and Garman; "White Man Jailed in Mix Death Try," *Jackson (Miss.) Clarion-Ledger*, August 20, 1965; U.S. Civil Rights Commission, 223; Motion for Supplemental Relief, September 1965, *Alexander v. Holmes County*, NAACPLDF Litigation Files; B. E. Bergesen III to Denison Ray, January 11, 1967, Lawyers Committee for Civil Rights Under the Law, Litigation Files, SCRLR, reel 129.

24. Wirt, *Politics of Southern Equality*, 208–9; Blackmon, interview; Barry and Garman; Motion for Further Injunctive Relief, [1965]; Eddie H. Tucker to Derrick A. Bell, September 27, 1965; and Affidavit of Randrough Miller, [1965], all in *Dian Hudson v. Leake County School Board*, NAACPLDF Litigation Files.

25. Rev. R. L. Stanton to Ruby Hurley, October 18, 1966, IV-C-17, NAACP Papers, LC; MEA Statistics, 1968–69, Attorney General's Record, RG 48, vol. 185, MDAH; Summary for Lincoln County, [1966?], Box 53, Office Files of S. Douglass Cater.

26. Summary for Lincoln County, [1966?]; Stanton to Hurley, October 18, 1966; MEA Statistics, 1968–69; memo on complaints (partial list) referred to HEW or Justice, [1966?], NAACPLDF General Office Files, SCRLR, reel 161. Kenneth Dean, in "An Evaluation of School Desegregation in Mississippi," found that only 3 percent of the black parents who sent their children to the white schools had ever received information about the choice procedures from their school districts.

27. District summaries (HEW enforcement proceedings initiated) for Poplarville and Pontotoc County, November 18, 1966, Box 53, Office Files of S. Douglas Cater; David S. Seeley to Robert Sanders, November 9, 1966, Box 124, William M. Colmer Papers, 2nd Accession.

28. "School De-segregation in Issaquena and Sharkey," SNCC Papers, 1959–72, reel 58; MFDP, "A Report on School Integration in Issaquena and Sharkey Counties, Mississippi," 1965, Box 3, Ed King Papers, TCA; MFDP WATS Report, September 1, 1965, Box 9, Mississippi Freedom Democratic Party Papers.

29. Gene Roberts, "Mississippi Law Bars Hundreds from Schools," *New York Times*, September 11, 1965; Consent Order, March 4, 1968, *Willie Earl Carthan and the United States of America v. Mississippi State Board of Education and the State of Mississippi*, Box 6, Rims Barber Papers. Although the legislature repealed the nonresident tuition law in 1966, the lawsuit continued, eventually resulting in an agreement that forced the state of Mississippi to refund the tuition payments to people who had to pay school districts under the provisions of the law while it was in effect.

30. "School De-segregation in Issaquena and Sharkey"; "A Report on School Integration in Issaquena and Sharkey Counties."

31. "School De-segregation in Issaquena and Sharkey"; NAACP Legal Defense and Educational Fund brochure, "Children and Schools," n.d., Box 3, Ed King Papers; NAACP Legal Defense and Educational Fund, *Report* 4, no. 1 (March 1966), Segregation-Integration Miscellaneous Collection; U.S. Civil Rights Commission, 22. Mae Bertha Carter and her children endured similar trials in Sunflower County

during the free-choice period. Their story is brilliantly recounted in Constance Curry's *Silver Rights*.

32. Leslie Trager to Denison Ray, September 11, 1966, Lawyers Committee for Civil Rights Under the Law, Litigation Files, SCRLR, reel 114; "Their Struggle Is Ours Too," brochure from Southern Conference Education Fund—Operation Freedom, December 1966, Facts on Film, July 1966–June 1967, reel 15.

33. For examples of intimidation of black parents in the 1967–68 and 1968–69 school years, see *U.S. v. Farrar* 414 F.2d 936 (1969) and the documents concerning school desegregation scattered throughout the SCRLR.

34. Porter and Harrington, interview; Student Research Project of the Mississippi Council on Human Relations, [1966?], Box 26, MCHR. This project surveyed twelve of the twenty-one black students who desegregated three Jackson high schools during the 1965–66 school year.

35. "Jackson Municipal Separate School District, May 3, 1967," NAACPLDF Litigation Files, SCRLR, reel 152; Student Research Project of the Mississippi Council on Human Relations; Barry and Garman; Johnnie Faye Inge, interview by Don Williams, November 28, 1998, transcript, Civil Rights Documentation Project: The Meridian Movement, TCA; Anthony J. Harris Civil Rights Memoir, 3, MCLA. See also Curry.

36. Iris Brest to Calvin R. King, January 21, 1967, *Alexander v. Holmes County*, NAACPLDF Litigation Files; Phil Draper to Constance Curry, May 2, 1966, AFSC.

37. Blackmon, interview; Student Research Project of the Mississippi Council on Human Relations; Inge, interview.

38. Motion for Supplemental Relief, September 1965; and Iris Brest to Calvin R. King, January 21, 1967, both in *Alexander v. Holmes County*, NAACPLDF Litigation Files; Motion for Further Injunctive Relief, [1965?], *Dian Hudson v. Leake County School Board*, NAACPLDF Litigation Files; Affidavit from black parents of children going to previously white schools, September 1966, case file, *Jeremiah Blackwell Jr., et al. v. The Issaquena County Board of Education, et al.*, U.S. District Court, Jackson.

39. Letter from NAACPLDF, October 27, 1966, Segregation-Integration Miscellaneous Papers, MSU; "278 Negro Students Are Suspended," *Greenville (Miss.) Delta-Democrat Times*, October 23, 1966; "Attorneys Ponder Next Move," *Greenville (Miss.) Delta-Democrat Times*, October 28, 1966; FBI report of observations at Parchman Penitentiary on October 24, 1966, FBI-GRN; "Negroes Yield in Grenada Pupil Boycott," *Washington Post*, November 3, 1966; "Boycotts in Grenada Are Prohibited," *Greenville (Miss.) Delta-Democrat Times*, November 8, 1966; Motion for Temporary Restraining Order and for Preliminary Injunction, October 27, 1966, *Rev. L. T. Cunningham v. Suggs Ingram*, Box 16, Charles A. Marx Papers, MCLA.

40. Wirt, *Politics of Southern Equality*, 226; D. M. Allen to Governor Johnson, May 27, 1964, Box 119, PBJ; "Jackson Municipal Separate School District, May 3, 1967," NAACPLDF Litigation Files, SCRLR, reel 152; "Bolivar County," December 20, 1967, Box 141, PBJ; Delta Ministry Reports, May 1968, Southern Regional Council Papers, reel 21.

41. Reuben to Paul and Melvyn, December 27, 1967; Answer to Motion to Enforce Decree, November 20, 1967; and J. Harold Flanney, Memorandum of Law, June 9, 1967, all in *Baird v. Benton County*, NAACPLDF Litigation Files; Stancill, interview.

42. Leventhal, Conference on Public Education, April 26, 1969; Ed King to Delta Ministry Staff, June 13, 1968, Box 7, Ed King Papers.

43. Peter H. Stewart, interview by author, August 20, 1997, transcript, vol. 712, MOHP; Brief for Plaintiffs, November 13, 1969, *Singleton v. Jackson Municipal Separate School District*, in Lawyers Committee for Civil Rights Under the Law, Litigation Files, SCRLR, reel 94; "A Summary of Reasons to Resist Every Effort to Add to Schools as Is Now Being Proposed," [1968?], Box 13, Ed King Papers.

44. *Mississippi Newsletter* (MFDP Paper), September 15, 1967, Box 141, PBJ; "Shelby and Boycotts," *F.I.S. Mississippi Newsletter*, June 7, 1968, in Lawyers Constitutional Defense Committee, Alvin J. Bronstein Files, SCRLR, reel 168. Information on the Leland boycott can be gleaned from a series of documents in Box 6, Rims Barber Papers. For information on the Indianola boycott, see letter from black parents and children to Superintendent of Indianola Public Schools and Board of Education, n.d., Box 3, Fannie Lou Hamer Collection, UM; and Linda Jenkins, interview by Robert Wright, July 13, 1969, transcript, Ralph Bunche Oral History Collection, Howard University, Washington, D.C.

CHAPTER 7

1. Appellant's Brief, March 13, 1970, Petition for a Writ of Certiorari, U.S. Court of Appeals, Fifth Circuit, *United States of America v. Tunica County School District, et al.*, Freedom of Information Act documents obtained from the U.S. Department of Justice, Civil Rights Division, in author's possession.

2. Jimmy H. Isbell at hearing before Judge Keady, May 21, 1970, *United States of America and Driver v. Tunica County School District*, case file, FDCOX; Transcript of Hearing before Judge Keady, May 21, 1970, *United States of America and Driver v. Tunica County School District*, case file, FDCOX; Complaint, February 18, 1970, *Driver v. Tunica County School Board*, case file, FDCOX. The two cases, *United States of America v. Tunica County School District, et al.* and *Driver v. Tunica County School Board*, were consolidated on May 5, 1970.

3. Complaint, February 18, 1970, *Driver v. Tunica County School Board*, case file, FDCOX; "Tunica County School District," February 16, 1970, Box 72, WHSP-SMOF: Leonard Garment; Appellant's Brief, March 13, 1970, Petition for a Writ of Certiorari, U.S. Court of Appeals, Fifth Circuit, *United States of America v. Tunica County School District, et al.*

4. "School Segregation: End It 'At Once,' Says the Supreme Court," *New York Times*, November 2, 1969; "School Integration 'At Once' Is Ordered by Supreme Court; Nixon Bid for Delay Rejected," *New York Times*, October 30, 1969; "Grim School

Blows Showered on State," *Jackson (Miss.) Daily News*, December 10, 1969; *Beatrice Alexander v. Holmes County Board of Education*, 90 S. Ct. 14. By the time of the NAACPLDF appeal of the delay granted to the Nixon administration in the summer of 1969, an additional eight school districts from the southern federal district of Mississippi had been added to the original twenty-five districts in the *Hinds County Board of Education* case.

5. Congressional Statement, "Freedom of Choice Is the Only Way to Save Quality Public Education," October 29, 1969, Box 46, Charles Griffin Collection, MSU; transcript of Statewide Television Address of John Bell Williams, January 3, 1970, RG 27, vol. 1144, MDAH; "No Statewide Solution to School Crisis—JBW," *Jackson (Miss.) Clarion Ledger*, January 4, 1970; James Eastland speech, *Congressional Record*, December 16, 1969.

6. Indiana Bailey, interview by William Wade Pulliam, [1970?], transcript, vol. 1, MHC; letter to the editor from "A Mississippi Citizen," *Jackson (Miss.) Clarion-Ledger*, March 11, 1970; letter to the editor from Felix Pace (Clinton, Miss.) to the *Jackson (Miss.) Clarion-Ledger*, March 10, 1970.

7. Jere B. Nash Jr. to Sonny Meredith and Buddy Grisham, May 22, 1973, RG 54, vol. 9, MDAH; Claude Ramsey to Mrs. Milton B. E. Hill, December 9, 1969, Box 2219, AFL-CIO.

8. Derrick Bell, *And We Are Not Saved: The Elusive Quest for Racial Justice* (New York: Basic Books, 1987), 103; Jerry DeLaughter, "In Crowded Coliseum, Quiet Hotel School Protest Calls Resound," *Memphis Commercial Appeal*, February 9, 1970; "Clarksdale Reaction to School Decision Varies," *Memphis Commercial Appeal*, January 24, 1970.

9. "JBW Plans 'Counter-Offensive,'" *Greenville (Miss.) Delta-Democrat Times*, December 11, 1969; Attorney General A. F. Summer on statewide television, December 1969, Lawyers Constitutional Defense Committee Files, SCRLR, roll 93; A. F. Summer to Members of the Mississippi State Bar, December 17, 1969, Box 48, Hattiesburg Municipal Records, MCLA; Senate Concurrent Resolutions, 1970, Box 161, William Colmer Papers, 2nd Accession; Newsfilm, F-4211 and F-4238, MDAH; "House Gives OK to 'Free Choice' in Mississippi," *Memphis Commercial Appeal*, January 12, 1971. The freedom-of-choice bill, modeled on a New York State law already declared unconstitutional by the federal courts, was eventually passed by the Mississippi legislature during the 1971 session.

10. Address of Governor John Bell Williams to the Joint Session of the Mississippi Legislature, January 13, 1970, RG 27, vol. 1144, MDAH; Charles M. Hills Jr., "Williams Calls for Support of Schools," *Jackson (Miss.) Clarion-Ledger*, January 14, 1970.

11. James M. Palmer Sr., "Mississippi School Districts: Factors in the Disestablishment of Dual Systems" (Ph.D. diss., Mississippi State University, 1971), 100; James M. Palmer Sr., "Resegregation and the Private School Movement," *Integrated Education* 9 (May–June 1971): 8; Michael W. Fuquay, "Civil Rights and the Private School Movement in Mississippi, 1964–1971," *History of Education Quarterly* 42 (Summer

2002): 176; Neil Maxwell, "Integration Irony: Supreme Court Ruling May Spur Segregation of Some Dixie Schools," *Wall Street Journal*, November 12, 1969; Laura Lynn McKnight, "Lessons in Freedom: Race, Education, and Progress in a Mississippi Delta Community since 1965" (master's thesis, University of Mississippi, 1996), 61–76.

12. "Instant Schools," *Newsweek*, January 26, 1970, 59; Richard Schweid, *Catfish and the Delta: Confederate Fish Farming in the Mississippi Delta* (Berkeley: Ten Speed Press, 1992), 96–97; *Memphis Commercial Appeal* article, January 7, 1970, in MCHR, Box 34; Wilson F. Minor, "Mississippi Schools in Crisis," *New South* 25 (Winter 1970): 33.

13. *Comparison of Enrollment by Race in Mississippi Public Schools for the Scholastic Years 1969–70 and 1970–71* (Jackson: State Department of Audit, n.d., 1971?); Council School Foundation Contract of Employment, May 29, 1973, MDAH; Alabama Council on Human Relations et al., *It's Not Over in the South: School Desegregation in Forty-Three Southern Cities Eighteen Years After Brown* (Atlanta: n.p., 1973), 125; "Jackson Municipal Separate School District," February 16, 1970, Box 72, WHSF-SMOF: Leonard Garment; Otho Monroe, interview by Michael Garvey, March 19, 1973, vol. 545, MOHP; R. B. Layton, interview by Thomas Healy, November 1, 1977, vol. 538, MOHP; Jacksonians for Public Education Records, 1970s, MDAH.

14. "JBW School Plan Cost Is Revealed," *Jackson (Miss.) Daily News*, August 20, 1969; James H. Downey, "Student Loan, Tax Credit Bills Pass," *Jackson (Miss.) Daily News*, September 11, 1969; "Instant Schools"; Edward L. Cates to Russell C. Davis, January 16, 1970, Box 43, Russell C. Davis Papers, MSU; "Private School System Urged," *Jackson (Miss.) Clarion-Ledger*, December 21, 1969.

15. Newsfilm, D-293, MDAH; "Address of Governor John Bell Williams to the Joint Session of the Mississippi Legislature," January 7, 1971, RG 27, vol. 1144, MDAH; Bruce Galphin, "State Strategy toward Integration Now Appears to Be 'Hunker Down,'" *Greenville (Miss.) Delta Democrat-Times*, January 19, 1970; Paul Pittman, "School Problem Hurting Economy," *Greenville (Miss.) Delta Democrat-Times*, August 5, 1970; telegram from John Bowman (Acting Director, Mississippi Council on Human Relations) to President Nixon, November 12, 1970, Box 15, WHCF, Subject Files—Human Rights, Nixon Project, NA.

16. Brian K. Landsberg to Jerris Leonard, September, 11, 1970, Box 72, WHSF-SMOF: Leonard Garment; Fred Clark Sr., interview by Leesha Faulkner, June 10, 1994, transcript, vol. 494, MOHP; "Leads on Private School Support," [1970?], Box 6, Rims Barber Papers; Charlotte Brown, interview by M. G. Tread, May 24, 1982, MC-CPL; Transcript of Hearing before Judge Keady, May 21, 1970, *United States of America v. Tunica County School District*, case file, FDCOX; John B. Farese to Attorney General Sumner, February 28, 1970, and A. F. Sumner to John B. Farese, March 2, 1970, both in RG 48, Box 17446, MDAH; *U.S. and Russell v. Greenwood Municipal Separate School District* 444 F.2d 544 (1971).

17. John Sparks, "14 Additional Schools Lose Tax Exemption," *Jackson (Miss.) Clarion-Ledger*, October 6, 1970; "High Court Rejects Schools' Tax Plea," *Jackson (Miss.)*

Clarion-Ledger, January 12, 1971; "End of Tax Exemption Ordered for 23 Mississippi Academies," *New York Times*, March 27, 1971; Southern Regional Council, *The South and Her Children: School Desegregation 1970–1971* (Atlanta: Southern Regional Council, 1971). For details on the politics of race in the careers of George Wallace and Richard Nixon, see Dan T. Carter, *From George Wallace to Newt Gingrich: Race in the Conservative Counterrevolution, 1963–1994* (Baton Rouge: Louisiana State University Press, 1996). Carter also recounts the effort by the Ronald Reagan administration in the early 1980s to reestablish the tax-exempt status of the South's segregated educational institutions.

18. Clark, quoted in Maxwell.

19. Quarterly Report, September–December 1971, Greater Jackson Area Committee of the Mississippians for Creative Public Education, Mississippians for Creative Public Education Records, TCA; C. R. Fulton, 152–53; Luther Munford, "Black Gravity: Desegregation in Thirty Mississippi School Districts" (bachelor's thesis, Princeton University, 1971), 165–67; "Report of the NEA Task Force III, School Desegregation: Louisiana and Mississippi," November 1970, in Box 6, Charles H. Ramberg Papers, MDAH. James F. Sheffield Jr. and Joseph Stewart Jr., "Fiscal Neglect as a Response to School Desegregation: Defunding Desegregated Schools," *National Political Science Review* 6 (1997): 192–204, in a statistical analysis of the relationship between school desegregation and school financing in Mississippi, found that "desegregated schools were defunded schools; the more desegregated, the greater the lag in funding."

20. Galphin; *Comparison of Enrollment by Race in Mississippi Public Schools for the Scholastic Years 1969–70 and 1970–71*; John Saunders and Mohamed El-Attar, *Mississippi Counties: Social and Economic Aspects, A Compendium of Statistical Data* (Starkville: Mississippi State University Department of Sociology and Anthropology, 1984); Willie Morris, *Yazoo: Integration in a Deep-Southern Town* (New York: Harper's Magazine Press, 1971), 122; Hodding Carter, interview by Jack Bass, April 1, 1974, transcript, SHC. While there was no exact black/white population ratio in a school district that triggered white flight, those districts with greater numbers of black students were more likely to experience more white flight. Luther Munford, in "Black Gravity," demonstrates that the white flight from Mississippi public schools in 1970 can be closely correlated with the number of blacks in a school district.

21. McPhail, 10–11, 119; Ruling of the Court, July 6, 1970, *U.S. v. Carroll County*, Lawyers Committee for Civil Rights Under the Law, Litigation Files, SCRLR, reel 94; William C. Keady, *All Rise: Memoirs of a Mississippi Federal Judge* (Boston: Recollections Bound, 1988), 106; G. E. Denley and others to John C. Stennis, February 25, 1970, Series 29, Box 8, JCS; MEA Statistics, 1968–69; Dave Bates, "Desegregation to Begin Oct. 31," *Jackson (Miss.) Clarion-Ledger*, October 19, 1977.

22. Jan Hillegas, "September School Situation—Jackson, Mississippi," *Southern Patriot*, September 18, 1970; Newsfilm, D-243, D-291, and D-328, MDAH.

23. McPhail, 21–24; Orfield, *Must We Bus?*, 22; Newsfilm, D-243, MDAH; Charles Reddin, "Dixie-Central Parents Vote for Sit-in Plan," *Hattiesburg (Miss.) American*,

August 25, 1970; "Sit-ins at Central and Dixie as Classes Open," *Hattiesburg (Miss.) American*, September 8, 1970.

24. Orfield, *Must We Bus?*, 22; Minor, "Schools in Crisis," 35; Newsfilm, D-244, MDAH; "The End of an Era," *Time*, January 19, 1970, 14.

25. Jack R. Reed, interview by Worth Long, November 15, 1999, transcript, vol. 746, pt. 2, MOHP; *Public Papers of the Presidents of the United States: Richard Nixon, 1970* (Washington, D.C.: Government Printing Office, 1971), 315–20; Orfield, *Must We Bus?*, 328; Newsfilm, D-255, MDAH.

26. Judge Robert Gillespie, interview by Orley B. Caudill, July 25, 1972, transcript, vol. 46, MOHP; Dave Dunaway, interview by R. Wayne Pyle, March 24, 1981, transcript, vol. 411, MOHP.

27. James T. Patterson, *Brown v. Board of Education: A Civil Rights Milestone and Its Troubled Legacy* (New York: Oxford University Press, 2001), 155–82; *Public Papers of the Presidents*, 315–20; "Integration: Polishing Up That Old Southern Strategy," *New York Times*, August 15, 1971.

28. Orfield, *Must We Bus?*, 244–71, 291–97, 328; Patterson, *Brown v. Board of Education*, 155–82.

29. John S. Hardin to President Richard M. Nixon, December 15, 1969, Box 195, Colmer Papers, 2nd Accession; F. W. Robertson and others to President Nixon, October 9, 1970, Box 12, WHCF, Subject Files—Human Rights, Nixon Project; letter to the editor from "A Mississippi Citizen"; Morris, 123; "Busing for Segregation Is Old Practice, HEW Says," *Greenville (Miss.) Delta Democrat-Times*, March 9, 1970; Harold E. Dacus to Representative Montgomery, March 25, 1970, RG 50, vol. 169, MDAH.

30. "Tallahatchie High Pupils All Busing," *Jackson (Miss.) Clarion-Ledger*, September 1, 1970; "Legislation, 1970," Lawyers Constitutional Defense Committee, General Office Files, SCRLR, reel 94.

31. Opinion of Judge Dan Russell, October 19, 1971, case file, *Singleton v. Jackson Municipal School Board*, U.S. District Court, Jackson; "Mississippi Chief Cuts School Aid," *New York Times*, September 12, 1971; Hugh Morgan, "Busing to Continue in Jackson Monday," *Jackson (Miss.) Clarion-Ledger*, September 13, 1971.

32. Opinion of Judge Dan Russell; "Court Busing Ruling 'Unbridled' Act—JBW," *Jackson (Miss.) Daily News*, October 20, 1971; Testimony of Peter H. Stewart and J. W. Hemingway before United States House of Representatives, Committee on the Judiciary, Sub-Committee Number 5, on H. R. 13196, Box 29, MCHR.

33. "Federals Reject City's School Plan; Full, Immediate Compliance Now or Federal Court Will Take Charge," *Picayune (Miss.) Item*, June 18, 1970; "Picayune School Board Announces Plan Integrating All Schools Here September 1," *Picayune (Miss.) Item*, July 2, 1970.

34. Hattiesburg School Board Minutes, May 1970; Mel Leventhal, June 24, 1970, U.S. Senate, Select Committee on Equal Educational Opportunity; Leonard Lowrey, "City Schools' Plan Okayed by Federal Judge," *Hattiesburg (Miss.) American*, July 16, 1970; Clarence Magee, interview by author, February 9, 1998, transcript, vol. 714,

MOHP; unsigned note [by Paul Grady?], June 17, 1970; Moran M. Pope to Mayor Paul E. Grady, July 22, 1970; and Proposed Plan for Developing a Unitary School System, n.d., all in Box 48, Hattiesburg Municipal Records; Moran Pope, interview by author, June 3, 1996, transcript in author's possession; Anonymous to Dr. Aaron Henry, August 18, 1970, Box 123, Aaron Henry Papers; "Laurel Schools Forced to Start Mixing Classes," *Jackson (Miss.) Clarion-Ledger*, December 17, 1977; "Biracial Group Fights Columbus Busing," *Memphis Press-Scimitar*, August 19, 1977, in Eugene Cox Papers, MSU.

35. "Laurel Schools Forced to Start Mixing Classes"; "Pairing Possible in City Schools as Order Result," *Laurel (Miss.) Leader-Call*, December 17, 1977; "Schools Open," *Laurel (Miss.) Leader-Call*, September 1, 1978. Enrollment statistics are from MEA Statistics, 1968–69; Annual Reports of the State Superintendent of Public Education for the years 1976–77, 1978–79, and 1979–80; and 1995–96 Mississippi Report Card, both available at www.mde.k12.ms.us/account/report/MRC.htm (accessed May 31, 2003).

36. Peggy Rector, "School Case Background," *Columbus (Miss.) Commercial Dispatch*, August 11, 1977; "Biracial Group Fights Columbus Busing"; Jess Hillman, "Parents to Take Action through the Courts," *Columbus (Miss.) Commercial Dispatch*, August 19, 1977. Enrollment statistics are from MEA Statistics, 1968–69; Annual Reports of the State Superintendent of Public Education for the years 1976–77, 1978–79, and 1979–80; and 1995–96 Mississippi Report Card.

37. Hattiesburg School Board Minutes, May 1970; Alabama Council on Human Relations et al., 122; "Blacks Seek Changes in City School Plan," *Hattiesburg (Miss.) American*, July 26, 1971; Sam Spinks, interview by author, September 15, 1997, vol. 693, MOHP.

38. Spinks, interview; J. Syd Conner, "Lawrence: Court Order Hurt Blacks," *Hattiesburg (Miss.) American*, February 25, 1987; "A Report on the Implementation of Desegregation, Hattiesburg Public Schools," Box 171, Hattiesburg Municipal Records; *United States v. Pittman By Pittman* 808 F.2d 385; Shirley Schofield, "Hattiesburg Solved Its First-Year Problems," *Hattiesburg (Miss.) American*, November 13, 1988; 1995–96 Mississippi Report Card.

39. Lucy Hutton-Seaberry-Moore, interview by author, September 11, 1999, transcript, vol. 748, pt. 1, MOHP; Bell, interview. Enrollment figures for the Cleveland schools for 2003 available at http://www.greatschools.net/modperl/browse_district/15/ms (accessed June 18, 2003).

40. "Mississippi Called 'Most Integrated,'" *Memphis Commercial Appeal*, June 26, 1970; Richard Nixon, *RN: The Memoirs of Richard Nixon* (New York: Grosset and Dunlap, 1978), 443–45. A number of historians have agreed with Nixon's self-assessment about his efforts to enforce school desegregation in the South during 1970. See Orfield, *Must We Bus?*, 327–28; A. James Reichley, *Conservatives in an Age of Change: The Nixon and Ford Administrations* (Washington, D.C.: Brookings Institution, 1981); Patterson, *Grand Expectations*, 730–31; and Joan Hoff, *Nixon Reconsidered* (New York: Basic Books, 1994). Desegregation statistics from Read and McGough, 614–16.

CHAPTER 8

1. NAACP Meridian Chapter to Frank A Taylor (President, Meridian School Board), May 9, 1972, Box 29, MCHR.

2. Ibid.

3. President's Address to the 33rd Annual Convention of the Mississippi NAACP, November 2, 1978, Box 2207, AFL-CIO.

4. T. R. M. Howard, July 30, 1954, III-C, NAACP Papers, reel 1; Newsfilm, D-250, MDAH.

5. Transcript of Pre-Trial Conference, November 6, 1969, RG 48, vol. 209, MDAH; Leventhal, June 24, 1970, U.S. Senate.

6. Hattiesburg School Board Minutes, entries from 1970; Proposed Plan for Developing a Unitary School System, n.d., Box 48, Hattiesburg Municipal Records; Stewart, interview; Middleton, 115.

7. News Release from Willie B. Long, September 3, 1969, Box 12, Delta Ministry Papers, MSU; Race Relations Information Center, *Majority-Black School Districts in the 11 Southern States* (Nashville: Race Relations Information Center, 1970), 11–18; Appeal from the United States District Court for the Northern District of Mississippi, *Dorris Edwards v. Greenville Municipal Separate School District*, 1970, Box 6, Delta Ministry Papers, MSU; *Edwards v. Greenville Municipal Separate School District*, 431 F.2d 365 (1970).

8. News Release from Willie B. Long, September 3, 1969; Race Relations Information Center, 11–18; Appeal from the United States District Court for the Northern District of Mississippi, *Dorris Edwards v. Greenville Municipal Separate School District*, 1970.

9. "Plaintiffs Protest Court Order," *Greenville (Miss.) Delta Democrat-Times*, April 8, 1970; Race Relations Information Center, 14.

10. Bennie S. Gooden to J. H. Wheatley, November 17, 1972; Semmes Luckett to Charles Stringer, June 17, 1974; and note written on back of envelope containing letter from Luckett to Stringer of June 17, 1974 (presumably written by Charles Stringer), all in Box 123, Aaron Henry Papers; Semmes Luckett, interview by Tom Healy, September 14, 1977, transcript, vol. 370, MOHP.

11. George Fleming, "Negro Educators Threaten Protests Over Mixing Role," *Jackson (Miss.) Clarion-Ledger*, December 21, 1969.

12. Newsfilm, D-250, MDAH; Billy Skelton, "Blacks Again Demand School Board Member," *Jackson (Miss.) Clarion-Ledger*, February 18, 1970; note dated January 12, 1970, Box 43, Russell C. Davis Papers.

13. Letter from City Council, Board of Supervisors, and Chamber of Commerce to Dr. C. E. Smith (Hattiesburg NAACP president), July 17, 1967, Box 36; C. D. "Red" Galey to Mayor Paul Grady and Commissioners Walter Parker and W. Ford Vance, December 24, 1969, Box 48; Clarence E. Magee to city officials, January 20, 1970, Box 70; Mrs. James "Eli" Massengale to Mayor Grady, February 9, 1971, Box 48; "Woman and Black Put on City School Board," unidentified newspaper article of February 14, 1972, Box 48; and Order of the Hattiesburg School Board (autobiography

of Jesse Parker attached), February 14, 1972, Box 48, all in Hattiesburg Municipal Records; "The City School Board Appointments," *Hattiesburg (Miss.) American*, February 4, 1971; letter to the editor by Julia M. Davis, *Hattiesburg (Miss.) American*, February 10, 1971.

14. "Boycotting Yazoo Blacks Demand Firing of Principal," *Jackson (Miss.) Clarion-Ledger*, September 10, 1977; Jimmy Langdon, interview by Chea Prince and Constance Curry, 2000, videotape, MCLA; Johnnie Johnson, interview by Chea Prince and Constance Curry, 2000, videotape, MCLA; Andy Kanengiser, "Ditto Asked to Put Black on Jackson School Board," *Jackson (Miss.) Clarion-Ledger*, March 3, 1994; "Jackson Schools: New Board Brings an Historic Moment," *Jackson (Miss.) Clarion-Ledger*, October 19, 1994.

15. Frank R. Parker, *Black Votes Count: Political Empowerment in Mississippi after 1965* (Chapel Hill: University of North Carolina Press, 1990).

16. Reecy Dickson, interview by author, September 24, 1999, transcript, vol. 743, MOHP.

17. Ibid.

18. W. Webb Burke to Sovereignty Commission Investigators, February 13, 1970; Fulton Tutor to Sovereignty Commission Director, December 29, 1969; and Weekly Report of Investigator Fulton Tutor, October 12–17, 1970, all in LF; Pearl Garrett, interview by Willie Wade Pulliam, May 26, 1970, transcript, vol. 6, MHC.

19. "Getting Together in Yazoo," *Time*, January 19, 1970, 15; "Federal Scatterload of Lawsuits Arouse Both Sides in School Mixing," *Memphis Commercial Appeal*, July 19, 1970; Munford, 120–21; Testimony of Winifred Green, June 16, 1970, U.S. Senate, Select Committee on Equal Educational Opportunity; Gloria J. Watkins Brown to Aaron Henry, February 23, 1970, in Lawyers Constitutional Defense Committee, Alvin J. Bronstein Files, SCRLR, reel 93; C. J. Duckworth, "Ferment in the Schools," *Mississippi Educational Journal* 46 (April 1970): 17.

20. "Report of the NEA Task Force III, School Desegregation: Louisiana and Mississippi," November 1970, Box 6, Charles H. Ramberg Papers; Alberta Burnett, interview by Alvin Thomas and June Johnson, July 29, 1971, transcript, vol. 3, MHC.

21. Mrs. Ernest M. Graham to William Colmer, November 14, 1969, Box 195, William Colmer Papers, 2nd Accession; *Bell v. West Point Municipal Separate School District*, 446 F.2d 1362 (1971); James M. Palmer Sr., "Mississippi School Districts: Factors in the Disestablishment of Dual Systems" (Ph.D. diss., Mississippi State University, 1971), 123. On the issue of black school closings in the South and black opposition to this process, see David S. Cecelski, *Along Freedom Road: Hyde County, North Carolina, and the Fate of Black Schools in the South* (Chapel Hill: University of North Carolina Press, 1994).

22. Madge Noble, "Crisis in Education," n.d., in author's possession; "General Face Lifting at South Side School," *Picayune (Miss.) Item*, July 9, 1970. For descriptions of other clean-ups of black schools, see Wilson F. Minor, "Mississippi Schools in Crisis," *New South* 25 (Winter 1970): 33; and Morris, 45. Noble was teaching at Canton High School (white) in the 1969–70 school year.

23. Lynda J. Davis, interview by Milan Green, July 23, 1971, transcript, vol. 5, MHC.

24. NEA Survey of Student Displacement, [1972?], Box 3, MCHR; Mississippi State Sovereignty Commission Minutes, March 19, 28, 1971; and James M. Mohead to Sovereignty Commission Director, [1971], all in LF; Rufus C. Huffman to Robert Hauberg (U.S. Attorney in Jackson), May 14, 1971, Box 123, Aaron Henry Papers; "300 Negro Students March in Support of 'Grievances,'" *Hattiesburg (Miss.) American*, March 2, 1971.

25. Penny Jenkins, "Court Order Reinforces School Procedure," *Greenville (Miss.) Delta Democrat-Times*, October 25, 1970; Dave Dunaway, interview by R. Wayne Pyle, March 24, 1981, transcript; and Dave Dunaway to Hodding Carter III, March 29, 1971, both in vol. 411, MOHP; Clarence Magee, interview by author, February 9, 1998, transcript, vol. 714, MOHP; Florence H. Levinsohn and Benjamin D. Wright, *School Desegregation: Shadow and Substance* (Chicago: University of Chicago Press, 1976), 188–90. Numerous oral histories detail the strict discipline common in Mississippi's segregated schools. For examples, see Magee, interview; E. S. Bishop Sr., interview by author, February 27, 1991, transcript, vol. 358; Zella Weathersby, interview by author, November 8, 1997, transcript, vol. 710; and Josephine Clemons Bell, interview by Amy McPhail, October 22, 1996, transcript, vol. 675, all in MOHP.

26. Newsletter, Mississippians for Creative Public Education, April 1973, Box 126, Aaron Henry Papers.

27. Charles Hardy, "Making the Extra Effort . . . Again," *Southern Exposure* 7 (May 1979): 96–97.

28. Edna Luckett and Aaron E. Henry to Leon Porter Jr., June 12, 1973, Box 123, Aaron Henry Papers; "$500.00 Reward," [1972], Eugene Cox Papers, 1974 Addition; L. C. Dorsey, interview by Chea Prince and Constance Curry, July 6, 2000, videotape, MCLA; "School Probe Finds Discrimination Evidence," *Jackson (Miss.) Clarion-Ledger*, July 17, 1980.

29. Newsletter, Mississippians for Creative Public Education, April 1973; Aaron Henry, "A Report on the Black History Week Episode, Clarksdale High School Officials and Black Student Confrontation, February and March 1973," March 27, 1973, Box 124; and Bennie S. Gooden to Robert M. Ellard, May 21, 1978, Box 123, both in Aaron Henry Papers.

30. Roger Mills and Miriam M. Bryan, *Testing . . . Grouping: The New Segregation in Southern Schools?* (Atlanta: Southern Regional Council, 1976), 45–46; Mrs. Chalmers E. Hobart to President Nixon, February 23, 1970, Box 15, WHCF, Subject Files–Human Rights, Nixon Project, NA; Fred J. Hurst to President Richard Nixon and others, January 27, 1970, Box 195, William Colmer Papers, 2nd Accession (emphasis added); Thomas J. Tubb, interview by Thomas Healy, August 30, 1978, MOHP; John Bell Williams, interview by Jack Bass and Walter de Vries, March 29, 1974, transcript, SHC.

31. Frederick M. Wirt, *"We Ain't What We Was": Civil Rights in the New South* (Durham, N.C.: Duke University Press, 1997), 128–29; Janet Ward Schofield, "Review of Research on School Desegregation's Impact on Elementary and Secondary School Students,"

in *Readings on Equal Education*, ed. Kofi Lomotey and Charles Teddlie, 13:84 (New York: AMS Press, 1996); Walter G. Stephan, "School Desegregation: Short-Term and Long-Term Effects," in *Opening Doors: Perspectives on Race Relations in Contemporary America*, ed. Harry J. Knopke et al., 106–10 (Tuscaloosa: University of Alabama Press, 1991); Rosemary C. Salomone, *Equal Education Under the Law: Legal Rights and Federal Policy in the Post-Brown Era* (New York: St. Martin's, 1986), 198.

32. Henry, quoted in Patricia Roberts, "School Desegregation: 'Damned If We Do and Damned If We Don't,' " *Mississippi Freelance*, September 1969. For examples of the tenacity of white belief in the hereditary nature of intelligence, see William S. Purvis, "Racial Bias Does Not Explain Away Poor School Performance By Blacks," *Citizen* (February/March 1989): 20–21, for a Mississippi perspective, and Richard J. Hernstein and Charles Murray, *The Bell Curve: Intelligence and Class Structure in American Life* (New York: Free Press, 1994), for a national explanation.

33. "Statement of Dr. Morris Kinsey," U.S. Congress, House of Representatives, Subcommittee on Civil and Constitutional Rights of the Committee on the Judiciary, 97 Congress, 2nd Session, September 30, 1982, 87; Langdon, interview.

34. Orlando Patterson, "For Whom the Bell Curves," in *The Bell Curve Wars: Race, Intelligence and the Future of America*, ed. by Steven Fraser, 187–209 (New York: Basic Books, 1995); Alabama Council on Human Relations et al., 111; "Statement of Dr. Morris Kinsey," 87; Herb Frazier, "Wrong Side of the Track," *Southern Exposure* 23 (Fall/Winter 1995): 28–30.

35. Newsfilm, F-4177, MDAH; Educational Resources Center, "Racism and the Desegregation Process," December 1970, Facts on Film, July 1970–June 1971 Supplement, reel 15; Bobby Gene Cooper, "The Effects of Desegregation on Black Elementary and Secondary Teachers in Mississippi, 1970–1973" (Ed.D. diss., University of Colorado, 1977).

36. W. S. Griffin, interview by Thomas Healy, July 19, 1978, transcript, vol. 414, MOHP; Langdon, interview; Don Hamil Harrison, "A Study of the Impact of the Desegregation-Integration Processes on the Public AA Size High Schools of Mississippi as Perceived by Selected Principals" (Ed.D. diss., University of Mississippi, 1978), 104–6.

37. *Armstead v. Starkville Municipal Separate School District* 461 F.2d 276 (1972). For another example of a school district using the cover of the NTE to eliminate black teachers in the wake of total school integration, see *Baker v. Columbus Municipal Separate School District* 329 F. Supp. 706 (1971). The Columbus school district also did not apply the supposedly objective standards of the NTE fairly, allowing a white teacher who failed to make the necessary score to retain her teaching job yet firing black teachers who scored low on the test.

38. The existence of such a list for Marshall County is revealed in the memo from Sovereignty Commission investigator Fulton Tutor to the director of the commission, December 29, 1969, LF.

39. L. O. Todd to C. A. Johnson, October 2, 1970, RG 50, vol. 176, MDAH; Complaint for Injunctive Relief, September 11, 1970; affidavit of Don E. Jennings, September 22, 1970; transcript of School Board Hearing, September 28, 29, 1970; and School Board's report to District Court on Jennings's Hearing, November 18, 1970, all in *Don E. Jennings v. The Meridian Municipal Separate School District, et al.*, case file, National Archives–Southeast Regional Center, Atlanta. Jennings lost his suit at the district court level, in a case presided over by longtime segregationist Harold Cox. He also lost on appeal to the Fifth Circuit. Another example of retaliation against black teachers for their support of civil rights can be found in *U.S. and Stephen Brown et al. v. Coffeeville Consolidated School District et al.*, case file, FDCOX.

40. Educational Resources Center; U.S. Congress, Senate, Committee on Equal Opportunity, *Hearings on Displaced and Present Status of Black School Principals in Desegregated School Districts*, 92nd Congress, 1st Session, June 1971, 4993, 5385.

41. "Statement of Dr. Morris Kinsey," 85–86; Report to the Court, Vicksburg Public Schools, October 1, 1976; and "We Seek Answers to the Following Inequities in the Vicksburg Municipal School System," [1976?], both in Box 125, Aaron Henry Papers; "School Probe Finds Discrimination Evidence"; Aaron Henry, interview by Jack Bass, April 2, 1974, transcript, SHC.

42. Fred Banks, interview by author, March 5, 1998, transcript, vol. 706, MOHP; Doretta Brown, interview by Nathan Baskin, May 28, 1970, transcript, vol. 2; and Hezakiah Braddock, interview by Willie W. Pulliam, May 26, 1970, transcript, vol. 3, both in MHC.

43. Rims Barber, "Swann Song from the Delta," *Inequality in Education* 9 (August 1971): 4–5; Derrick Bell, "The Remedy in *Brown* Is Effective Schooling for Black Children," *Social Policy* 15 (Fall 1984): 8; Harry Bowie, interview by Jack Bass and Walter De Vries, March 31, 1974, transcript, SHC.

EPILOGUE NOTES

1. Andrew P. Mullins Jr., *Building Consensus: A History of the Passage of the Mississippi Education Reform Act of 1982* (self-published, 1992); William Winter, interview by author, August 29, 2001, transcript, MOHP; transcript of *Sunday Morning on CBS*, January 9, 1983, in RG 27, vol. 1255, MDAH; "How a Governor's Efforts Brought New Hope to Education in His State," *Lexington (Ky.) Herald-Leader*, February 27, 1983, in RG 27, vol. 1255, MDAH; James C. Simpson, interview by author, May 11, 1992, transcript, vol. 497, MOHP; Cecil Herbert to Governor Winter, December 22, 1982, RG 27, vol. 1255, MDAH. Vol. 1255 of RG 27 contains many additional letters of support and praise for Winter's education reform efforts.

2. "Public School Enrollment as a Percentage of Total Enrollment," Southern Regional Education Board's Elementary and Secondary Enrollment statistics, available at

www.sreb.org/main/EdData/DataLibrary/03/secondaryed/enrollment/enrollment
.asp (accessed July 29, 2004).

3. Brynece Smith to Lt. Gov. William Winter, June 6, 1974, RG 54, vol. 8, MDAH;
Winter, interview; Cecil Herbert to Governor Winter, December 22, 1982, RG 27,
vol. 1255, MDAH; "How a Governor's Efforts Brought New Hope."

4. "How a Governor's Efforts Brought New Hope"; transcript of *Sunday Morning on
CBS*, January 9, 1983; Mullins.

5. John A. Salmond, *"My Mind Set on Freedom": A History of the Civil Rights
Movement, 1954–1968* (Chicago: Ivan R. Dee, 1997), 157, suggests that the school systems in small towns throughout the South are among the most integrated school
systems in the country.

6. For examples, see "Meridian School Board Moves toward Handling Racial Balance,"
Jackson (Miss.) Clarion-Ledger, May 6, 1991; "Protesters Demand Baldwyn Schools
Hire Black Principal," *Jackson (Miss.) Clarion-Ledger*, August 12, 1991; Donald V.
Adderton, "Covington County Public Schools Will Answer Bias Charge,"
Hattiesburg (Miss.) American, February 23, 1993; Nikki Davis Maute, "Lawsuit
Accuses Forrest Schools of Discrimination," *Hattiesburg (Miss.) American*, March
23, 1993; "Yazoo Boycott Continues: Decision Not to Rehire School Superintendent
Sparks Protest," *Jackson (Miss.) Clarion-Ledger*, April 14, 1993; Lora Hines, "3
Decades Later, Desegregation Issue in McComb Schools Again," *Jackson (Miss.)
Clarion-Ledger*, February 3, 2004.

7. Raymond Walters, "From *Brown* to *Green* and Back: The Changing Meaning of
Desegregation," *Journal of Southern History* 70 (May 2004): 322; Diana Jean Schemo,
"U.S. Schools Turn More Segregated, a Study Finds," *New York Times*, July 20, 2001;
Greg Winter, "Schools Resegregate, Study Finds," *New York Times*, January 21, 2003.

8. State Educational Finance Committee, "School District Reorganization and School
Consolidation Report," May 20, 1985, Box 126, Aaron Henry Papers.

9. Middleton, 125–37; Banks, interview; Nicholas Lehman, *The Promised Land: The
Great Black Migration and How It Changed America* (New York: Alfred A. Knopf,
1991), 321–23; Robert M. Ellard to Biracial Advisory Committee, November 1, 1984,
Box 124, Aaron Henry Papers; Tony Tharp, "Neighborhood Schools Get Another
Try," *Jackson (Miss.) Clarion-Ledger*, September 4, 1984.

10. Monica P. Carter, "School Plan Ends Long Bus Rides," *Hattiesburg (Miss.) American*,
March 28, 1998; Monica P. Carter, "Hattiesburg Forms Biracial Committee to Monitor
Progress of School Plan," *Hattiesburg (Miss.) American*, March 28, 1998.

11. Such sentiments can be gleaned from numerous oral histories. See, for example,
W. J. Jones, interview by Kim Lacy Rogers, July 17, 1998, transcript, Delta Oral
History Project; and Roscoe Jones, interview by Michael Vaughn, May 9, 1997,
transcript, vol. 740, MOHP.

12. Derrick Bell, *Silent Covenants: Brown v. Board of Education and the Unfulfilled
Hopes for Racial Reform* (New York: Oxford University Press, 2004).

INDEX